PROBLEMS AND SOCIAL ADJUSTMENT IN OLD AGE
A SOCIOLOGICAL ANALYSIS

PROBLEMS AND SOCIAL ADJUSTMENT IN OLD AGE

A Sociological Analysis

Saraswati Mishra

GIAN PUBLISHING HOUSE
NEW DELHI-110002

GIAN PUBLISHING HOUSE
4-C Ansari Road
New Delhi 110002

ISBN 81—212—0250—7

PRINTED IN INDIA

Published by Mrs. Gayatri Garg for Gian Publishing House, New Delhi and Printed at Godwall Printers, Delhi.

PREFACE

Scientific interest in social adjustment in old age, in terms of determining the correlates of good adjustment began with the earliest period of modern gerontology, owing to the compelling pressures of the social problem of old age, particularly in western countries. In India also, gradually, the problem of old age is becoming a social problem due to the rising proportion of the aged people in the population and their declining role and status in the changing Indian society. Consequently, the need of finding out the correlates of 'good adjustment' in old age in the Indian background is being increasingly felt. As far as the knowledge of researcher goes, no scientifically systematic specific sociological study has been conducted so far, regarding the correlates of good adjustment in old age. In the present investigation an effort has been made in this direction through a comparative study of the retired Government employees living in Chandigarh and Jabalpur.

The information regarding retirees of Chandigarh was collected in the year 1973 for the Ph. D. Thesis, which was submitted in the Panjab University, Chandigarh in the year 1976. But the findings of the study could not be generalized for the whole Indian urban society due to the typical characteristics of newly built, highly developed and most modern city of Chandigarh. We really did not know, what the state of affairs would be, in the context of social adjustment in old age, in the less developed, traditional and changing cities of India. All the three states were possible in such cities, the problem of adjustment and the correlates of good adjustment may be the same as in Chandigarh. If it is so, the findings can easily be generalized for the whole of Indian urban society. But it was also possible that the problem of adjustment may be more or less quite due to difference in the financial and socio-cultural factors, and the correlates of adjustment may be different. Therefore the collection of identical data in a less developed old city of Jabalpur was considered useful to make comparison of the different situations, problems and the patterns of adjustment. As a matter of fact Jabalpur represents a very large section of the Indian society, because India as such is considered a traditional and under-developed country in the world.

The information regarding the retirees living in Jabalpur was collected in the year 1983 for the purpose of present comparative study. Although we find a gap of ten years in the collection of information in Chandigarh and Jabalpur but it makes no difference regarding the facts and trends in various issues under consideration. On the contrary, this difference in period of data collection, which has to be kept in mind all the time, makes the study more interesting. The state of modernization and development which Chandigarh had achieved ten years earlier, has not been achieved by Jabalpur even now. This fact makes the conditions and situations more suitable and the findings more applicable as far as the comparison between the respondents of both the cities is concerned.

Along with finding the correlates of good adjustment in old age, an effort has been made to find out the applicability and desirability of two opposite theories of successful aging, i.e. 'activity' and 'disengagement' theories established by western gerontologists. Apart from this, by considering the criticism of both the theories for oversimplification of the issue and the need of adopting a developmental approach in this regard, some effort has been made to find out the characteristics and activities of well adjusted aged people adopting two different life styles or choosing a mid-way for successful aging.

Lastly on the basis of findings of the study some conclusions have been drawn and some suggestions have been given for making the policy and programme for the welfare of the

Indian aged. In this way, along with theoretical significance, the findings of this study have relevance for policy formulation and programme design in the interest of the aged people. It is hoped that this study will certainly add to the knowledge in georontological literature.

First of all, I am extremely grateful to my supervisor of Ph. D. Thesis, Professor Dr. V.S. D'Souza, Ex-Head of the Sociology Department, Panjab University, Chandigarh, for guiding me patiently. Then I am grateful to Professor Dr. P. Chandra, Ex-Head of the Department of Sociology, Rani Durgawati Vishva-Vidyalaya, Jabalpur, for giving me advice to take up this comparative study for my D. Litt. thesis. I wish to record my gratitude to the Ex-Vice Chancellor, Shri Kanti Choudhary, Dean, Faculty of Social Sciences, Dr. K.N. Sinha and all the members of Research Degree Committee for appreciation and approval of the subject and approach of the present study. I would also like to express my sincere thanks to Professor and Head of the Department of Sociology, Rani Durgawati Vishwa-Vidyalaya, Jabalpur, Dr. R.K. Gupta for his encouragement and helpful attitude, without, which the work would never have been completed. I am also thankful to our present Vice-Chancellor Dr. Amaresh Awasthy for his great concern towards the University teachers' annual academic achievements which encouraged me to complete my work as soon as possible. Last but not least, I am greatly obliged to all the concerned Government officials of various offices and institutions and the respondents of Chandigarh and Jabalpur for their cooperation by furnishing the required information.

SARASWATI MISHRA

CONTENTS

LIST OF TABLES

INTRODUCTION

Scientific interest in social adjustment in old age, in terms of determining the correlate of good adjustment, began with the earliest period of modern gerontology. Since then, it has remained a matter of great concern, particularly in the western countries, owing to the compelling pressures of the social problem of old age (Rosow, 1963 : 195). The problem of old age is becoming a social problem, though gradually, in Indian society also. Consequently, the need for finding out the correlates of 'good adjustment' in old age in the Indian background is being increasingly felt. The present investigation is a step in this direction.

A problem is considered social when difficulties met by a group of people, (a) result from the functioning, organisation or structure of society, (b) may endanger society at large, and (c) can and should be solved through social policies and political initiative (Philibert, 1968 : 23). The declaration of 1982 as the "International Year of the Aged" by the United Nations itself shows the seriousness of the problem of old age which needs immediate social attention.

The problem of old age has emerged as a social one, to some extent, owing to the rising proportion of the aged people in the population (International Encyclopedia of the social sciences, 1968, Volume I, P. 186), but, to the large extent, owing to the declining roles and status of the aged people in the industrial society of the present world (Burgess, 1951 : 7-8 ; Crawford, 1973 : 447 ; Desai and Naik, 1973 : 2-3 ;

Russell, 1979 : 2 ; Lowy. 1978 : 5 ; Marray and Flynn ; 1938 : 404).

Advancement in medical science, improvement in living conditions and public facilities have prevented epidemics and brought the general diseases under control. This has increased the life expectency of people all over the world (Woltereck, 1960 : 3 ; Burgess, 1960 : 3 ; Tibbitts, 1964 : 301 ; Burns, 1954 : 385 ; Chowdhry, 1981 : 54 ; Parthasarthy, 1980 : 385 ; India, A Reference Annual, 1981 : 6). Average life expectancy in the world was only 47 years in 1950 which is expected to be 70 years in 2025. For the first time in history, we will be seeing the world wide emergence of a new generation—The over 60s. Total population is expected to trable within this period but United Nations predicts a five fold increase in the population of over 60s, and over 80s will increase seven times their present number. It means that one person in every seven will be over 60 years of age in 2025 is comparison to just one in every twelve in 1950 (The Economic Times, 23rd May, 1982 : 45). As cited by Taylor (1982 : 5), the United Nations points out "As a consequence of social development and achievement of the twentieth century, long life has become a reality for hundreds millions of people throughout the world. In the coming decades it will become a reality for millions more. In the past only a few people attained old age. In future only a few will not reach it".

The data of World Health Organization indicates, as noted by Neysmith and Eawardh (1984 : 24), that between 1980 and 2000 the number of persons over 65 will increase by 138 million and approximately 100 million of these people will be living in third world countries. According to the population projections by the United Nations, highlighted at a Inter-Governmental preparatory meeting in Manila in 1981 for the World Assembly on Aging in 1982, by 2000, the total number of old people, aged above 60 years, will increase by 175 per cent, total of 590 million, and in India it will increase by 77 to 80 per cent, total of 57 million (Taylor, 1982 : 5). It was concluded in this meeting that the aged above 60 years will represent 9.7 per cent of the world population and two-thirds of them will be in developing world, with quite a high percentage in India (Raju, 1982 : 16). It shows that aging is no longer a phenomenon of the western industrialized world now. The discrepancy in life expectancy between less developed and more developed regions at age 65 was 1.8 years in 1975. This gap will reduce by 0.3 years in 2000. Therefore, in the third world countries there will be more persons over 60 than their counterparts in industrialized countries (Heysmith and Edwardh, 1984 : 34).

About the percentage of the aged above 65 years, the population projections made by the United Nations indicated as cited by Aggrawal (1972 : 5), that it will increase in the world from 5 per cent in 1965 to 5.5 per cent in 1985. In the more developed regions it will increase from 8.9 per cent to 10.4 per cent and in less developed regions from 3.3 per cent to 3.8 per cent. Regarding the United States of America, population projections made by U.S. Bureau of the census reveal that the proportion of the aged above 65 years will increase from 4.0 per cent in 1900 to 15.4 per cent in 2025 (Lowy, 1979 : 23). These population projections have emerged out as the facts of the present world. In general, in most of the western countries, the percentages of aged above 65 years was 4 or 5 per cent in the beginning of 20th century which has increased to 10 to 12 per cent in 1970 (Havighurst, 1978 : 15). In the United States the percentage of people aged 65 years and above has increased from 4.1 in 1900 to 9.8 in 1970 (Pathak, 1973 : 34-42). Based on death rates in 1974 in U.S.A., average remaining years of life, at the age of 65 years were 15.6 (Lowy, 1979 : 26). In 1975 there were 22 million people, i.e. 10 per cent of the population, aged above 65 years and life expectancy has expanded to over 70 years for the average person in the United States (Russell, 1979 : 26-27, 62).

In India, the percentage of people above 65 years has increased from 1.98 in 1881 to 3.36 in 1981 (India, A Reference Annual, 1981 : 116), and according to the population figures of 1981, 5.63 per cent, 5.96 per cent and 6.49 per cent of Indian population was in the age group of 60 years and above in 1961, 1971 and 1981 respectively (Census of India, 1981, Series I, Part II, P. 26). Within the period of 10 years i.e.

1971 to 1981, life expectancy has increased from 46 years to 54 years in India (Stach, 1982 : 17). In 1975, the estimated population of persons above 60 years was around 37 million (Chowdhry, 1981 : 54-55) which increased to 40 million in 1981 (Stach, 1982 : 17). With this rate it will certainly reach upto 57 million by the turn of twentieth century as projected by United Nations. The population of India, aged above 70 years, is expected to be 19.9 million in 1991 as compared to its level of 9.9 million in 1971. Expectation of life as noted by Bose (1982 : 14-17), between 1960 to 1970, at the age of 75 years, was 7.8 years for males in India. According to the statement given by the Chairman of "Age Care India', the population of the people aged 60 years and above will reach upto 28 crores in 2800 in India (Nav-Bharat, 9th July, 1984, P. 4, Col. 1). Thus we find that this is the 'age of aging' and all over the world including India the proportion of aged people is increasing quite considerably.*

In addition to the rise in the percentage of old people, the more important factor is that the roles and status of the old people are declining in the present society. It deprives them of the satisfaction of their physical and socio-psychological needs. The drives or needs of the old people listed by some gerontologists (Kaplan, 1960 ; 49 ; Arthur, 1954 : 33-34 ; Borts, 1963 : 172 ; Burgess, 1951 : 16-17 ; Simmons, 1959 : 4 ; Havighurst, 1956 : 22 and 1959 : 440 ; Lowy, 1979 : 116-117 ; Chowdhry, 1981 : 56) may be summed up as : financial and physical security, recognition as useful and significant persons in their own world, association and relation with others, social and creative activities, passing the leisure time in satisfying ways, etc.

In the pre-industrial society the old people used to get enough opportunities to satisfy their various needs. In the societies dominated by agricultural and handicraft economics they participated in the productive activities as specialists (Simmons, 1960 : 72-77), directly or indirectly, depending on their physical health, and remained financially independent.

---

*The percentages of the aged population in selected countries including India are given in Appendix-A.

Until 1900 there was no widespread practice of compulsory retirement at a set age and people used to continue their occupational activity till they were physically unfit or incapacitated (Burns, 1954 : 384). Moreover. it was regarded as a moral duty of the children to provide financial and physical security to their parents in old age (International Encyclopedia of the Social Sciences 1968, Vol. I, P. 187). The children were the 'eyes, ears, hands and feet' to the aged parents (Sim ..ons, 1960 : 81). As such, even the deteriorating health was not an obstacle in leading a comfortable life in old age. They were given the leadership roles and powerful positions of decisionmakers and advisers in the joint family and community because their knowledge and experience were considered to be of great value in the proper functioning of society (Simmons, 1945 : 16 ; Tibbitts, 1960 : 3 ; Russell, 1979 : 98). Thus, the pre-industrial social order provided full opportunities to its aged members for the satisfaction of their various needs. But the present society does not provide opportunities to its aged members to load a comfortable, respectful and socially useful life. With the modernisation and industrialisation of society the roles and status of the old people decrease (Kooy, 1963 : 59 ; Russell, 1979 : 98). The knowledge and experience of the old people lose significance in the proper functioning of society. The younger generation replaces the aged people in their powerful positions, leaving them in a weakened and functionless situation (Simmons, 1959 : 7, International Encyclopedia of the Social Sciences, 1968, Vol. I, P. 188 ; Rogers. 1979 : 199-218). Modern industrial society has shifted responsibility of the elderly people away from the family and they in turn have moral and legal claims on society (Havighurst, 1978 : 21). The aged are the new 'Harizans' in the present society (Sethi, The Economics Times, 30th May, 1982).

Aging becomes more disturbing in a society whose culture provokes irreverence toward the aged and where the economic competition works to their disadvantages (Barron, Streib, and Suchman, 1952 : 479-482). Owing to the rapid advance in industrial technology for the expansion of productivity through high energy system, in the 20th century, the American society restricted the participation of older employees in the labour market (Burns, 1954 : 385 ; Orbach, 1962 : 624 ; Hauser, International Encyclopedia of the Social Sciences, 1968, Vol. I, P. 191). And it is only for the last few decades that the retired people are being regarded as a new category of persons in society (Donahue et al., 1960 : 334). With the social 'retirement' aging quickers and the anxiety psychosis starts working feverishly (Nair, 1980 : 20). In the present society the aged people are ascribed to the terminal sick role (Lipman and Sterne, 1969 : 200) and low status (Prancher, 1969 : 29-36; Burgess, 1951 ; 10-13 ; Palmore and Whittington, 1971 : 90). They do not get higher status even in the family (Talmon, 1961 : 284-295). With the emergence of the nuclear family system in the present society, the roles played by them in the family during the joint family system of the pre-industrial society have been transferred to various institutions (Kooy, 1963 : 58; Baumert, 1960 : 210). They do not get proper care and protection from their children (Burgess, 1960 : 286 ; Kurian, 1972 : 286 ; Gordon, 1963 : 209). They have become relatively an independent generation (Tibbitts, 1963 : 345), having an 'extra familial' status in the nuclear family system, which is the obstacle in satisfying even the consumatory needs of the aged people (Messer, 1968 : 277-278). Thus, the environment of the present industrial society is not conducive to the old people to get satisfaction of their physical and socio-psychological needs. Since they have to depend on their own capacity and resources, they are exposed to the vulnerability of the aging process. So aging has become a complex and challenging proposition for the individuals to face it personally. As Talmon (1961 : 284-285) has found out, growing old is not smooth process but a difficult and the painful one in the modern industrial society. Quite a few of the aged, therefore, suffer in the process of growing old and become overwhelmed by the threatening environment when they find themselves unable to solve their problems of financial and physical security, utilisation of leisure, loneliness, isolation, etc. Owing to the absence of norms and lack of socializing facilities for the old people, they do not find any guideline for their actions and thereby experience the lost feeling (Bongston, 1973 : 24-31; Orbach, 1962 : 62 ; Mani, 1980 : 4). In this situation, these people become the 'social problem cases' because the burden of looking after their interests and taking care of them falls on society. With the industrialisation and modernization, the proportion of such socially problematic people increases. Therefore. in the highly industrialized countries like America the problem of old people has become a big social problem (Desai and Naik, 1973 : 21). As cited by Russell (1979 : 2), the perception of old age as a social problem had emerged by the 1930s, and there was growing recognition of the need for collective action on behalf of the aged.

In the pre-industrial agrarian Indian society also most of the old people used to remain financially independent till they lived. They retained ownership of landholding and other occupational establishments and participated in productive activities according to their physical fitness. The traditional social and cultural values did not permit the grown-up children to leave their financially or physically insecure old parents alone. Moreover, the prevailing economic, political and values systems of the pre-industrial social order, which were based on the preservation of inherited inequality enabled the aged people to enjoy leadership roles and powerful positions of decision-makers and advisers in the joint family, caste group and the village community (D'Souza, 1971 : 302; Bhatia, 1964 : 5).

With the advent of industrialisation, urbanisation and modernisation in Indian Society, the education and employment opportunities have been extended to all levels of people in society. Consequently, the spreading practice of compulsory retirement from services at a fixed age has also affected a growing group of aged people in terms of loss of income, activity, social interaction, social status, etc. (Pinge, The Economic Times, 30th May 1982 ; Hardikar and Bhatia 1983 : 87). Every year three to four lakh employees retire and with ten years as acturial life span there are 40 lakh pensioners in the country at a time. With five persons in the family on an average, it becomes a problem of two crore population (Tripathi, 1980 : 5-6). Because along with himself the aged of the eastern culture remains worried about the welfare of his family members also (Parthasarathy, 1980 : 385). As cited by Russell (1979 : 192), retirement is an ambiguous 'roleless role' to play in old age (Donahue, Orbach and Pollak, 1960 ; Blau, 1973; Rossow, 1974). So much so that at the time of financial crisis the services of middle aged people are terminated even before the retirement age, as has happened in France in many industries recently (Gaullier, 1982 ; 165-182).

Owing to the changing Indian social structure the old people have been dislodged from the leadership positions in the family, caste group and community (D'Souza, 1971 : 303 ; Bhatia, 1964 : 6 ; Singh, 1969 : 118-124). With the growth of new economic, political and value systems, the integrity and compactness of the joint family and caste group have been weakened and for the leadership in the community, achieved properties like wealth or education have become more important than the ascribed properties like age and seniority in the modern society. Information available in some studies indicates that the status of the old people is declining gradually, creating many problems for them (Merula-Siddaiah, 1966 : 180 ; Kurian, 1972 : 225 ; Jagjit Singh, 1962 : 40-42 : Narang, 1968 : 102 ; Indra, 1963 : 70 ; Gursharan Kaur, 1964 : 73; D'Souza, 1982 : 55 ; Hardikar and Bhatia. 1983 : 91). The old people have become aware of the greater significance of the acquired rather than ascribed attributes to get status in the new industrial social order based on the equalitarian ideals (D'Souza, 1971 : 303). This is confirmed by the fact that wherever older persons are in the positions of leadership, it is mainly due to their education and wealth rather than their age (Jagjit Singh, 1962 : 40-42). Thus, aging is not only biological in nature but also a cultural process. Physical, social and emotional changes at this age require readjustments in interpersonal relations in different situations with the members of family and society (Chowdhry, 1981 : 53).

The emergence of new force affecting the roles and status of the older people has become a source of utter frustration and thereby maladjustment for an ever larger group of socially problematic older people in the present Indian society too. It is because, as Kuhlen (1959 : 853) has said, the adjustment of the aging person depends upon the degree to which his personal and environmental circumstances offer opportunities or pose as threats to the satisfaction of his needs. It is so, because the meaning of aging itself and impact of changes occurring at this age may differ from culture to culture (Russell, 1979 : 9). Thus, the environmental contributes to success or failure of the process of aging (Hardikar and Bhatia, 1983 : 87-91). Therefore, the problems of adjustment may have different characters in societies which may be developed or undeveloped, urban or rural, Western or Indian. As discussed earlier, the present technological society creates such an environment for the aged people, which compared to that of the primitive society, provides less opportunities of need satisfaction and, therefore, as Simons (1959 : 7) has pointed out, is less conductive to good adjustment in old age. Since they have to depend on their own resources for the same purpose, many unresourceful old people become maladjusted. As Havighurst (1956 : 22) has cited Buhler's statement, that the time, when an individual feels that the fundamental motive or drive of life, that is 'continued expansion' or 'ongoingness' with regard to his various needs has ceassed, represents a critical times with respect to his adjustment.

The term 'adjustment' in gerontological literature tantamounts to the internal and external equilibrium of human organism (Rosow, 1963 : 197). It has been used mostly to refer to the States of harmony not only within itself but also with its environment (Kuhlon, 1959 : 852). Whereas Havighurst (1957 : 172) has said that there is no difference between these two harmonies and the meaning of the word 'adjustment' should be obtained as a state of harmonious living. The concept of adjustment has been used in the context of the practical purpose of gerontology. The practical purpose of gerontology is to help people in leading a better life in later years (Verzer, 1969:98; Havighurst, 1963:299), so that they can 'add life into years, not years into life' (Cheliam, The Economic Times, 30th May 82). Speaking about the importance and requirement of the studies regarding adjustment in old age, Havighurst (1957:173) has stated that for making the welfare policies and programmes of social assistance to the aged people the knowledge about the symptoms of good living and the determining conditions of good living is necessary. Therefore, we find that a great deal of research has been devoted especially by the western gerontologists to identifying some operational criteria for the evaluation of the quality of adjustment and finding out the correlates of good adjustment in old age.

Review of the Studies on Adjustment

A practical difficulty in presenting a review of the studies on adjustment in old age, conducted in the Western countries, is the lack of such gerontological literature in India. This is because the research interest in the field of gerontology has gained importance in India only recently. Owing to the non-availability of the first-hand source of information regarding adjustment in old age, very often their citations in secondary source of information have also been utilised in the short review of the studies regarding adjustment in old age in the following pages. According to Donchue, Orbech and Pollak (1960 : 379), the first major studies of adjustment in old age were those of Folsom and Morgan in 1937 and Landis in 1942. Folsom and Morgan (1937 : 223-229) have used the present life happiness as the index of adjustment and reported that factors like good health, freedom from liabilities, pleasent social and emotional relations with friends and family members hobbies, work like activities and independent living in own homes are positively associated with good adjustment of the recipients of old age assistance in New York. Landis (1942 : 468-70) by emphasising the factors from the post life and using the activities and attitudes of the aging individuals for the measurement of adjustment, has found that economic independence, high education, marriage at the right time, small family, low death rate of children, infrequent residence and job change, life insurance, good health, employment, hobby, visits to friends and church and preference for living with children are the variables corresponding positively with the adjustment of the aged people.

While reviewing the findings of the studies, conducted between 1950 and 1958 on adjustment in old age, Donahue et al. (1960 : 379) have cited that in the studies of Burgess and his associates in 1950 at the University of Chicago using the scale 'your activities and Attitudes' prepared by Caven et al. in 1949, it is found that the factors, positively associated with good adjustment in old age are : satisfactory health, married, life, good family relationships and friendship, participation in leisure time and other activities, membership of an organization, absence of unhappy experience, self-concept of being middle aged, feeling of permanent security, social status equal to that held previously, plans for future, religiosity and belief in rebirth. Further, they have mentioned that by employing the Chicago scale Shanes in 1950, Britton and Britton in 1951, Albrecht in 1951, Britton in 1951, Havighurst in 1953 and Morrison and Kristjenson in 1958, by using a scale of morale Kutner et al. in 1956 and by employing a scale of fantasy escape from non-rewarding role Phillips in 1957, all have found with a little variation, more or less the same type of factors of Burgess et al. in 1950. Shanes (1958 : 55) has also isolated a complex of items associated with a high adjustment score on the basis of the findings of the studies conducted till 1953 which include most of the above mentioned factors.

Pan (1951 : 379-81) and Schmidt (1951 : 33-42) using the Chicago scale have also reported more or less the same set of factors as the correlates of adjustment. By the evaluation of adjustment of the retired people through the measures of happiness and usefulness taken from the attitude index of the Chicago scale prepared by Cavan et al. in 1949, Burgess (1954 : 352-360) has found positive association between group activities and adjustment. And by the application of the dejection scale and the life satisfaction scale for the measurement of adjustment Fetreib and Thompson (1958 : 180-197) have found health condition, financial condition and pre-retirement positive attitudes towards retirement as the correlates of adjustment after retirement. Havighurst (1957 : 152-162) has also found that people getting the higher adjustment score from the attitude inventory tended in their leisure to be autonomous, creative, active and gregarious to seek new experience and to find ego integration. In a longitudinal study using the activity and attitude inventories of the Chicago scale separately as the indicators of activeness and morale, respectively, a positive association has been found between the activity and adjustment of the non-institutionalized people both the time (Naddox and Bisdorfer, 1952 : 254-260 ; Maddox, 1963 ; 195-204). However. another longitudinal study of older people measuring the adjustment through morale has showed that the positive association of social interaction with adjustment diminishes in the later years of life (Cumming and Henry, 1961 : 209). Yet another intensive study of retired urbanmen measuring adjustment to aging and retirement through the indices of life satisfaction and well-being has established that passitvity, inactivity and low interaction, i.e., the 'rocking chair pattern' may be perfectly consistent with satisfactory psychological adjustment (Reichard et al. : 1962). Recently in one study of the adjustment of the retired university faculty members, applying the happiness index of adjustment, it has been found that factors like a long period of retirement, living in family, better education, higher income and good health are positively associated with good adjustment (Skrabanek ; 1969 : 65-69). But Poorkaj (1972 : 289-300) measuring adjustment through life satisfaction has found no ralationship between the factors like health condition, education status, degree of religiosity and attitude towards death on the one hand and the level of adjustment on the other. It has also been noticed in the same study that a low level of activity does not necessarily cause lower level of morale.

The review of these studies concerning adjustment in old indicates two important facts. Firstly, it shows, as Rosow (1963 : 198) has also pointed out, that for the measurement of adjustment in old age, activities or social participation and life satisfaction or happiness have dominated the gerontological literature. It is so, because the attitudinal definition of successful adjustment leads to the measurement of adjustment through the inner feelings of happiness and satisfaction with the present life and the functional definition of successful adjustment puts stress upon the competent behaviour of individual which most nearly conforms to the norms and expectations of society to which he belongs (Eaton, 1947 : 77). Havighurst (1963 : 300) has also expressed the same reasons for the selection of these two criteria, with a little variation, for measurement of successful aging. Secondly, it shows that old people's socio-economic status, health status, their relationship and interaction with various group of people and their activities related to occupation, hobbies, religion, etc. are the most popular and frequently—

selected factors to determine their relationship with the level of adjustment in later years. For convenience these factors may be divided into two broad categories and termed as the situational and behavioural factors. The situational factors are those which indicate the social, economic and physical situation of the old people. With the increasing importance of achieved properties like education, income, etc. the study of these factors with regard to adjustment in old age become more important. As cited by Estroib and Thompson (1957 : 191) there seems to be a fairly wide agreement in gerontological literature. There are two very important variables related to adjustment and they are socio-economic status and physical health. Therefore, they should be regarded as basic variables in any analysis. On account of their importance we find that in most of the studies of adjustment, the gerontologists have studied these factors to find out their relationship with adjustment in old age.

The behavioural factors are those which are concerned with the behaviour of the aged people such as their interaction and relationship with different groups of people and various other activities. Great importance has been given in the gerontological literature to two types of 'life style' of the aged people, i.e. 'active' and 'disengaged' with respect to adjustment. So much so that on the basis of the contradictory findings about the association of various activities with the adjustment of the old people, the gerontologists have developed two opposite theories of successful aging. They are the activity theory and the disengagement theory. As cited by Rosow (1967 : 106) and Russell (1979 : 104), while the first one emphasizes on the desirability of high activity and high interaction, the latter suggests low activity and low interaction to lead a satisfactory life in old age. Although as cited by Russell (1979 : 20), Maddox and Wiley (1976) have noted that systematic theory development has been 'strikingly absent' in gerontology. About both the theories mentioned above, it is said that they offer an over simplified view of aging and its effects on the individual. According to the latest thinking on the issue, a developmental approach is preferable, since it recognises both, stability and change. Individuals want to maintain previous patterns of living but aging places constraints on the ability to maintain continuity. Each individual develops his own style of aging in light of his personal history and current context. As cited by Rusell (1979 : 105) some impirical investigations indicate a number of patterns of aging and apparently several ways to age 'Successfully'.

As far as the interest on the problem of old age in India is concerned, it is only in the last few years that this problem has attracted the attention of social reformers, social scientists and the Central and State Governments. The need for scientific studies on old age, as Saxena and Bose (1984 : 33-39) have said, is being increasingly felt these days because such information is an important pre-requisite for social and economic planning. In India first academic recognition to gerontology was accorded in the late 1960s when the Indian Gerontological Association was established in India and few articles were published in the Indian Journal of Gerontology during the period of 1969 to 1972. After this unfortunately due to some unavoidable circumstances the association as well as the journal lost their existence. The studies on old age in India are still in an infant stage and in most of the studies efforts have been confined only to the exploration of the problems of the old people. No scientifically systematic sociological study has been conducted so far on the adjustment of the old people in terms of determining to correlates of good adjustment, to the knowledge of researcher at least. While in a psychological study Ramamurti (1968) has dealt with psychological factors, in a sociological study Bhatia (1976) has touched almost all the aspects of the life of the aged people very simply. Considering, it appears very necessary that information about various factors positively related to the adjustment of the old people in Indian society, be gathered so that some social assistance may be provided for the maladjusted or socially problematic categories of older people to lead a more satisfying life. The present study makes an attempt in this direction.

Considering the possibility that even in one society the problem of adjustment may have different characters in more and less advanced communities. The cities of Chandigarh and Jabalpur have been selected for the study. Both the cities are existing at two different levels of development and represent two different socio-cultural ethos. It was felt that a comparison of the situations and problems in these two towns might suggest some issues which the social policymakers and programme-planners would like to utilize.

The objective of the investigation is to attempt a comparative study between the correlates of "good adjustment' of the retired Government employees living in Chandigarh and Jabalpur. The retired people have been chosen because compulsory retirement, which is becoming increasingly common in the modern society, brings most of the problems of old age suddenly and earlier in the life of the retirees. Hence the problem of the retired people may be expected to be more severe in nature thereby creating more 'social problem cases' among them than the self-employed people who can keep themselves financially independent and socially active as long as they have the will and physical fitness to do it.

The term 'adjustment' as used in the present study, refers to a state of harmonious living of the retired people. It includes the internal as well as external harmony of an aged person. The assumption here is that the attainment of the inner harmony is not possible without maintaining the external harmony. As a matter of fact, the inner harmony shows the effects which the harmony with the environment produces in the internal state of mind of an individual.

The adjustment of the retirees has been called social adjustment because it refers to their harmonious living in the social situation in which society places them by giving the 'terminal sick role of old age'. The concept of successful adjustment, i.e. the harmonious living in old age, has been operationally defined in the present study as the state of personal happiness and satisfaction with the present life. In other words, it can be said, as suggested by Gottrell (1942 : 617), that the amount of frustration, tension and anxiety created by playing a given social role of a retired person, has been considered as an index of the individual's adjustment to his role.

It is thought desirable to measure the adjustment through satisfaction because in the absence of systematic knowledge of specific social norms regarding the expected activities or behaviour of the aged people in the changing society like India, it becomes difficult to measure social acceptability of their behaviour correctly. Moreover, it is observed that people find pleasure and displeasure within the normative structure of behaviour. Therefore, happiness has been used quite often directly or indirectly as the indicator of adjustment in the field of sociology (Bright 1942 : 414) and Gerontology Donahue et al., 1960 : 379).

For the evaluation of the quality of adjustment of the retirees, an index, measuring their present life satisfaction has been developed with the help of the life satisfaction indices of successful aging (Havighurst, 1963 : 305-320).* Regarding the correlates of 'good adjustment' in old age, positive indications, which would have served as the sources of hypotheses for the present study are not available due to the absence of any systematically conducted research work, specially of the comparative nature, in the sociological field, in India.

In these circumstances it is not possible to derive hypotheses to be tested in the present study. Therefore, the most popular and frequently-tested situational and behavioural factors in the studies of the Western countries regarding the adjustment in old age have been selected to examine their relationship with the level of adjustment of the retired Government employees of the developed and under-developed regions of Indian society. Apart from these factors, considering the changing values, norms and thereby the social structure of Indian society some attitudinal factors, such as attitudes towards various social changes, non-interference in the personal affairs of grown-up children and popular religious beliefs, have also been examined against the adjustment of the retired people.

The factors like attitudes towards social changes and non-interference have not been tested in the studies of adjustment in old age conducted in the Western societies. The reason may well be understood by keeping in view the fact that the earliest studies on the subject commenced around 1940 and by

* The symptoms of harmonious living which have been used as the basis of the measurement of adjustment of the retirees will be described in detail while discussing the research methodology.

this time the impact of industrialization, which took place in the 19th century, had already stabilized in the new social order. These factors have special significance for the Indian aged people because here industrialization is a very recent process and society is passing through a transitional period. In any changing society aging becomes more problematic because it becomes very difficult for the aged people to depart from the traditional values and norms and adopt the modern values and norms. In this condition their attitudes towards new functions and structure of society in terms of acceptance or rejection of the new values and norms reflect their reactions to the new situation in which they are placed and become relevant to their adjustment. Their attitudes towards popular religious beliefs are also taken into consideration because religion may also play a very important role for adjustment in later years of life especially in the context of the changing attitudes of younger generation towards the elder generation in the present society.

Thus, the factors taken into consideration to examine their relationship with the level of adjustment of the retired people may be divided, for the sake of convenience, into three broad categories viz, situational, attitudinal and behavioural factors. The situational factors include the retirees' educational qualification, pre-retirement occupational status, present financial condition, physical condition, age. The attitudinal factors consist of their attitudes towards various social changes, non-interference in the personal affairs of the grown-up children and religious beliefs. The behavioural factors include the retirees' relationship and interaction with the family members living in the same house-hold and the children living separately, with relatives, friends, neighbours, and members of voluntary organisations, their involvement in occupational activities, hobbies, religious activities, overall activeness and interaction with non-family members, etc. Bose (1982, 1-19) has also recognized more or less same factors as very important to be taken into consideration in any meaningful study of elderly population.

The present study is an exploratory one which attempt to find out 'what exists' rather than to predict the relationships that will be found, though the findings may bring the knowledge about the important relationships between the variables (Katz, 1953 : 74). In the context of social adjustment in old age, we really do not know about the different state of affairs, in these two developed and undeveloped regions of Punjab and Madhya Pradesh in Indian society. All the three States are possible, the correlates of good adjustment may be the same in both the communities. If it is so, the findings can be generalized for the whole Indian society. It is also possible that in the less developed regions the problem of adjustment may be less acute due to religiosity and the existence of traditional values and norms, conforming the higher status of the aged in the family, or it may be more serious due to limited financial resources, poor health and the rigidity in certain matters on the part of the older people.

This study has theoretical significance and policy relevance for providing the social welfare services to the aged people. Although direct testing of the two opposite theories of successful aging through controlled observation has not been intended, but still while discussing about the behavioural factors as correlates of adjustment, an effort has been made to find out tentatively that which type of life style i.e. active or disengaged, is more desirable and acceptable to the aged for lending a satisfying life. Apart from this, by considering the criticism of both the theories for over-simplification of the issue and the suggestion of adopting a developmental approach, in this regard, effort has been made to find out its adoptability or possibility by considering together, the characteristics and activities of well adjusted people, choosing two different life styles or adopting a mid-way for good adjustment. On the basis of findings some conclusions have been drawn and some suggestions have been given for making the policy and programmes for the social assistance to the Indian aged people. Thus the findings of this study, apart from adding to the knowledge in gerontological literature, will provide valuable information that may help in the proper functioning of the Government and voluntary social service organizations in the interest of the aged people.

METHODOLOGY

The present study was conducted in Chandigarh and Jabalpur cities of Punjab and Madhya Pradesh respectively. Before discussing the universe and sample, it is relevant to mention some characteristics of both these cities.

The city of Chandigarh is an example of a modern township whose population is recently created agglomeration of migrants from the different parts of Punjab after the great holocaust of 1947 post-independence disturbances in India. Dr. Rajendra Prasad, first President of India inaugurated this systematically planned and newly constructed 'City beautiful' on October 7, 1953. It got the name of 'Chandigarh' due to the existence of old temple of Chandi-Devi in this area. Although the main object of planning Chandigarh was to rehabilitate the displaced persons from West-Punjab and to have a capital of East-Punjab, as, Lahore, which was the capital of undivided Punjab, went to Pakistan, the people from other neighbouring states have also migrated to stay here due to its attraction. Thus, the entire community is composed of immigrants.

Originally Chandigarh was designated as the capital of erstwhile Punjab. After the division of the old Punjab State into two States of Haryana and Punjab, Chandigarh became a centrally-administered Union Territory. It continues to be the capital of both the States, i.e. Punjab and Haryana besides being the capital of the Union Territory. So, a large number of Government offices are located here. Thus, Chandigarh is mainly an administrative city having 715 Government or Quasi-Government establishments (Census of India, 1971, 41)*. An overwhelming majority (70.2%) of the total workers are employed in Government or Semi-Government establishments as shown in the study of the 'social structure of Chandigarh city' (D' Souza, 1968-69). Therefore, the people in services are constantly coming in and going out of the city. A large number of the private residential houses are owned either by the retired or the serving Government employees. The facilities provided by the Government to purchase plots and construct houses, systematic character, beauty and cleanliness of the city have attracted people, retired from Chandigarh as well as from other places, to settle down here. The population of Chandigarh in 1971, was 2,18,743 (District Census Hand book, Chandigarh 1971, Series-25, Part K-B, P. 32) which has increased to 421, 256 in 1981 (Census of India, 1981, U.T. Chandigarh, Population Table I, P. 168). The growth rate of population between 1971 to 1981 was 80.84 (Census of India 1981, Series I, Provisional Population Totals, P. 66).

Owing to its peculiar origin, the urban culture there, has the stamp of newness, and changes in the traditional social norms and values are discernible in Chandigarh. It may be regarded as a representative of the Indian urban communities in the context of changing social structure. For instance, the number of joint families are very less (4.10%) and the average size of the family is vary small (3.91 persons) in this city (D' Souza, 1968 : 47, 25). The literacy rate of Chandigarh Union Territory was 64.68 in 1981 and for males it came to 68.82 per cent (India, A Reference Annual, 1981, P. 10). A large number of Government officials from higher-cadre of services have settled down here after retirement. Their life style is

* As it has already been stated in preface, the information regarding Chandigarh and the retirees living there was collected in early 70s. It can very well be imagined that the 'City beautiful' must have advanced quite further in the Path leading towards the absolute modernism within the period of last ten years. This fact has to be borme in mind all the time while making comparisous between the situations of Chandigarh and Jabalpur.

highly influenced by the western culture and value system. Most modern life style with materialistic and individualistic attitudes can easily be seen in this highly developed and most modernized city.

In contrast to it, Jabalpur is a very old city of India. So far as the evidence goes the earliest inhabitants of Jabalpur were perhaps the palacolithic men. The widespread traces of their settlements are noticed at various places, particularly in Bheraghat, Tilwaraghat and Lametaghat. There is evidence to show that the banks of river Narmada and its tributaries were inhabitated as early as in the stone age i.e. in about the second nillennium B.C. (M.P. District Gazetteers, Jabalpur, 1968, P. 1). About the assumption of the name 'Jabalpur' there seems to be a difference of opinion. Some historians including Rai Bahadur Hiralal shared the view that the place was named after Javali, a Brahmin sage who did 'Tapassya' (Penance—the act of self mortification) at the bank of Narmada here. It has also been suggested by others that it derived the name from Arabi word 'Jabal' meaning stony hills, as they are spread all over the city (M.P. District Gazetteers, Jabalpur, 1968, P. 1).

Acharya Vinova Bhave has called this city 'Sanskardhani' due to its very rich cultural heritage. The dawn of the history of Jabalpur opens with the period of 'Ashok the Great'. After the fall of Mouryas, the Kanvas succeeded them and then the rule of Gupta dynasty followed. Archaeological excavations have revealed that this place enjoyed the status of capital during the Kalchuri and Gond dynasties. The Gond queen Durgawati laid her life while fighting against Asaf Ali Khan and defending the glory and honour of her motherland. Later on Jabalpur endured the rigid grip of Marathas and subsequently atrocities of British rule.

The city has played a very important role in the National Freedom Movement. In the middle of 19th century itself, as a part of Indian Mutiny of 1857, Indian soldiers stationed in Jabalpur cantonment revolted against the British officers and hundreds of them alongwith the British officers lost their lives in the battle. Then in the 20th century, in 1930 hundreds of Congressmen from this place took an oath to free motherland from the British rule and in 1939 Tripuri session of Indian National Congress was held in Jabalpur. Quite India Movement followed and quite a few citizens of Jabalpur laid their lives for the motherland (M.P. District Gazetteers, Jabalpur, 1968, P. 59). Jabalpur has produced quite a few literary stalwarts and philosophers of world fame. It appears as a town on the tourist map of the world for the scenic beauty of Marble Rocks at the River Narmada's bank. Jabalpur is the Central district of the Central Province i.e. Madhya Pradesh, of India. The Tropic of cancer passes through the middle of the Jabalpur district and divides it into nearly equal halfs.

This culturally rich city falls in the under-developed region of the country. Madhya Pradesh is the largest State of the Indian Union but it ranks 12th in respect of industrial development. Its population in 1981 was 5.21 crores in comparison to 1.66 crores and 1.22 crores in Punjab and Haryana respectively (India, A Reference Annual 1981, P. 6). Due to economic backwardness and widespread unemployment here wage rates are very low for the workers. Per-capita income in Madhya Pradesh was Rs. 1217 in 1981 as against the all India average of Rs. 1749.5. In 1983 the percentage of the Government employees having their monthly income below Rs. 500 was 18.99 per cent in comparison to 1.72 per cent of those getting above Rs. 1500 per month (Employees in Government services, issued by Directorate of Economics & Statistics, 1983, P. 11-13). Literacy percentage which is 27.82 in 1981 also lags far behind the all India average of 26.12 per cent (Pocket compendium of Madhya Pradesh Statistics, 1982, M.P. in Indian Economy, Table 125, P. 283).

The Jabalpur city's population of 5,34,845 in 1971 (District Census Hand Book, Jabalpur, 1971, P. 160) has increased to 7,57,726 in 1981 (Census of India 1981, Series II, M.P. Bhopal, P. 57). The growth rate of population between 1971 to 1981 in Jabalpur was 41.67 (Census of India, 1981, Series I, Provisional Population Totals, P. 125). The literacy rate of Jabalpur Tehsil in 1981 was 44.93 and for males it came to 55.29 per cent (District Book of Statistics, Jabalpur, 1982 : 33). Only 27.76 per cent of the population of the city was found economically active in 1981. The population of Jabalpur in 1971 consisted of 75.79 per cent Hindus, 10.79 per cent Muslims, 2.73 per cent Christians, 2.02 per cent Sikhs, 1.88 per cent Jains and others (District Census Hand Book, Jabalpur, 1971, P. 160).

Jabalpur has provided employment opportunities to a very large number of people of surrounding areas, specially through defence industries, which were established and strengthened to fulfil the requirements of two world wars.* There was a noticeable increase in industrial labourers between 1931 to 1951, which constituted 8.3 per cent of the total population of the city in 1961. Apart from permanent migration of the people from rural areas to this city, daily movements of people to and from Jabalpur is also significant between this place and 25 Kilometers around it. Thousands of people come early with dawn and go back by sunset. Thus, a large number of unemployed persons of rural areas have been absorbed in this place in the establishments of Central Government. In 1981 there were 84,751 Central Government employees in comparison to 20,604 State Government employees (District Book of Statistics, Employment in Government Establishments, P. 75). Apart from this School education upto matriculation during the British regime produced a large number of school teachers and clerks in this region. In 1983 there were 1,684, i.e. 7.25 per cent, Government employees in the Gazetted posts in comparison to 21,569, i.e. 92.75 per cent, employees in the Non-Gazetted Post in Jabalpur District (Directorate of Economics & Statistics, Madhya Pradesh, Employment in Government Services, 1983, P. 3). Among Hindus, higher agricultural and artisan castes dominate the Class I, II and III Government services whereas the serving castes of the traditional Hindu society have taken up Class IV Government services. According to the treasury office records 70 per cent, 25 per cent, 4.5 per cent and 0.5 per cent of the Pensioners,

* Gun Carriage Factory and Ordnance Factory located in Jabalpur manufacture Gun parts, mountings, shells and variety of arms and ammunitions for war purposes as well as civillian needs. Apart from these factories, Heavy Vehicle Factory, Grey Iron Foundry, Post & Telegraph Workshop, Central Ordnance Depot etc. have also absorbed a large number of workers.

settled down in Jabalpur, have retired from the class IV, III, II and I Government services respectively. It is also observed that in the absence of any ties with their hometowns in the form of property specially, the class IV workers having rural background have a tendency to settle down permanently in the city after their retirement from services.

Residents of this city, specially the old and middle aged population is still believing in the values and norms of the traditional Indian society. Performance of various 'Sanskars' and rituals according to the traditional method can easily be seen here. It is common for a man to live with his wife, children and some lineally related dependents in the same household (M.P, District Gazetteers, Jabalpur, 1968, P. 154).

In this way we find that Chandigarh and Jabalpur are existing at two different levels of development and represent atleast two different socio-cultural ethos. As a matter of fact Jabalpur represents the larger section of Indian society because India as such is considered an under-developed country in the world.

These factors can creat different types of situations and problems for the same category of people namely the retired Government employees. Thus, the persons belonging to the same category have to face different types of problems of socio-cultural and economic adjustment in two different places because of the regional differences.

It was felt that a comparisons of the situations, problems, and the patterns of adjustment by the aged people might suggest some new issues which will be useful for the welfare authority while making the programmes in the interest of the aging people. Therefore, the study was proposed to be conducted in these two places. The information regarding the retirees staying in Chandigarh was collected in the year 1973 for the Ph.D. Thesis.* But the findings of the study could not be generalized for the whole Indian Urban society due to the typical characteristics of highly developed and most modernized Chandigarh city. We really did not know, what

* A Thesis 'Social Adjustment in Old Age' (A Case Study of Retired Government Employees Living in Chandigarh) was submitted in Punjab University in the year 1976 for the degree of Ph.D.

the State of affairs will be, in the context of social adjustment in old age, in the less developed cities like Jabalpur. Therefore, the collection of identical data in the city of Jabalpur was considered useful to facilitate a comparative study of the problem and consequently generalization of the facts if possible.

Universe and Sample

The universe of this study is the entire number of male retired Central and State Government employees living in the cities of Chandigarh and Jabalpur. The retired people have been selected for the investigation because compulsory retirement, as a major consequence of industrialization and modernization of society, brings most of the problems of old age earlier and rather suddenly in the life of the Government employees. Therefore, the problems of the retired people may be expected to be more serious in nature, creating more 'social problem cases' among them than the self employed aged people who can keep themselves away from atleast some of the problems as long as they wish. For the purpose of the study, all the retired Government employees have been treated as aged people because, in the social sense, old age begins in an individual's life at a point where he ceases to perform the duties and enjoy the rights of middle age (Burgoss, 1960 : 204 ; International Encyclopedia of the Social Sciences, Vol. I, P. 177) which needs adjustment (Chowdhry, 1981 : 53). In the census report also people above the lowest age of retirement in most of the Government services, that is above 55 years, are classified as elderly people.

In the case of Chandigarh the names and addresses of the retired people, who were drawing their pensions from the local treasury offices, were recorded from the treasury offices in the month of March 1973. Whereas in Jabalpur the treasury office as well as the authorised banks were utilised for this purpose, coincidently again in the month of March 1983.*

* Government of India has introduced a new system of the distribution of the pensions from 1st April 1977. According to it, for the convenience of the pensioners, there is a provision of transferring the pension cases to the branches of authorised banks nearer to their residences.

For the sake of lowering down the mortality rate of the sample and convenience of interviewing, only those people have been included in the universe of both the places who have drawn their last pensions during the six months prior to drawing the sample. Women employees are not included in the universe because their number is insignificant.* The numbers of male retirees included in the universe was 936 and 1553 in Chandigarh and Jabalpur respectively. By adopting the random sampling method, 300 retirees from Chandigarh and 500 retirees from Jabalpur were drawn from the universe of these cities as samples. In this way almost one-third proportion of the universe is chosen as the sample in both the places. The sample has been drawn with the help of tables of randam numbers. While deciding the adequacy of the number of units for sample to be studied, it has been borne in mind that the sample should be sufficiently large to enable us to arrive at satisfactory and significant conclusions and at the same time, it should be sufficiently small to be manageable by a single researcher. In conformity to these requirements, the samples as the units of the study in both the places have been considered appropriate to draw valid conclusions.

Procedure of Data collection

A presentation of the procedures of data collection by the researcher is useful to make sure that the data have been collected by fairly well-established standards (Hyman, 1960 : 142). The nature of the present study is such that only personal interviews with respondents can be expected to yield fruitful and reliable information. Because it is only through the interview method that the investigator can read the sub-liminal

---

*This fact can be understood by keeping in view the lack of tradition among women of Indian society to work. A study conducted by the Punjabi University Centre for research in economic change in 1971 the percentage of the working women in 1971 in India was 13.18 ('The Tribune' dated 9th May, 1976, page 3, column 1). In the period of 10 years also this percentage has not increased much. Out of the main workers in India, females have constituted only 13.99 per cent (Census of India, 1981, Series I, Part II, Chapter 3, P. 27).

clues of the respondents besides their replies to the questions. Moreover, to get reliable information about the personal details of individuals it is necessary to establish a good rapport with the respondents. So, for collecting the data of the present study an interview schedule was prepared, pre-tested and modified before starting the actual field work. The interview schedule includes a large number of questions regarding the background characteristics, situational factors showing the social, financial, and physical situation of the ratirees, attitudinal factors showing their attitudes towards various social changes, non-interference in the personal affairs of grown-up children and popular religious beliefs, and the behavioural factors showing their routine activities, relationship and interaction with the family members and relationship and interaction with friends, relatives, neighbours and members of voluntary organizations etc. It also includes 30 statements which constitute the index of adjustment on the basis of the respondent's feelings of happiness and satisfaction with the present life.* All the information has been collected by interviewing the respondents at their residence with the help of the interview schedule by the researcher. In the interview schedule many personal questions about various aspects of the retired life have been included which people generally do not discuss with a stranger. Therefore, before starting the interview the repondents have been assured that all the information would be kept confidential and used for research purpose only. On the whole, the response of the retired people has been quite satisfactory in both the places. The reason for the good response in Chandigarh may be that almost all the respondents were atleast matriculates and able to understand the purpose and utility of this type of study. As far as the respondents of Jabalpur is concerned they, specially those retired from class IV services were found too keen to talk about their past experiences and to discuss their present problems with the researcher. In Chandigarh 23 and in Jabalpur 52 retirees could not interviewed because of untraceability, non-availability, refusal to give the required

* Interview schedule has been given in Appendix C.

information and death. Thus, the total number of the respondents have come down to 372 and 443 in Chandigarh and Jabalpur respectively. Each interview has lasted from an hour to two hours in both cases. The field work was completed in eight months in Chandigarh whereas it took a little more then half year in Jabalpur, while the number of Jabalpur respondents was more than the Chandigarh respondents.*

Index of Adjustment

The present study is aimed at knowing the correlates of 'good adjustment' in old age. Therefore, adjustment is the important and the main variable of this investigation. With a view to judging the levels of adjustments of the respondents, an index of adjustment has been prepared.** Since it is the major index used in the study, it needs a detailed discussion. The terms 'adjustment' in the study refers to the state of harmonious living and it has been defined operationally as the state of respondents' personal happiness and satisfaction with the present life.

After a careful consideration of several measuring indices of life satisfaction, used by gerontologists in this field, it has been decided to develop a pilot measuring device for this investigation. Thus, a total of 34 items have been designed to measure the satisfaction or happiness of the retired people. These statements have been prepared on the basis of five components of the life satisfaction indices suggested by Havighurst (1963 : 299-320) to measure successful aging. These components of life satisfaction are : resolution and fortitude, goodness of fit, positive self-concept, mood tone and zest for living. Happiness of the individuals is influenced by the cultural background of society. Therefore, most of the statements of the existing indices of successful aging have been

* The reasons for this hurried data collection in Jabalpur were, firstly that the researcher with the intention of finishing the work in a shortest possible time, exerted much more than earlier this time and secondly, the class IV retired employees were easily available at a time in large number at the places of their settlements.

**Categorization of various levels of adjustment and the distribution of the respondents into different levels are given in Chapter II.

modified or replaced keeping in view the social structure and culture of Indian society. The Likert type of scaling method is used in the construction of the life satisfaction index. Each component consists of three positive and three negative statements. All the statements regarding the five components of life satisfaction have been mixed up and arranged in the index to get reliable information. Each item has five point response categories, ranging from strongly agree to strongly disagree. The score of each item ranges from one to five in negative statements and five to one in positive statements. In this way the total scores of all the 30 items of index add to 150.

It is now in order to discuss briefly the five components of life satisfaction to know how the scoring has been done and how they indicate the inner happiness and higher morale of a person in old age. All the components of life satisfaction represent almost overlapping themes and it is difficult to keep these items distinctively separate but some effort has been made to differentiate one from the other.

Resolution and Fortitude

A person may be called satisfied and gets higher score if he thinks that old age and its consequences are inevitable and accepts them sportingly, thinks that his life is meaningful, believes in trying again and again to achieve something, faces the problems with courage and confidence and is not afraid of death.

Goodness of Fit

Here it has to be seen to what extent the respondent feels that he has achieved his goals and fulfilled his ambitions. Higher scores have been given to those who feel that whatever is important for them and they desire to get in this period of life they are getting and who think that they have managed to fulfil their responsibilities and get rid of their liabilities of life to a greater extent.

Positive Self-concept

We are concerned here with the respondent's image of his own physical and psychological attributes. High scores have been given to those who have positive image about their younger appearance, wisdom, mellowness, accomplishment and importance for others.

Mood Tone

The retired people, who have expressed happy and optimistic attitudes and mood, used spontaneous and positively toned affective terms for people and things and expressed pleasure in life, have been given higher score on this component.

Zest for Living

The respondents who have enthusiastic and optimistic attitudes towards life, have some future plans, interest in various activities, persons and ideas have been rated higher on all the statements regarding this component.

Item Analysis

After completing the field study work in Chandigarh 100 interview schedules out of 272 have been randomly selected and the upper and lower quartiles for each item score have been worked out. Both the quartiles consist of 25 interview schedules. It is assumed that these two groups provide the criteria groups in terms of which each statement of an index can be evaluated by deriving its 't' ratio. As Edward (1969 : 1953) has written the value of 't' measures the extent to which a given statement differentiates between the high and low groups. Further, he has said that as a crude and approximate rule of thumb, the 't' value equal to or greater than 1.75 may be regarded as indicating that the average response of the high and low groups to a statement differs significantly, provided 25 or more subjects have been kept in both the groups. In the present study also, with the help of 't' ratio, the difference between the mean response of each statement in the upper and lower quartiles has been tested for significance. Any statement having a 't' ratio less than 1.75 is required to be removed while preparing the final index. But the average response of the high and low groups to all the 30 statements of the life satisfaction index differ significantly. Therefore, no item has been rejected after its analysis.* It was not thought necessary to reanalyse the items for the study of retirees at Jabalpur due to the comparative nature of the study and same interview schedule including index of adjustment was used in Jabalpur also.

Processing of Data

All the relevent information received on the interview schedule has been meaningfully coded and transferred on the cards. With the help of these coding cards frequency tables have been prepared and after applying the test of association, wherever required, the data analysed. To present a very clear picture of the different state of affairs about the various aspects of retirees' life in Chandigarh and Jabalpur, separate tables regarding the same variables in both the places have been prepared and kept side by side for the comparison. This form of presentation of data was considered better than inserting the data of both the groups in one single table.

Test of Association

In the present investigation an attempt is made mainly to examine the association that exists between various factors on the one hand and the level of adjustment on the other. Since we have the ordinal level of data, Goodman's and Kruskal's Gamma(r) test of association has been applied for examining the association between any two variables. Since 'r' measures the degree of agreement or association between any two ordinal level variables, the value of 'r' shows the percentage of error which gets reduced in the mutual predictability of those two variables (Champion, 1970 : 219-224). Further, the value of 'r' has been converted into the value of 'z' to find out its statistical significance by applying the conservative asymptotic test suggested by Goodman and Kruskal (1963 : 310-364). The 'z' values equal to 1.92 and 2.33 are considered statistically significant at .05 and .01 levels respectively. Owing to the qualitative nature of the data, .05 level has been set to test the statistical significance of

---

* Item analysis is shown in appendix II.

association between any two variables in the present study. From the different values of 'r' between the same variables on one hand and the level of adjustment on the other, in Chandigarh and Jabalpur, the relative importance of those variables for the adjustment in old age in developed and undeveloped regions of society can easily be understood.

Since the nature of the variables concerned is largely qualitative, a multiple correlational analysis could not be adopted and researcher has to content with only a single factor association between any two variables in both the eities.

1

SPECIAL FEATURES OF THE SAMPLE

Before examining the relationship that exists between various factors on the one hand and the adjustment in old age on the other in Chandigarh and Jabalpur, it will be better to have some knowledge about the special characteristics of the respondents of both these places. It will serve as a background in understanding their attitudes and activities.

Immigration

Chandigarh being a newly-built city all the retired Government employees living here are immigrants. D'Souza's study of the social structure of Chandigarh city reveals some facts about the migration of the people residing here. It shows that all the heads of the households here are migrants. A substantial number of them are displaced persons from Pakistan, the majority of them have migrated from the urban communities and most of them belong to the nearby areas of Chandigarh. Among the various reasons for migration, while transfer and lack of economic opportunities are the most important reasons, the latter is more prevalent in the case of immigrants from rural areas (D'Souza, 1968, 216-235).

As far as the structure of Jabalpur city is concerned no

such study has been done so far. From the 'M.P. District Gazetteers, Jabalpur, 1968' mainly we get some ideas about the migratory aspect of the population. Although Jabalpur is a very old city, at the beginning of the 20th century its population was only 90,316. Significant developments, that is, various Government establishments provided increasing employment opportunities to the people of surrounding areas (Pandit, 1982). Now it is one of the most populous city of Madhya Pradesh, ranking 4th in 1961. Following the partition of the country in 1947, considerable displacement of population occurred and Jabalpur had its own share of 28,642 refugees. In 1957 Jabalpur city sheltered nearly 1.05 lakh immigrants on account of its being an important business and industrial centre. This is predominantly a Hindu city. Between 1941-51 due to the partition the number of Muslims decreased and the number of Sikhs increased in this place. It has also become an important centre of the Christian community since the advent of British in the region (M.P. District, Gazetteers, Jabalpur, 1968, P. 157). In this way we find that the migration of people from rural areas to Jabalpur is responsible to a large extent for the rapid increase of the city's population.

In middle age, sometimes people can only stay in the place of their own choice due to the compulsion of economic activity, especially, in the case of Government services. But at the time of retirement people have the option to settle down anywhere they like. It is observed that normally people prefer to settle down in their own home communities in old age. It is a well known fact that the people, specially of rural areas have a very strong emotional attachment with their ancestral or self-earned property, may be agricultural land, residential house or cattles. In Chandigarh all the respondents and in Jabalpur most of the respondents are the migrants and therefore, it seems desirable to have information about the location of their hometowns, their urban/rural background and the main reason for not settling down in their home communities, after retirement. This information will also give us some idea as to why these retirees have selected these cities for settling down permanantly.

The distribution of the respondents according to the location of their hometowns and their rural/urban background in Chandigarh and Jabalpur is given in Table 1.1 side by side. About Chandigarh it reveals the presence of more or less the same background characteristics among them as have been found among the migrants in the D'Souza's study of Chandigarh city (D'Souza, 1968 : 216-235).

The Table 1.1-A shows that a considerable number, i.e. 38.60 per cent, of the respondents of Chandigarh have their hometowns in Pakistan. The explanation of this finding is, that one of the main objectives in planning Chandigarh was to rehabilitate the displaced persons from Pakistan. The facilities provided by the Government to construct houses might have attracted them to settle down in Chandigarh. Although Chandigarh is also the capital of Haryana, some how, this State is not adequately represented among the retirees settled down here. Comparatively a larger section, that is 47.06 per cent, of the respondents belong to Punjab. The reason for the concentration of the respondents in this category may be that Chandigarh is expected to be the exclusive capital of Punjab in future.

It also gives strength to the fact that generally people like to live in the culturally homogeneous community in old age. Only 39 respondents constituting 14.34 per cent of the sample belong to the rest of the States of India which is worth noting. Among these, 21 belong to Haryana, five to Himachal Pradesh, four to Delhi, five to Uttar Pradesh and one each to Gujarat, Madhya Pradesh, Maharashtra and Jammu and Kashmir.

The distribution of the respondents of Chandigarh according to their rural/urban background shows that majority, i.e. 53.68 per cent, of them belong to the urban areas. The respondents from the urban areas of both Pakistan and Punjab State are more in number than the rural areas of these places. Only in the case of immigrants from other States of India we have found more retirees having rural background than those having urban background but their number is not significant.

The distribution of the respondents of Jabalpur according to the location of their hometowns and their rural/urban

TABLE 1.1

Distribution of the Respondents of Chandigarh and Jabalpur According to the Location of Home Town and Rural/Urban Background

Location of Home Town	(A) Chandigarh Rural/Urban Background: Rural areas	Urban areas	Total	Location of Home Town	(B) Jabalpur Rural/Urban Background: Rural areas	Urban areas	Total
Pakistan	45	60	105 (38.60)	Uttar Pradesh	30	18	48 (10.71)
Punjab State of India.	60	58	128 (47.06)	Madhya Pradesh	153	163	316 (70.53)
Other States of India.	21	18	39 (14.34)	Other States of India.	55	29	84 (18.76)
Total	126	146	272 (100.00)	Total	238	210	448 (100.00)
	(46.32)	(53.68)	(100.00)		(53.12)	(46.88)	(100.00)

(The percentages are given in parentheses)

background (Table 1.1-B) shows that an overwhelming majority, i.e. 70.53 per cent, of the respondents have their home towns in Madhya Pradesh itself. The explanation of this finding lies in the fact that Jabalpur is a very old city and it has provided employment opportunities to the people of surrounding areas. Apart from the old residents of this city, the migrants from the rural areas and the smaller towns have also settled here after their retirement. It is often observed that after working for a quite long time in a particular place, a person develops liking for that place and becomes used to the urban lifestyle and therefore, decides to settle down there permanently. Next state which has been represented by the retirees, although not prominantly, is Uttar Pradesh, 48 respondents which is 10.71 per cent of the sample belong to this State. Cultural similarity between these two States seems to be the reason behind their decision to settle down in Jabalpur. Rest of the respondents have their hometown in Punjab, Bihar, Rajasthan, Bangal, Andhra Pradesh, Maharashtra and Kerala. Madhya Pradesh being the central province of India, people from all the States, specially the adjoining ones, are found here. Jabalpur falls in the central region of Madhya Pradesh hence its population consists of people belonging to various States.

The distribution of the respondents of Jabalpur according to their rural/urban background shows that the majority, i.e. 53.12 per cent, of them belong to the rural areas. It again indicates towards the employment opportunities provided by Jabalpur to the rural people of surrounding areas as well as of the other States. Most of the respondents belonging to Uttar Pradesh and other States of India are from the rural areas of these States. But in the case of Madhya Pradesh majority of them are from urban areas. This is because quite a considerable number of the respondents, that is 90 (20.09%), belong to Jabalpur itself, being an old city.

While comparing the data between Chandigarh and Jabalpur the striking fact we find that while in Chandigarh displaced persons from Pakistan constitute a large proportion of the sample, no one, by chance, has represented this section of the society among the respondents of Jabalpur. The second difference we notice that in Chandigarh majority of the retired persons belong to urban areas whereas in Jabalpur majority of them belong to the rural areas. This difference in their background itself explains the modernity and traditionality of the attitudes and behaviour of the aged people residing in both of these cities. While all the respondents of Chandigarh, due to its being the new city, are outsiders, one fifth proportion of the respondents of Jabalpur are the original residents of this city.

By further probing into the reasons for not living in the home communities after retirement according to the rural/urban background of the respondents of both the cities (Table 1.2), it has been found that in Chandigarh the predominant reason is partition of India, which is quite understandable. About 38.60 per cent of the respondents have left behind their hometowns in Pakistan and due to their changed citizenship the question of settling down there, after retirement, does not arise. Since they had to settle down some where in India, they found Chandigarh quite suitable for living in old age.

The lack of medical, educational, recreational, cultural and other facilities in the hometown is the second main reason mentioned by 35.66 per cent of the respondents for not staying there after retirement. This may be understood in the light of the various facilities available in Chandigarh. The lack of opportunities for re-employment, business or private practice of the profession after retirement in their own home towns is the next reason more frequently mentioned (17.65%). It again shows that these retirees wanted to continue their economic activities even after retirement and due to its expansion they found better prospects of earning money in Chandigarh. Absence of intimate ties with the home towns in terms of relatives or property has been mentioned by 8.09 per cent of the respondents, as the reason for not settling down in their home towns.

If we exclude the respondents who are displaced from Pakistan and their reason that their home towns are in Pakistan, we find that the relative prominence of the various reasons is somewhat different in the case of the respondents having the rural and urban background. The reason of lack

TABLE 1.2

Distribution of the Respondents of Chandigarh and Jabalpur According to the Main Reason for not Staying in Home Town After Retirement and the Rural/Urban Background

(A) Chandigarh				(B) Jabalpur			
Main Reason for not Staying in Home Town After Retirement.	Rural/Urban Background: Rural background	Urban background	Total	Main Reason for not Staying in Home Town After Retirement.	Rural/Urban Background: Rural background	Urban background	Total
Home Town in Pakistan	45 (35.71)	60 (41.09)	105 (38.60)	Employment of the sons in Jabalpur	54 (22.69)	27 (12.85)	81 (18.09)
Lack of better educational, medical, cultural, recreational and other facilities	47 (37.30)	50 (34.25)	97 (35.66)	Construction of the house during service in Jabalpur	79 (33.20)	18 (8.60)	97 (21.65)
Lack of opportunities for reemployment, business or private	21 (16.67)	27 (18.49)	48 (17.65)	Lack of better educational, medical, cultural, recreational	18 (7.56)	19 (9.04)	37 (8.25)

practice of one's profession after retirement				and other facilities in home town			
No bonds with home town in terms of property or relatives etc.	13 (10.32)	9 (6.16)	22 (8.09)	Lack of opportunities for reemployment, business and private practice of the profession in home town	26 (10.92)	20 (9.52)	46 (10.27)
				No bonds with home town in terms of property or relatives etc	61 (25.63)	36 (17.14)	97 (21.65)
				Not applicable	0	90 (42.85)	90 (20.09)
Total	126 (100.00)	146 (100.00)	272 (100.00)	Total	238 (100.00)	210 (100.00)	448 (100.00)

(The percentages are given in parentheses)

of various facilities is relatively more frequent among the respondents having the rural background whereas lack of economic opportunities after retirement is more frequent among the respondents having the urban background, although the difference is not very striking. These facts may be understood by keeping in view that quite a few persons coming from the rural areas own some agricultural land in their home towns and it remains one of the sources of income even after retirement, but they do not get various other facilities there. People from the urban areas may get various facilities in their home towns, but they do not find the same prospects of earning money there as in Chandigarh. The lack of ties with the home towns in terms of property and relatives has also been mentioned more frequently by the respondents belonging to the rural areas than those from the urban areas, which indicates the trend of urbanization in Indian society.

In the case of Jabalpur quite a considerable number of the respondents, i.e. 20.09 per cent, belong to the Jabalpur itself and the question is not applicable to them. Among others more or less the same number of the respondents, that is 97, have mentioned construction of own house in Jabalpur during the service period and no bonds with home town in terms of property or relatives as the main reason for not staying in home town after retirement from service. Both these reasons show that quite a few people, while in service, had planned their retirement and decided about their permanent settlement in Jabalpur. Therefore, probably they had disposed off their property in home town and constructed the houses in Jabalpur for living during the service period as well as the retirement period. The employment of the sons in Jabalpur is the next most frequently mentioned reason (18.09%) for not staying in home town after retirement. This indicates towards the fact that they expected their sons to look after them in old age. Probably they feel secured while living among their near and dear ones. It suggests the existence of traditional values and norms among the residents of Jabalpur city. Lack of opportunities for reemployment, business and private practice of the profession after retirement in their home towns is the reason which has been mentioned only by 10.27 per cent respondents. It shows the aged people are not very keen to involve themselves in the economic activities again after retirement. The lack of better educational, medical, cultural recreational and other facilities in home town has got the last priority among all the reasons given by the retired people in Jabalpur. It shows that they are not giving much importance to these activities.

By excluding the old residents of Jabalpur when we look at the rural/urban background of the respondents, we find that the relative prominence of the various reasons is somewhat different in the case of the migrants from rural areas and urban areas. The reason of construction of own house during service period in Jabalpur is relatively more frequent among the respondents having the rural background, whereas no bonds with home towns, lack of various facilities and re-employment opportunities are the reasons, more frequently mentioned by the respondents having the urban background. These facts show that most of the migrants from rural areas leave their home towns for ever. They do not want to settle down in the village, even if they have got some property or relatives there. That is why they construct their houses in city as soon as they settle down in service, although they do not attach much importance, to various facilities or economic activity in retired life. This is not so in most of the cases of educated persons having urban background. They leave their home towns permanently either due to the absence of any ties in the form of property or relatives or they want to avail the facilities and reemployment opportunities of the big city. They want to remain active and economically independent even in old age. Equal importance, given by the respondents having both types of background, to the employment of sons in Jabalpur as the main reason for not staying in home town shows again the dependence of people on their grown-up sons in old age.

While comparing the data of Chandigarh and Jabalpur we find that while a large number of respondents of Chandigarh have mentioned lack of various facilities and reemployment opportunities as the main reasons for not settling down in home towns, the respondents of Jabalpur have mentioned no bonds with the home town, construction of the house in Jabalpur as the important reasons, behind their decision of settling down in Jabalpur. It seems that behind the migration of Chandigarh respondents the push factors that is the attraction of the beautiful city and in the case of Jabalpur respondents the push factors of unemployment and poverty in villages have remained responsible. The most striking difference between the immigrants of these cities is that while quite a few of them in Jabalpur are depending economically upon their grown up sons and living with them as they have mentioned the employment of sons in Jabalpur as the main reason for not settling down in their home towns after retirement, whereas not even a single immigrant of Chandigarh has mentioned this reason. While majority of Chandigarh respondents have urban background, the majority of Jabalpur respondents have the rural background. All these factors indicate the developmental stage of these two places of Indian society. When Chandigarh seems to be a most modern city, Jabalpur is just stepping out of the traditionalism.

Religion and Caste

About the religious affiliations of the community of Chandigarh city, both, the Census report (District Census Hand-Book, Chandigarh, 1971, Series-25, Part-X-B, P. 33) and the Chandigarh study (D'Souza, 1968 : 53) show that Hindus and Sikhs are the two major religious groups and all other religious put together, constitute only a small percentage of the population.

As far as Jabalpur is concerned it is predominantly a Hindu city. In 1971, 75.79 per cent population of this place was following Hindu religion. Among the non-Hindus, the largest religious community of this city is of Muslims. 10.79 per cent persons of the city's population were the followers of Muslim religion. Among other religious communities were, 2.73 per cent Christians, 2.02 per cent Sikhs and 1.88 per cent Jains in this city (District Census Hand Book, Jabalpur, 1971, P. 160).

The distribution of the Chandigarh respondents according to their religious affiliations (Table 1.3-A) shows that an overwhelming majority, i.e. 65.44 per cent, of the respondents belonging to the Hindu religion. Among the non-Hindus, the largest group that is 32.72 per cent of the total respondents are Sikhs. We have only four Christian and one Jain respondents in the sample.

TABLE 1.3

Distribution of the Respondents of Chandigarh and Jabalpur According to the Religion

	(A) Chandigarh			(B) Jabalpur	
Religion	Frequency	Percentage	Religion	Frequency	Percentage
Hindu	178	65.44	Hindu	395	88.17
Sikh	89	32.72	Muslim	27	6.02
Others	5	1.84	Christian	14	3.12
			Others	12	2.69
Total	272	100.00	Total	448	100.00

The Table 1-3-B shows that the overwhelming majority, that is 88.17 per cent, of the Jabalpur respondents are Hindus. Among the non-Hindus the largest group, although not very prominent, i.e. 6.02 per cent of the total respondents, is of Muslims, 3.12 per cent of the respondents are the Christians and rest 2.69 per cent of the sample consists people of other religions.

A comparative look at the religious affiliation of the respondents of Chandigarh and Jabalpur makes it clear that while in Chandigarh although Hindus are in majority, Sikh community makes a significant contribution among retirees, in Jaba'pur no other religion than Hindu has a very prominent place among the pensioners.

About the castes among the Hindus and Sikhs, the social grading according to their relative social prestige in this region, has been developed by D'Souza for the Chandigarh study (D'Souza, 1968 : 33-36). In that study it is found that the higher castes among the Hindus and Sikhs constitute the majority of the sample population (D'Souza, 1968 : 288-289).

Among the Hindus the caste hierarchy in District of Jabalpur may be classified into three broad categories, first, the higher agricultural castes, second, the higher artisan castes and third the serving castes. Brahmin, Kshatriya and Vaishya are the principal castes while the rest are covered as others (M.P. District Gazetteers, Jabalpur, 1968, P. 142) Kayasthas or 'Lalas' got important posts under the Gond regime in this region, specially in urban areas whereas 'Lodhis' and 'Kurmis' constituted a considerable proportion of rural areas. Higher agricultural and artisan castes dominate urban elites whereas the serving castes of rural areas have taken up the lower classes of services in the urban areas. There are 50 thousand people of various Schedule Castes in the Jabalpur city (Census of India, 1981 Series-II, M.P., P. 57).* Due to the shorter distance from the tribal district of Mandala quite a few tribal people can easily be seen here.

For the present study in the case of Chandigarh, all the Hindu castes and Sikh castes, found in that region, are divided separately into three caste groups, consisting equal number of hierarchically arranged castes and named as Higher, Middle and Lower caste groups according to their relative social status. Regarding the Jabalpur respondents only Hindus were divided into three caste groups according to their relative social status. The reasons for this decision are, as we have seen earlier, that Hindus constitute an overwhelming majority of the sample and the caste system is prominently prevalent and observed among Hindus. All the Hindu castes have been divided into three groups according to their relative social status in Jabalpur. In this Mahakoushal region of Madhya Pradesh the number of Brahmins is larger in comparison to other places, and due to the existence of traditional values and norms they continue to enjoy higher status in the society. Teaching as their profession in traditional society is quite favourite among the Brahmins even now. Therefore, the Brahmins have been kept in the upper caste group. The Kshatriyas, Vaishyas and the Kayasthas have been put together in the middle caste group and rest of the castes belong to the lower caste group.

* Provisional Population Totals Issued by Director of Census Operations, M.P. Bhopal.

TABLE 1.4

Distribution of the Respondents of Chandigarh and Jabalpur According to the Religion and Caste Group

Caste Group	(A) Chandigarh Religion					(B) Jabalpur Religion				
	Hindu religion	Sikh religion	Total	Other religion	Grand Total	Hindu religion	Muslim religion	Chris-tian religion	Other religion	Total
Upper caste group	159 (89.33)	58 (65.17)	217 (81.27)	—	217	98 (24.81)	—	—	—	98 (21.88)
Middle caste group	19 (10.87)	31 (34.83)	50 (18.73)	—	50	126 (31.89)	—	—	—	126 (28.12)
Lower caste group	0	0	0	—	0	171 (43.30)	—	—	—	171 (38.17)
Not applicable	—	—	—	5	5	—	27	14	12	53 (11.83)
Total	178 (100.00)	89 (100.00)	267 (100.00)	—	272	395 (100.00)	27 (100.00)	14 (100.00)	12 (100.00)	448 (100.00)

(The percentages are given in parentheses)

The distribution of the Chandigarh respondents according to upper, middle and lower caste groups and religion shows (Table 1.4-A) that among the respondents of both, the Hindus and Sikh religions, an overwhelming majority, i.e. 81.27 per cent, of the respondents belong to the higher caste group. This may be because that people having higher socio-economic status alone can afford to live in a costly city like Chandigarh after retirement. The table shows that the percentage of the respondents from the higher caste group is comparatively higher among the Hindus than the Sikhs. It may be due to the fact that majority of the Hindu retirees coming from the states other than Punjab and Haryana incidently belong to the higher caste group.

The above table reveals that among the Hindu respondents of Jabalpur city almost one-fourth of them, i.e. 24.81 per cent, are Brahmins, although relatively a larger section (43.30%), is from the lower caste group here. Respondents from the middle caste group constitute 31.89 per cent of the Hindu retired people living in Jabalpur.

While comparing the facts about the caste groups of the respondents of Chandigarh and Jabalpur we find that while in Chandigarh, majority of the respondents are from the higher caste group, in Jabalpur, among Hindu respondents, quite a considerable proportion is from the lower caste group although Brahmins have a considerable number. This explains the social structure of both these cities to some extent atleast. This also explains to a great extent the fast and slow speed of development in both these places. In Chandigarh the upper strata of the urban areas has immigrated whereas for Jabalpur mostly the lower strata of rural society has migrated from the beginning of this century.

Mother-tongue

According to the Chandigarh study, Hindi and Punjabi constitute the mother-tongue of 53.8 and 42.9 per cent of the sample respectively (D'Souza, 1968 : 110), whereas Jabalpur is linguistically a homogeneous city because 90 per cent of its population have Hindi as their mother-tongue (M.P. District Gazetteers, Jabalpur, 1968, P. 142).

But the distribution of the Chandigarh respondents of present study on the basis of their mother-tongue (Table 1.5-A) shows that an overwhelming majority, i.e. 85.66 per cent have Punjabi and only 12.13 per cent have Hindi as their mother-tongue. The obvious reason for this is that in middle age people have to stay in various places due to the occupational activity but after retirement they want to settle down in their own communities. In the Bombay study of retired people also the majority of the respondents have Marathi as their mother-tongue (Desai and Naik, 1973 : 117).

TABLE 1.5

Distribution of the Respondents of Chandigarh and Jabalpur According to their Mother-tongue

(A) Chandigarh			(B) Jabalpur		
Mother-tongue.	Frequency	Percent-age.	Mother-tongue.	Frequency	Percent-age.
Punjabi	233	85.66	Hindi	401	89.50
Hindi	33	12.13	Urdu	27	6.02
Others	6	2.21	Others	20	4.48
Total	272	100.00	Total	448	100.00

Same is the finding about Jabalpur respondents regarding their mother-tongue. 89.50 per cent i.e. an overwhelming majority of them have Hindi as their mother-tongue and only 6.02 per cent have urdu as their mother-tongue which again demonstrates that the people want to live in the culturally homogeneous group specially in old age.

The most striking difference between Chandigarh and Jabalpur is that while in the earlier one most of the respondents have Punjabi, in the latter one, they have Hindi as their mother-tongue.

Age and Pariod of Retirement

The age of the respondents refers to their age at the time of the interview and the period of retirement is the length of time after the date of their retirement and before the interview.*

The distribution of the Chandigarh respondents according to their age and the period of retirement (Table 1.6-A) shows most of them were not very old at the time of interview. A higher proportion, that is 47.07 per cent, of the respondents are in the age group of 61 to 65 years and about a little more than one fourth of them are in the age category of 60 years and below. None of the respondents is below 58 years. In all 72.80 per cent of the respondents are in the age group of 65 years and below. As far as the period of retirement is concerned it is found that the majority, i.e. 57.35 per cent, of the respondents have retired during the last five years before the date of interview.

Table 1.6-A clearly shows the decreasing percentage of the retirees with the increasing period of retirement. A closer look of the table reveals a positive association between the two variables, i.e. age and the period of retirement. As the age of the retirees increases the period of retirement also increases which is quite obvious and may reasonably be expected.

One of the possible reasons for higher concentration of the retirees in the lower age groups and shorter period of retirement could be the special characteristic of Chandigarh being a newly built city. Most of the people retired after Chandigarh came into being might have settled down here and the people retired earlier might have settled down in other places of this region.

The distribution of the Jabalpur respondents according to their age and the period of retirement in Table 1.6-B shows that relatively a large number of the respondents, i.e., 35.93 per cent, falls in the age group of 66 to 70 years and quite a considerable proportion of them, that is 27.90 per cent, are in the age category of above 70 years. Only a little more than one fourth of them have come in the age group of 61 to

* The data regarding the Chandigarh respondents were collected between July 1973 and February 1974, whereas the data about the respondents in Jabalpur were collected between March 1983 to September 1983.

TABLE 1.6

Distribution of the Respondents of Chandigarh and Jabalpur According to the Age-Group and Period of Retirement

Age Group	(A) Chandigarh Period of Retirement					(B) Jabalpur Period of Retirement				
	5 years and below	6 to 10 years	11 to 15 years	Above 15 years	Total	5 years and below	6 to 10 years	11 to 16 years	Above 15 years	Total
60 Years and below	66 (42.31)	4 (7.84)	0	0	70 (25.73)	34 (27.41)	10 (7.87)	2 (1.36)	0	46 (10.27)
61 to 65 years	89 (57.05)	33 (64.70)	6 (12.76)	0	128 (47.07)	88 (70.98)	25 (19.69)	3 (2.04)	0	116 (25.90)
66 to 70 years	1 (0.64)	14 (27.45)	24 (51.06)	2 (11.11)	41 (14.70)	2 (1.61)	92 (72.44)	67 (45.58)	0	161 (35.93)
Above 70 years	0	0	17 (36.17)	166 (88.88)	33 (12.60)	0	0	75 (51.02)	50 (100.00)	125 (27.90)
Total	166 (100.00) (57.35)	51 (100.00) (19.85)	47 (100.00) (16.91)	18 (100.00) (5.89)	272 (100.00) (100.00)	124 (100.00) (27.63)	127 (100.00) (28,34)	147 (100.00) (38.81)	50 (100.00) (11.17)	448 (100.00) (100.00)

(The percentages are given in parentheses)

65 years. In all 63.83 per cent of the respondents are in the age group of above 65 years.

Regarding the period of retirement also we find that the largest number of the respondents, i.e. 32.81 per cent, falls in the category of period of retirement from 11 to 15 years, 27.68 per cent of them have recently retired and 28.34 per cent of the retirees have experienced 6 to 10 years of retired life. The reason for this finding lies in the fact that Jabalpur is a very old city and apart from the original residents of the city immigrants are staying here since a very long time.

While comparing the age and period of retirement of the respondents of Chandigarh and Jabalpur we find that the retirees of Chandigarh are comparatively younger than the retirees of Jabalpur. This difference of the age between these two groups of study can easily be explained by the special characteristics of Chandigarh and Jabalpur being a newly built city and a very old city respectively.

Pre-retirement Type of Service, Class of Service and the Level of Education

There are four broad occupation prestige classes in the Government services ranging from class I at the top to class IV at the bottom. While class I and class II services fill at the gazetted posts, class III and class IV services fill all the non-gazetted post. In Punjab in 1974, 0.75 per cent, 0.86 per cent, 81.96 per cent and 15.43 per cent of the permanent Government employees belonged to class I, II, III and IV services respectively, and gazetted and non-gazetted posts were held by 2.61 per cent and 97.39 per cent of the permanent employees (Statistical Abstract of Punjab, 1975, Economic and Statistical Organisation's Publication, Pp. 214-215). This information gives us some idea about the approximate proportions of various classes of Government services in Punjab.

The study of social structure of Chandigarh city shows that 65.7 per cent of the workers in the city are Government Employees (D'Souza, 1968 : 69). According to the prestige classification of various occupation developed by D'Souza in the same study, it is found that the majority of the male employed persons belonged to the occupational grade IV, in which clerical staff of the offices has been included (D'Souza, 1968 : 71). Since they form the class III of Government services, it shows that among the working Government employees the proportion of class III worker is much more than other classes.

In Madhya Pradesh also, in 1981 the percentage of Government employees was 0.79, 3.72, 83.01 and 12.48 in class I, II, III and IV services respectively. In Jabalpur division the number of Government employees in class I, II, III and IV services was 592, 2675, 57362 and 8363 in the year 1981 which comes to 0.86, 3.88, 83.14 and 12.12 per cent respectively (Pocket Compendium of Madhya Pradesh Statistics 1982, Pp. 140-141). It is a well known fact that the number of class III and IV services is always more than the number of I and II services anywhere. One may reasonably expect that among the retirees also the proportion of the Government employees retired from class III and IV services, will be more than class I and II in any city.

The distribution of the Chandigarh respondents according to their pre-retirement class of service (Table 1.7-A) shows that the percentage of the retirees from class I and II services is very much higher and the percentage of the retirees from class III and IV services is much lower than their percentages in the Government services in general, therefore, in the present study they constitute 33.82, 30.51, 31.98 and 3.68 per cent of the total number of the Chandigarh respondents respectively. This table also shows that a majority, i.e. 64.43 per cent, of the respondents have retired from the gazetted posts and only 35.67 per cent of them had been serving in non-gazetted posts in the pre-retirement period.

It shows that most of the people retired from the lower classes of service probably cannot afford to stay in Chandigarh after retirement and, therefore, they have shifted to their home towns. People retired from the higher classes of service prefer to stay in Chandigarh because it is modern, beautiful, neat and clean city and also that they can financially afford to stay here.

TABLE 1.7

Distribution of the Respondents of Chandigarh and Jabalpur According to the Pre-retirement Type of Service, Class of Service and the Level of Education

(A)

Chandigarh

Pre-retirement Class of Service		Level of Education: Less than matriculation	Matriculation	Upto graduation or professional diploma	Upto post-graduation or professional degree	Total
Non-Gazetted Posts	Class IV Service	10 (100.00)	0	0	0	10 (3.68)
	Class III Service	0	52 (61.18)	26 (26.80)	9 (11.25)	87 (31.97) 35.67
Gazetted Posts	Class II Service	0	23 (27.06)	38 (39.17)	22 (27.50)	83 (30.51)
	Class I Service	0	10 (11.76)	33 (34.03)	49 (61.25)	92 (33.82) 64.33
	Total	10 (100.00) (3.58)	85 (100.00) (31.24)	97 (100.00) (35.67)	80 (100.00) (39.41)	272 (100.00) (100.00)

(B)
Jabalpur

Pre-retirement Class of Service		Level of Education: Uneducated	4th and below	Less than matric	Matriculation	Upto graduation or professional diploma	Upto Post-graduation or professional Degree	Total
Non-gazetted Posts	Class VI Service	105 (100.00)	122 (94.57)	25 (30.86)	0	0	0	252 (56.25)
	Class III Service	0	7 (5.43)	56 (69.14)	28 (57.14)	21 (39.62)	0	112 (25.00)
								31.25
Gazetted Posts	Class II Serviee	0	0	0	19 (38.77)	23 (43.39)	16 (51.61)	58 (12.94)
	Class I Service	0	0	0	2 (4.09)	9 (16.99)	15 (48.39)	26 (5.81)
								18.75
	Total	105 (100.00) (23.43)	139 (100.00) (23.80)	81 (100.00) (18.10)	49 (100.00) (16.93)	53 (100.00) (11.93)	31 (100.00) (6.91)	448 (100.00) (100.00)

(The percentages are given in parentheses)

The educational categories, as presented in the Chandigarh study (D'Souza, 1968, 79) have been merged here into four broad categories as : below matriculation, matriculation, upto graduation or prefessional diploma and upto Post-graduation or prefessional degree. The distribution of the Chandigarh respondents in these categories (Table 1.7-A) shows that most of them are atleast matriculates. Comparatively a higher proportion, i.e. 35.67 per cent, of the respondents have studied upto graduation or have professional diploma and 29.41 per cent of them have studied upto Post-graduation or have professional degrees, which is worth noting. The reason for the relatively advanced educational qualifications of the respondents lies in the fact that except the class IV Government service, one cannot get service even in the clerical cadre, if one is not a matriculate specially in the administrative city like Chandigarh. The Bombay study of retired people also shows that an overwhelming majority of the retired people are atleast matriculates (Desai and Naik, 1973 : 20). D'Souza's study of Chandigarh city shows that the proportion of the male employed persons educated upto matric, upto graduation or professional diploma and upto Post-graduation or professional degree constitute 63.8, 26.2. and 10.0 per cent, respectively, of the total male employees in the sample (D'Souza, 1968 : 74). Since the majority of the workers in Chandigarh are Government employees (D'Souza, 1968 : 60). We may infer to some extent that comparatively higher proportion of Government retirees from the higher educational levels and lower proportion from lower educational levels may be due to the tendency of less educated people to shift from Chandigarh to their home towns after retirement. It also perhaps reveals the fact that highly educated people, retired from places other than Chandigarh, have a tendency to migrate from these places to this city after retirement.

Table 1.7-A also shows the association between the educational level and the class of pre-retirement services of the respondents. All the respondents retired from class IV services are either uneducated or non-matriculates whereas most of the matriculates respondents have worked in the class III services in the pre-retirement period and the retirees who have studied upto graduation or professional diploma, also constitute a higher percentage in class II pre-retirement services.

When we look at the distribution of the Jabalpur respondents, according to their pre-retirement class of service in the above table it shows that the majority, i.e. 56.25 per cent, of the respondents have retired from class IV Government services. Exactly one-fourth proportion of the sample, that is 25 per cent, were working in the class III services before their retirement. The fact worth noting is that only 12.94 per cent and 5.81 per cent of the Jabalpur respondents have retired from class II and I Government services. Table 1.7-B also shows that an overwhelming majority, i.e. 81.25 per cent, of the Jabalpur respondents have retired from the non-gazetted posts and only 18.75 per cent of them had been serving in gazetted posts in the pre-retirement period.

Regarding the educational qualifications of the Jabalpur respondents Table 1.7-B reveals that a considerable number of the respondents, that is 23.43 per cent, are uneducated, whereas 28.80 per cent of them have studied upto 4th class or less than that. In all 70.33 per cent of the pensioners in the Jabalpur sample come under the educational category of less than matric. Comparatively small porportions, that is 10.93 per cent, 11.83 per cent and 6.91 per cent of the respondents fall in the categories of matriculation, upto graduation or professional diploma and upto Post-graduation or professional degree respectively.

Distribution of the Jabalpur respondents according to the class of service and education in table 1.7-B clearly reveals that majority of them have retired from class IV Government services where education is not required as a qualification to get the service. As a matter of fact most of them were working as the industrial labourers in the Government defence industries, like Gun Carriage Factory and Ordnance Factory located in Jabalpur. Probably they did not have any bonds with their home towns in the form of property specially, therefore, either they have constructed the cheap houses here during service or after retirement, or living with their sons.

By keeping in view the proportion of class III Government

services, which is the largest among all classes, the number of respondents retired from class III Goverment services is quite less. The reason for this may be that the people from middle strata of nearby rural societies do normally have some landed or residential property in their home towns. By taking education they come to urban societies to have additional source of income. During service period either they come to city at sunrise and go back to village at sunset or they stay in the city temporarily and finally after getting retired from service settle down permanently in their respective home communities. Due to the shorter distance between the city and their villages, they can avail all the facilities of city while staying in home town. Jabalpur probably has not provided much attraction for the retirees of upper classes of Government services of other cities to settle down here, although their proportion in the sample is more than their proportion in Government services.

While comparing the educational and service background of the Chandigarh and Jabalpur respondents, we find a great difference between the two cities. Most of the retirees living in Chandigarh are highly educated and have retired from upper classes of service, whereas most of the retirees living in Jabalpur are either uneducated or very little educated and have retired from lower classes of service. Thus these two cities consist of two quite different sections of the retired people. This finding itself demonstrates quite clearly the stage of development and the level of modernization of these two cities. This information confirms our assumption that Chandigarh and Jabalpur represent two different socio-cultural ethos.

Class of Service Before Retirement and the Monthly Income at Present

The economic condition of an individual plays a vital role in leading a satisfying life in old age in the modern society. Therefore, it is useful to know about the economic condition of the respondents. All the respondents of present study have retired from the Government services and they are entitled to pension throughout their life, therefore, all of them have some monthly income of their own. The fact worth finding is, that what amount of money including income from other resources also, they are getting per month.

The distribution of Chandigarh respondents according to their own monthly income (Table 1.8-A) shows that a higher proportion, i.e. 43.01 per cent, of the respondents have a monthly income of Rs. 400 and below and 35.40 per cent have a monthly income of their own ranging from Rs. 401 to Rs. 800. The point worth noting here is, that a considerable number, that is 20.59 per cent of the respondents are getting above Rs. 800 every month even after retirement. When we look at the present income of the Chandigarh respondents according to their pre-retirement class of service we find a positive relationship between two variables. Owing to the insignificant number of respondents, retired from class IV services, they have been put together with the respondents retired from class III services. An overwhelming majority, i.e. 79.38 per cent, of the respondents, retired from class III and class IV services have a monthly income of Rs. 400 and below whereas majority, i.e. 50.60 per cent and 50.00 per cent of the respondents retired from class II and I services have monthly income of Rs. 401-800 and above Rs. 800, respectively. It shows that quite a few of the Chandigarh respondents have sufficient income to remain financially independent even in old age, which can easily be understood by keeping in mind their educational and occupational background.

The distribution of the Jabalpur respondents according to the pre-retirement class of service the monthly income at present shows that a considerable number, i.e. 33.48 per cent, of them have monthly income of Rs. 200 and below and the monthly income of 36.38 per cent respondents is ranging between Rs. 201 to Rs. 400. In all, an overwhelming majority, i.e. 69.86 per cent, of the Jabalpur respondents are having their monthly income of Rs. 400 and below. Among the Jabalpur respondents 14.95 per cent and 8.70 per cent of them are getting monthly amount of money as their own income of Rs. 401 to Rs. 600, Rs. 601 to Rs. 800 respectively. The point worth noting is that only 6.49 per cent of the respondents in Jabalpur are having their monthly income above Rs. 800.

TABLE 1.8

Distribution of the Respondents of Chandigarh and Jabalpur According to Pre-retirement class of Service and the Monthly Income at Present

(A) Chandigarh

Monthly Income	Pre-retirement Class of Service III & IV	II	I	Total
Rs. 400 and below.	77 (79.38)	31 (37.35)	9 (9.78)	117 (43.01)
Rs. 401 to 800	20 (20.62)	42 (50.60)	37 (40.22)	99 (36.40)
Above Rs. 800	0	10 (12.05)	46 (50.00)	56 (20.59)
Total	97 (100.00)	83 (100.00)	92 (100.00)	272 (100.00)

(B) Jabalpur

Monthly Income	Pre-retirement Class of Service IV	III	II	I	Total
Rs. 200 and below	131 (54.13)	19 (16.98)	0	0	150 (33.48)
Rs. 201 to 400	101 (41.74)	55 (49.10)	7 (10.31)	0	163 (36.38)
Rs. 401 to 600	10 (4.13)	27 (24.10)	28 (41.17)	2 (7.69)	67 (14.95)
Rs. 601 to 800	0	11 (9.82)	18 (26.47)	10 (38.46)	39 (8.70)
Above Rs. 800	0	0	15 (22.5)	14 (53.55)	29 (6.49)
Total	242 (100.00)	112 (100.00)	68 (100.00)	26 (100.00)	448 (100.00)

(The Percentages are given in Parentheses)

When we look at the present income of Jabalpur respondent according to their pre-retirement class of service, we find here also, the positive relationship between these two variables. We find no retiree from class IV Government service having fallen in the monthly income categories of Rs. 601 to Rs. 800 and above Rs. 800 whereas no respondent, doing class III service before retirement has monthly income above Rs. 800. In the same way no respondent, having class I service background, has appeared in first two income categories, and no respondent having class II service background has come in the first category of income as Rs. 200 and below. Majority, i.e. 54.13 per cent, of the respondents, retired from class IV have concentrated in the income category of Rs. 200 and below whereas the majority of the respondents, that is 53.55 per cent, retired from class I services have monthly income above Rs. 800. This association between monthly income and class of service is obviously expected due to the difference in pay scales during service and pensions after retirement.

Regarding the monthly income also we find a lot of difference between respondents of Chandigarh and Jabalpur. In Chandigarh 43.01 per cent respondents were found to have monthly income of Rs. 400 and below whereas in Jabalpur 69.86 per cent respondents have come in this category. In the same way while in Chandigarh 20.59 per cent of the sample was having monthly income above Rs. 800, in Jabalpur only 6.49 per cent of it gets above Rs. 800 per month as their own income. This difference between the financial condition of the two groups can easily be understood by keeping in mind the difference of educational and occupational background of the retirees living in these two places. Most of the Chandigarh respondents seem to be in the financially comfortable position whereas most of the Jabalpur respondents as it appears may be leading a miserable life due to shortage of money. It again depicts the difference between the levels of development in these two places.

Marital Status and Living Arrangements

Family is a major institution for providing long lasting intimate primary, social and emotional ties with others. The marital relationship is particularly important because of the intimacy and sharing its employs. Marital status and living arrangement of an individual plays important role in the later years of his life, specially after retirement, due to his total dependence on family for the fulfilment of all the inter-personal needs (Rusell, 1979 : 307). This distribution of the Chandigarh respondents according to this information (Table 1.9-A) shows that only 10.29 per cent of them are widowers and an overwhelming majority, i.e. 89.71 per cent, are leading a married life. The reason for the concentration of the retirees in this category is that the majority of the respondents are not very aged as we have seen earlier. We did not find any unmarried or divorced respondent in our Chandigarh sample. In the Bombay study also 80.0 per cent of the respondents are married (Desai and Naik, 1973 : 25).

When we look at the living arrangements of the respondents we find that a higher proportion, i.e. 44.35 per cent, of the retirees are staying with unmarried children along with spouses or without spouses. But the point worth noting here is that 27.93 per cent of the respondents are living apart from their children either alone or with spouses if married. Relatively a small section (23.16%) of the respondents are staying with married children. And the proportion of the respondents living with married children is higher among the widowers (46.42%) than the married respondents (20.49%). A very small percentage of the respondents belong to the households where other relatives are also living with them and none of the retirees is living with non-relatives.

This information reveals that the joint families of the traditional Indian society, which facilitated older people to live with their married children, are gradually disappearing and the nuclear families are emerging, especially in the urban areas. The reasons for the nuclear families of the majority of the respondents may be that Chandigarh being a modern city is more responsive to social changes and hence represents the Indian urban life, especially in the context of the changing family structure of Indian society. The study of Chandigarh also shows that the average number in the family is 3.91 persons in this city (D'Souza, 1968 : 25). This study also

TABLE 1.9

Distribution of the Respondents of Chandigarh and Jabalpur According to the Living Arrangement and Marital Status

Living Arrangement	(A) Chandigarh Marital Status			(B) Jabalpur Marital Status		
	Married	Widower	Total	Married	Widower	Total
Self	0	6 (21.43)	6 (2.20)	0	3 (20.63)	3 (2.90)
Self with unmarried children	0	5 (17.86)	5 (1.84)	0	9 (14.31)	9 (2.00)
Self with married children	0	11 (39.28)	11 (4.04)	0	31 (33.32)	21 (4.70)
Self with unmarried and married children	0	2 (7.14)	2 (.73)	0	5 (23.80)	15 (3.34)
Self with miscellaneous living arrangements	0	4 (14.22)	4 (1.48)	0	5 (7.93)	5 (1.11)
Self and wife	70 (28.69)	0	70 (25.73)	72 (20.1)	0	72 (16.00)
Self and Wife with unmarried children	117 (47.95)	0	117 (43.01)	142 (36.90)	0	142 (31.70)

Self and Wife with married children	34 (13.93)	0	34 (12.50)	80 (20.77)	0	80 (17.85)
Self and Wife with unmarried and married children	16 (6.56)	0	16 (5.89)	77 (20.00)	0	77 (20.00)
Self and Wife with miscellaneous living arrangements	7 (2.87)	0	7 (2.58)	14 (3.63)	0	14 (3.12)
Total	244 (100.00)	18 (100.00)	272 (100.00)	385 (100.00)	63 (100.00)	448 (100.00)

(The percentages are given in Parentheses)

reveals that kinship tie is almost the only basis for two or more members to live together in households, that 66.0 per cent of the households have only one married couple and that only 4.10 per cent of the househod's have two or more married couples (D'Souza, 1968 : 47). In the Bombay study of retired people also, the number of retired people living with unmarried children is more than those living with married children (Desai and Naik, 1973 : 25).

The distribution of the Jabalpur respondents according to the living arrangement and marital status (Table 1.9-B) shows that here also an overwhelming majority, 35.93 per cent of them are leading a married life, and only 14.06 per cent of them are widowers. Coincidently we did not find any unmarried or divorced respondent in our Jabalpur sample also. In Jabalpur the reason for very large proportion of married respondents inspite of their being quite aged may be firstly, the traditional child marriages of girls of lower social strata and secondly, the fact that the life span of women is longer then the men in India. Therefore, we find more widows than the widowers in the society. This finding can be understood by the fact that the percentage of urban aged widowers in the age categories of 60 to 64 years, 65 to 69 years and 70 years and above was 14.0 per cent, 17.5 per cent and 27.9 per cent respectively in 1971 (Bose, 1982 : 5).

As far as the living arrangement is concerned the same table demonstrates that 33.70 per cent of the respondents are staying with unmarried children along with spouses or without spouses. Comparatively a larger section (43.08%) of the respondents are living with married children. The point worth noting here is that only 16.74 per cent of the Jabalpur respondents are living apart from their children either alone or with spouses, if married. The proportion of the respondents living with married children is higher among the widowers (57.14%) than the married respondents (40.77%). A very small percentage of the respondents belong to the households where other relatives are also living with them and no one is living with non-related persons here also. From the findings it is evident that family protection to the aged by the family network is still available. It resembles with the findings of the survey of aged persons in Madras and Bombay as cited by Bose (1982 : 6). Desai and Naik (1973 : 154) have also found the same fact in Bombay city.

While comparing the data about marital status and living arrangement of the Chandigarh and Jabalpur respondents we find that in both the places an overwhelming majority of the respondents are married, although the proportion is little less in the case of Jabalpur due to their occurrance in the higher age groups. About living arrangements of the respondents of both the places we find that in Jabalpur comparatively a small section of the respondents is living with unmarried children. While in Chandigarh 23.16 per cent of the respondents are living with married children, in Jabalpur 43.08 per cent of the sample is living with the married children. In Chandigarh comparatively a larger section of the respondents are living apart from their children either alone or with spouses if married.

This information shows the difference between the living arrangements of the aged people in these two cities. In Chandigarh the number of joint families is less than Jabalpur although the trend has started setting in here also. But still old traditions of protection and service to the old parents by the grown up sons seems to prevail here considerably. Whereas in Chandigarh existence of modern values and norms, affecting the family structure can easily be observed. One more reason may be added to this fact, as shown in the Bombay study of the problem of retired people (Desai and Naik, 1973 : 25), that the children of the economically well off respondents stay apart after their marriage because financially independent parents can afford to stay without them. Most of the Chandigarh respondents are having comfortable financial position whereas most of the Jabalpur respondents are getting a very little amount of money every month. Probably, they are compelled by the circumstances to live with their sons.

Age and the Living Arrangements

Age of the old people is important in determining their living arrangements. The distribution of Chandigarh respondents according to their living arrangements and their age groups (Table 1.10-A) reveals that while larger proportions, i.e. 60.00 per cent and 51.57 per cent of the respondents, falling in both the age groups, i.e. 60 years and below and 61 to 65 years, respectively, are staying with the spouses and unmarried children. Comparatively higher section, i.e. 36.43 per cent, of the respondents aged above 65 years are staying with their spouses only. This information tends to show that once the children become independent and get married they go away from their parents due to various reasons.

The distribution of the Jabalpur respondents according to the living arrangement and the age in Table 1.10-B demonstrates the fact that in all the three age groups relatively larger proportions of old people are living either with the unmarried children or with the spouses only. The reasons for the unmarried children at this age may be that due to illiteracy and ignorance most of the Jabalpur respondents might have produced very many children and even in extreme old age some of the responsibilities such as marriage of the younger children have remained unfulfilled. But at the same time we find that quite a considerable number of those, aged above 65 years is living with the married children also. Shortage of resources and the existence of traditional values both must have contributed towards their living with their sons even after their marriages. Although we do not find a clear trend of family disorganisation in Jabalpur with advancing age but we certainly find as Table 1.10-B also shows, the increasing number of the respondents with the advancing age, living apart from their children. Among the respondents living alone or with spouses, 13, 24 and 48 have fallen in the age groups of 60 years and below, 61 to 65 years and above 65 years respectively. This information shows that once the children become independent and get married they go away from their parents. Most of the characteristics of our Jabalpur respondents resembles with the features of urban poor aged in Delhi (D'Souza, 1982 : 53-61) and the aged of the traditional city of Meerut (Garg et al., 1980 : 6-9).

While comparing the data of Chandigarh and Jabalpur on this issue we find that the number of the aged people of

TABLE 1.10

Distribution of the Respondents of Chandigarh and Jabalpur According to the Living Arrangement and Age

Living Arrangements	(A) Chandigarh Age				(B) Jabalpur Age			
	60 years and below	61 to 65 Years.	Above 65 Years.	Total	60 years and below	61 to 65 Years.	Above 65 Years.	Total
Self	2 (2.86)	0	4 (5.52)	6 (2.20)	2 (4.34)	3 (2.59)	8 (2.79)	13 (2.90)
Self with Unmarried children	1 (1.43)	4 (3.12)	0	5 (1.84)	7 (15.21)	2 (1.72)	0	9 (2.00)
Self with married Children	1 (1.43)	4 (1.35)	6 (8.11)	1 (4.04)	1 (2.17)	7 (6.03)	13 (4.54)	21 (4.69)
Self with Unmarried and Married Children	1 (1.43)	0	1 (1.35)	2 (0.73)	2 (4.34)	10 (8.48)	3 (1.04)	15 (3.34)
Self with Miscellaneous Living Arrangements	0	2 (1.57)	2 (2.76)	4 (1.48)	0	1 (0.87)	4 (1.39)	6 (1.11)
Self and Wife	9 (12.85)	34 (26.57)	27 (36.49)	70 (25.73)	11 (23.91)	21 (18.10)	40 (13.98)	72 (16.10)

Self and Wife with Unmarried Children	42 (60.00)	66 (51.57)	9 (12.18)	117 (43.01)	17 (36.95)	45 (38.89)	80 (27.97)	142 (31.70)
Self and Wife with Married Children	3 (4.28)	15 (11.71)	16 (21.62)	34 (12.50)	2 (4.34)	9 (7.75)	69 (34.12)	80 (17.87)
Self and Wife with Unmarried and Married Children	10 (14.29)	0	6 (8.12)	16 (5.39)	3 (8.51)	16 (13.80)	58 (20.27)	77 (17.19)
Self and Wife with Miscellaneous living Arrangements	1 (1.43)	3 (2.34)	3 (4.05)	7 (2.58)	1 (2.17)	2 (1.72)	11 (3.84)	14 (3.12)
Total	70 (100.00)	128 (100.00)	74 (100.00)	272 (100.00)	46 (100.00)	116 (100.00)	286 (100.00)	448 (100.00)

(The percentages are given in parentheses)

Chandigarh, living in the nuclear families is more than the respondents in Jabalpur. The reason for this may be that Chandigarh being a modern city is more responsive to social changes especially in the context of the changing family structure in the Indian society. But quite a considerable number of the Jabalpur respondents are also living in the nuclear families. This shows that joint families of the traditional society are gradually disappearing and the nuclear families are emerging, especially in urban areas. These findings in the urban setting are not very surprising because even in the rural setting it has been found that very few extended families are in existence these days (Marula Siddaiah, 1966 : 181-183).

While summing up, the main features of the Chandigarh respondents in brief are : most of them belong to the nearby areas of Chandigarh, a substantial number of them are displaced persons from Pakistan, relatively higher proportion of them belong to urban communities, partition of India and lack of various facilities are the main factors behind their decision for not staying in their home communities after retirement, most of them are Hindus, and belong to relatively higher caste groups of this region, have Punjabi as their mother-tongue, are aged upto 65 years, have retired during the last five years before the date of interview, have education above matriculation, have retired from relatively higher grades and gazetted posts of Government services, are financially well off, married and living with spouses and unmarried children. Whereas the main features of the Jabalpur respondents in brief are : Most of them belong to the nearby areas of Jabalpur, a substantial number of them are the old residents of Jabalpur, relatively higher proportion of them belong to rural communities, no bonds with home town, and construction of residential house in Jabalpur during service period, are the main factors behind their decision for not staying in their home communities after retirement, an overwhelming majority of them are Hindus, relatively a higher proportion of them belong to the lower caste group of this region, most of them have Hindi as their mother-tongue, are aged above 65 years, have retired during the last fifteen years before the date of interview, have education below matriculation, have retired from relatively lower grades and non-gazetted posts of Government services, are not financially well off, married and relatively higher proportion of them are living with spouses and unmarried children.

In this way we find that both the groups of respondents of Chandigarh and Jabalpur are quite different in their socio-economic background. On the basis of characteristics of these two groups we can say that while Chandigarh respondents are quite advanced, the Jabalpur respondents are quite backward in various aspects of life. We can also assume that while Chandigarh is a modern city, Jabalpur is passing through the transitional stage between traditionality and modernity. But it is more of a traditional than the modern one, because it shows more symptoms of traditionalism than the modernism.

2

SITUATIONAL FACTORS AND ADJUSTMENT

After considering the characteristics of the respondents of Chandigarh and Jabalpur, now we move on to the analytical task of examining what factors are correlated with good adjustment of both the groups of aged people in the present study. An attempt has been made in this chapter to deal with those factors which indicate the social, financial and physical situation of an aging individual. The study of these factors regarding adjustment in old age seems to be quite significant by considering the fact that the present industrial society does not provide extraneous opportunities to the aged people for the satisfaction of their physical and socio-psychological needs. With the changing attitude of youth towards the aged people and the emergence of the nuclear family system, the aged have to depend on their own resources rather than on group resources. Hence, the situational factors, which determine the resources of an aged individual to satisfy his needs, play an important role in his life. Owing to the increasing importance of achieved rather than ascribed properties in the present society, the factors like socio-economic and health status determine the capability of the old people to lead a satisfying life.

There occurs to be a fairly wide agreement among gerontologists as cited by Streib and Thompson (1957 : 191) that the two situational factors, i.e. socio-economic status and health status, are the basis and very significant variables regarding the adjustment in later years of life.

In this study the most popular and frequently tested situational factors in the studies of adjustment in old age, conducted by the Western gerontologists, have been selected to examine their relationship with the adjustment of the retired people of Chandigarh and Jabalpur. The factors are the educational and pre-retirement occupational background, present financial and health condition of the respondents. Before examining the relationship that exists between various situational factors on the one hand and on the other the level of adjustment of old people of developed and under-developed regions of Indian society, it will be proper to discuss the patterns of adjustment of the respondents of both the groups first.

Patterns of Adjustment

The level of adjustment of the respondents has been measured through the life satisfaction index. The total score of a respondent on the life satisfaction index has been taken as the indicator of his level of adjustment. Based on the five point response categories of the 30 statements, the possible total score an individual can obtain on this index ranges from 30 to 150. This range of score has been equally divided into five categories as 30 to 54, 55 to 78, 79 to 102, 103 to 126 and 127 to 150. Higher score on this index shows the better level of adjustment. All the respondents have been appropriated in these categories indicating their levels of adjustment as very poor, poor, average, good and very good as shown in table 2.1.*

Distribution of the respondents of Chandigarh according to the level of adjustment (Table 2.1-A) shows that 32.72 per cent of the respondents have scored enough to achieve good

* Reichard et al. (1962) have also qualified the five categories of adjustment as very poor, poor, average, good and very good.

TABLE 2.1

Distribution of the Respondents of Chandigarh and Jabalpur According to the Level of Adjustment

(The range of the total score, one can achieve on the adjustment index is 30-150)

Division of the Range of Total Score	(A) Chandigarh Total Number of Respondents	Percentage	Qualification of the Categories	(B) Jabalpur Total Number of Respondents	Percentage	Qualification of the Categories
30-54	45	16.91	Very poor	180	40.17	Very poor
55-78	50	18.38	Poor	77	17.19	Poor
79-102	69	25.37	Average	38	8.49	Average
103-126	89	32.72	Good	63	14.06	Good
127-150	18	6.62	Very good	90	20.09	Very good
Total	272	100.00		448	100.00	

level of adjustment and 25.37 per cent fall into the category of average level of adjustment. Although the percentage of very poorly adjusted respondents is higher than those who have achieved very good level of adjustment, the overall pattern of adjustment of the respondents shows that a large section of them are moderately adjusted. Since the term 'adjustment' is used in gerontology in the context of welfare programmes for the 'Social problem cases' in the older population, it allows the classification of older people according to their good or bad adjustment, into social problem categories. It means that a well-adjusted aged persons does not become socially problematic because he does not require social assistance and vice versa. Considering the distribution of the respondents into various categories of adjustment it can be commented that relatively a larger proportion of the retirees do not need much social assistance for leading a satisfying life. This fact may appear reasonable in view of the special characteristics of the Chandigarh respondents of the present investigation as discussed in Chapter-I.

The distribution of the respondents of Jabalpur in Table 2.1-B reveals that quite a considerable number, i.e. 40.17 per cent, of the respondents are very poorly adjusted whereas only 20.09 per cent of them have come in the category of very good adjustment. As the above table shows the proportion of respondents having poor adjustment is relatively higher than those having good adjustment. The overall pattern of adjustment of the respondents of Jabalpur shows that a large section of them are poorly adjusted. Considering the distribution of the Jabalpur respondents into various categories of adjustment it can be commented that relatively a large proportion of the retirees may be categorized as the socially problematic cases who need social assistance for leading a satisfactory life. This fact may appear reasonable in view of the special characteristics of the Jabalpur respondents as discussed in the last chapter.

While comprising the overall pattern of adjustment of the Chandigarh and Jabalpur respondents we find that while a considerable number of Chandigarh respondents are well adjusted in their life and do not need much social assistance, a majority of the Jabalpur respondents are not being able to adjust themselves in the social situation and need social assistance for leading a satisfactory life in this period. This difference in the state of affairs regarding adjustment between the two groups may easily be understood by keeping in mind the fact that most of the Chandigarh retirees are highly educated, retired from higher posts of services and financially well off, whereas most of the Jabalpur respondents are either illiterate or little educated, retired from lower posts of services and financially in miserable condition.

Educational and Pre-retirement Occupational Background

The educational and pre-retirement occupational backgrounds of the respondents of Chandigarh and Jabalpur have already been discussed in Chapter I. The percentages of the respondents retired from class I, II, III and IV services are 33.82, 30.51, 31.58 and 3.68 in Chandigarh, whereas in Jabalpur they constitute 5.81 per cent, 12.94 per cent, 25.00 per cent and 56.25 per cent respectively. While the retirees in Chandigarh, educated less than matriculation, matriculation, upto graduation or professional diploma and post-graduation or professional degree constitute 3.63 per cent, 31.24 per cent, 35.67 per cent and 29.41 per cent, in Jabalpur the percentage in these categories are 70.33, 10.93, 11.83 and 6.91 respectively. This information clearly indicates that most of the Chandigarh respondents have higher educational and occupational background whereas most of the Jabalpur respondents have lower educational and occupational background.

Regarding the role of education and social status for adjustment in old age, Simpson (1961 : 134) has cited Anderson's statement that education increases an individual's reportoire of skills and interests, with the result that, when he faces a difficult transition period, he has a greater variety of activities to which he can turn to, and, therefore, makes a better adjustment. So, education is functionally significant for the social class and this relationship manifests itself in a higher co-efficient of adjustment for the better educated and socially privileged persons.

For the purpose of examining the association between the

TABLE 2.2

Distribution of the Respondents of Chandigarh and Jabalpur According to the Education and the Level of Adjustment

Level of Adjustment	(A) Chandigarh — Level of Education				(B) Jabalpur — Level of Education				
	Upto Matri-culation	Upto gradua-tion or profesional diploma	Upto Post-gradua-tion or profes-sional degree	Total	Upto 4th class	Upto Matri-culation	Upto gradua-tion or profes-sional diploma	Upto Post-gradua-tion or profes-sional degree	Total
Very poor	30	12	4	46	142	37	1	0	180
Poor	19	22	9	50	44	28	3	2	77
Average	20	27	22	69	7	15	10	6	38
Good	21	30	38	89	10	22	21	10	63
Very good	5	6	7	18	31	28	18	13	90
Total	95	97	80	272	234	130	53	31	448

(r=.37, z=2.35) (r=.67, z=4.18)

level of education and the level of adjustment, educational background of Chandigarh respondents has been divided into three categories as upto matriculation, upto graduation or professional diploma and upto post-graduation or professional degree. These educational categories are hierarchically arranged and cross tabulated with the five hierarchically arranged levels of adjustment. The distribution of the Chandigarh respondents according to their level of educational attainment and the level of adjustment (Table 2.2-A) shows that there is a positive association between education and adjustment. The retirees, who have studied upto post-graduation or have professional degrees are likely to achieve a good level of adjustment, whereas, the retirees having studied upto matriculation are likely to achieve a very poor level of adjustment. When we applied the Gamma test of association and tested the significance of the value of this test, it is found that a moderate positive association exists between these two variables which is statistically significant at .01 level (r=.37 z=2.35).*

Regarding the Jabalpur respondents, to present a clear picture of their educational background, it has been divided into four categories as upto fourth, upto matriculation, upto graduation or professional diploma and upto post-graduation or professional degree. These four educational categories are cross tabulated with five hierarchically arranged level of adjustment. The distribution of the Jabalpur respondents according to their level of educational attainment and the level of adjustment (Table 2.2-B) also very clearly shows that there is a positive association between these two variables, i.e. education and adjustment. The majority of retirees, who have studied upto class fourth, have fallen in the category of very poor adjustment, whereas the retirees who have studied upto graduation or professional degrees are more likely to achieve a good and very good levels of adjustment. On applying the

* The value of 'r' ranging between .1 to .3, between .3 to .4 and above .4 is considered to indicate the weak, moderate and high association between any two variables respectively. The values ranging between 1.92 to 2.33 and above 2.33 are considered statistically significant at .05 and .01 level respectively.

Gamma test of association and testing the significance of the value of Gamma, we find that between these two variables a positive association which is statistically significant at .01 level exists, in the case of Jabalpur (r=.67, z=4.18).

While considering the association between educational attainment and level of adjustment among the Chandigarh and Jabalpur respondents we find that in both the groups positive association which is statistically significant at .01 level, exists between these two variables. This finding resembles with the finding of the study of Ramamurti (1968 : 78). The only difference we find that while in Chandigarh they are moderately associated whereas in Jabalpur they are highly associated in the positive direction. This difference of degree of association may probably be due to the fact that almost all the respondents of Chandigarh are educated upto matriculation atleast, hence we do not find there the groups of respondents having a large gap between their educational qualifications. But in Jabalpur on one end we find a large number of uneducated respondents whereas on the other end quite a few are having graduate or post-graduate degrees with them. Therefore, we find a clear difference of levels of adjustment achieved by the Jabalpur respondents.

Occupational Background

There are four broad occupational prestige classes in the Government services ranging from class I at the top to class IV at the bottom. For examining the association between the pre-retirement occupational status and the level of adjustment the respondents have been divided into three hierarchical categories according to their pre-retirement class of services. The Chandigarh respondents retired from classes I, II and III services have been considered as having high, medium and low pre-retirement occupational status. Owing to the very little number of the retirees from class IV services, they have been kept in the low status category along with the respondents retired from class III services.

The distribution of the Chandigarh respondents according to their pre-retirement occupational status and level of adjustment (Table 2.3-A) reveals that higher the pre-retirement

TABLE 2.3

Distribution of the Respondents of Chandigarh and Jabalpur According to the Pre-Retirement Occupational Status and the Level of Adjustment

Level of Adjustment	(A) Chandigarh Pre-Retirement Occupational Status				(B) Jabalpur Pre-Retirement Occupational Status			
	Low	Medium	High	Total	Low	Medium	High	Total
Very poor	34	9	3	46	147	33	0	180
Poor	28	15	7	50	41	24	12	77
Average	14	23	32	69	20	16	2	38
Good	20	29	40	89	18	14	31	63
Very good	1	7	10	18	16	25	49	90
Total	97	83	92	272	242	112	94	448

(r=.50, z=3.19) (r=.65, z=4.12)

occupational status higher the score on the index of adjustment. While the majority of the respondents having low pre-retirement occupational status are concentrated in the categories of very poor and poor levels of adjustment, most of the retirees having high pre-retirement occupational status have achieved average and good levels of adjustment. On application of the test of association to the two variables, it has been found that a high degree of positive association exists between them which is statistically significant at .01 level ($r=.50$, $z=3.19$).

Regarding the Jabalpur respondents' pre-retirement occupational background, they have also been divided into three hierarchical categories. The Jabalpur respondents retired from class IV, III and II+I services have been considered as having low, medium and high pre-retirement occupational status. Owing to the smaller number of respondents retired from class I services they have been kept in the high status category along with the respondents retired from class II services. The distribution of Jabalpur respondents according to their pre-retirement status and the level of adjustment (Table 2.3-B) also reveals that higher the pre-retirement occupational status, higher the score on the index of adjustment. Here very clearly we find that majority of the respondents having low and high pre-retirement occupational status have achieved low and high levels of adjustment respectively. On application of the test of association to the two variables, it has been again found that a high degree of positive association exists between them which is statistically significant at .01 level ($r=.65$, $z=4.12$).

While looking at the association between these two variables in both the groups of present study, we find that in both the places a high degree of positive association which is statistically significant at .01 level, exist between pre-retirement occupational status and the level of adjustment.

Financial Condition

Financial hardship is the most important and genuine problem among the older people (Tissue, 1972 : 331-344). Because of the great importance of the financial condition after retirement, the retirees have been asked various questions about

TABLE 2.4

Distribution of the Respondents of Chandigarh and Jabalpur According to the Monthly Income and the Source of Income

Monthly Income	(A) Chandigarh Source of Income					
	Pension	Pension and rent	Pension and present occupation	Pension and interest on savings	Miscellaneous	Total
Rs. 400 and below	52 (88.13)	29 (38.67)	28 (40.88)	3 (8.11)	5 (15.62)	117 (43.01)
Rs. 401 to 800	7 (11.87)	37 (49.33)	23 (33.33)	18 (48.65)	14 (43.75)	99 (36.40)
Above Rs. 800	0	9 (12.00)	18 (26.09)	16 (43.24)	13 (40.62)	56 (20.59)
Total	59 (100.00) (21.69)	75 (100.00) (27.58)	69 (100.00) (25.37)	37 (100.00) (13.60)	32 (100.00) (11.76)	272 (100.00) (100.00)

(B) Jabalpur

Monthly Income	Source of Income					
	Pension	Pension and rent	Pension and present occupation	Pension and interest on savings	Miscellaneous	Total
Rs. 400 and below	212 (95.92)	10 (18.51)	66 (70.96)	5 (12.82)	20 (48.78)	313 (89.86)
Rs. 401 to 800	9 (4.8)	35 (64.81)	22 (23.68)	26 (66.66)	16 (34.14)	106 (23.66)
Above Rs. 800	0	9 (16.66)	5 (5.39)	8 (20.52)	7 (17.08)	29 (6.48)
Total	221 (100.00) (49.33)	54 (100.00) (12.05)	93 (100.00) (20.75)	39 (100.00) (8.70)	41 (100,00) (9.18)	448 (100.00) (100.00)

(The percentages are given in parentheses)

their monthly income, sources of income, number of dependents, sufficiency of the income, and their ways of handling the financial situation if their income is less than their required expenditure and so on.

The distribution of the Chandigarh respondents aecording to their monthly income and the sources of income after retirement (Table 2.4-A) bring out some important and interesting facts. Of the retirees 43.01 per cent and 36.40 per cent have a monthly income of Rs. 400 and below and between Rs. 401 and Rs. 800 respectively. The point worth noting is that a little more than one-fifth of the respondents are getting above Rs. 800 a month.

A little more than one-fifth of the retirees have no other source of income then their pension and overwhelming majority of them, i.e. 88.13 per cent, are from the lower income group having a monthly income of Rs. 400 and below. About 27.58 per cent and 25.37 per cent of the pensioners have mentioned house rent and the present occupation as their additional sources of income, respectively. Comparatively a smaller proportion of the pensioners have invested their savings to get interest every month. This table indicates that besides taking up the occupational activity again, rent and the interest on investment are the common sources of income. It appears from the table that the type of additional source of income does not make remarkable difference in the income level of the respondents. From this finding it may be understood that the older people exert to earn extra money only to the extent perhaps where their pressing requirements are met.

The distribution of the Jabalpur respondents according to the monthly income and the sources of income after retirement (Table 2.4-B) show that a great majority, i.e. 69.86 per cent, have a monthly income of Rs. 400 and below and only 6.48 per cent of the Jabalpur respondents are getting above Rs. 800 per month.

The point worth noting about the Jabalpur respondents is that almost half of them, i.e. 49.33 per cent, have no other source of income than their pension and an overwhelming majority of them i.e. 95.92 per cent, are from the lower income group having a monthly income of Rs. 400 and below. Only 12.05 per cent and 20.75 per cent of the pensioners have mentioned house rent and the present occupation as their additional sources of income respectively. While 8.70 per cent of the retirees have invested their saving to get interest every month, 9.15 per cent of them have mentioned that they have got various other sources of income along with the pension. Here also we find that the type of additional source of income does not make remarkable difference in the income level of the respondents.

On comparing this data between Chandigarh and Jabalpur respondents we find that while in Chandigarh a considerable number of the respondents have monthly income of Rs. 400 and below, in Jabalpur, a great majority of the respondents fall in this category.*

In Chandigarh one-fifth proportion of them depending only on their pensions, whereas in Jabalpur almost half of them are not having any other source of income than pension. A considerable number of Chandigarh respondents have mentioned 'rent of the house' as their source of income, but in Jabalpur very few pensioners are in the position to earn money from this source. On the whole this information shows that most of the Chandigarh respondents are in a comfortable financial position, whereas Jabalpur respondents are suffering from financial hardships.

The monthly income alone can not be regarded as an indicator of the retirees' financial condition because the number of dependents also make a difference in the financial situation. A person may have higher income but with a large number of dependents his financial position will be as stringent as a person having lower income with small number of dependents. So, the number of dependents have to be taken into consideration while talking about their financial position.

---

* The difference in the monthly income between the two groups of respondents can be understood more precisely by keeping in mind the purchasing power of a rupee ten years earlier. Even in the same category of income the Chandigarh respondents would have remained more comfortable than the Jabalpur respondents.

The distribution of the Chandigrah pensioners according to their income and the number of dependents (Table 2.5-A) shows that 58.82 per cent of the retirees have only one or two dependents. This fact may be understood by keeping in view that a large number of respondents are married and living with their spouses.

This table reveals that apart from their wives, a considerable number of retired people still have dependent children, quite a few have three to four and some have even five and more dependents. As cited by Bhatia (1968 : 254) in a study pensioners conducted by Bharat Pensioner's Samaj also it was found that near about 56 per cent of the pensioners have student children and family responsibility. The table also shows that the retirees having monthly income of above Rs. 800 have a lesser number of dependents than those having an income of Rs. 400 and below. It indicates that the lower class of people have a larger number of children than higher class of people and hence they are unable to settle their children before retirement. Most of the people who have no dependents are widowers and in the lower income group. They do not make any extra effort to earn more as they do not require it.

When we look at the distribution of the Jabalpur respondents according to their monthly income and the number of dependents (Table 2.5-B), it shows that 34.15 per cent of them have one or two dependents. The point worth noting here is that about one-fifth of the proportion, i.e. 18.08 per cent of the Jabalpur respondents have five and more dependents. This table in the case of Jabalpur also shows that the retirees having a monthly income of above Rs. 800 have a lesser number of dependents than those having an income of Rs. 400 and below. It again indicates that the lower class of people have a larger number of children to whom they cannot settle before their retirement.

While comparing the data on the number of dependents of both the groups of present study we notice some interesting rather surprising differences. In the case of Jabalpur the percentage of the respondents, having no dependents, is higher than the percentage of Chandigarh respondents in this cate-

TABLE 2.5

Distribution of the Respondents of Chandigarh and Jabalpur According to the Monthly Income and the Number of Dependents

Income Group	(A) Chandigarh Number of Dependents					(B) Jabalpur Number of Dependents				
	Nil	1-2	3-4	5 and Above	Total	Nil	1-2	3-4	5 and Above	Total
Rs. 400 and below	16 (76.20)	65 (40.62)	29 (41.43)	7 (33.33)	117 (43.01)	72 (74.22)	102 (66.66)	76 (64.95)	63 (77.78)	313 (69.86)
Rs. 401 to Rs. 800	3 (14.28)	62 (38.76)	94 (34.28)	10 (47.62)	90 (36.39)	15 (15.46)	38 (24.83)	36 (30.77)	17 (20.99)	106 (23.86)
Above Rs. 800	2 (9.52)	33 (20.62)	17 (24.29)	4 (19.05)	56 (20.60)	10 (10.32)	13 (8.53)	5 (4.28)	1 (1.23)	29 (6.48)
Total	21 (100.00) (7.72)	160 (100.00) (58.82)	70 (100.00) (25.74)	21 (100.00) (7.72)	272 (100.00) (100.00)	97 (100.00) (21.65)	153 (100.00) (34.15)	117 (100.00) (26.11)	81 (100.00) (18 08)	448 (100.00) (100.00)

(The percentages are given in parentheses)

gory. Along with the larger number of widowers, the fact that great majority of the Jabalpur respondents of this category have monthly income of Rs. 400 and below, probably explains the above mentioned difference. As we have discussed earlier majority of Jabalpur respondents belong to the lower strata of the society. Normally, it is observed that even during the service period of the husbands the wives of this class of people have to work somewhere, since the husbands' income is not sufficient for meeting expenditure. It is quite possible that quite a few wives of the Jabalpur respondents must be working somewhere even now to add income in the house. Second difference which we find between the two groups is, that the percentage of Jabalpur respondents having one or two dependents is lower than the Chandigarh respondents in this category. This may be firstly due to the higher percentage of the respondents, having five and more dependents and secondly due to the employment of wives, we have discussed above.

Streib and Thompson (1957 : 192-193) have suggested that in the studies of adjustment an individual's own feeling of economic deprivation or own appraisal of the adequacy of his income is more meaningful than his objective income. It is an expression of an individual's values in a given situational context. Therefore, it varies with the individual and situation. As they maintain that the reduction in income after retirement may not mean necessarily an increase in the economic deprivation for all the retirees due to different personal values. Keeping this in mind it is thought desirable to know the respondents' feeling about the adequacy of their income, i.e. whether their monthly income is less, or the same or more than the required expenditure every month. Apart from this, the respondents have also been asked about their ways of handling the situation if their income is less than their expenditure.

The distribution of the Chandigarh respondents according to the adequacy of income and the ways of handling the situation in the case of inadequate income (Table 2.6-A) reveals some important facts. The majority, i.e. 59.19 per cent, of the respondents feel that their monthly income is less than required for expenditure. The point worth noting is that 22.79 per cent

TABLE 2.6

Distribution of the Respondents of Chandigarh and Jabalpur According to Adequacy of the Income and the Ways of Handling the Situation if the Income is Inadequate

(A)
Chandigarh

Adequacy of Income	Ways of Handling the situation if the Income is less than the Expenditure: Withdrawal from Saving	Help from the Son/ Sons	Cutting down the Expenditure	Not Applicable	Total
Income less than expenditure	26 (16.15)	88 (54.66)	47 (29.19)	—	161 (59.19) (100.00)
Income same as expenditure	—	—	—	62 (100.00)	62 (100.00)
Income more than expenditure	—	—	—	49 (100.00)	49 (18.02) (100.00)
Total	26 (9.56)	88 (32.35)	47 (17.28)	111 (40.81)	272 (100.00) (100.00)

(The percentages are given in parentheses)

(B)
Jabalpur

Adequacy of Income	Ways of Handling the Situation If the Income is Less than the Expenditure					
	Withdrawal from Saving	Help from the Son/Sons	Cutting down the Expenditure	Borrowing	Not Applicable	Total
Income less than expenditure	17	80	18	18	0	299 (66.74)
	(5.70)	(26.75)	(63.21)	(4.34)		(100.00)
Income same as expenditure	—	—	—	—	121	121 (27.00)
					(100.00)	(100.00)
Income more than expenditure	—	—	—	—	28	28 (6.26)
					(100.00)	(100.00)
Total	17	80	189	13	149	448 (100.00)
	(3.79)	(17.86)	(42.19)	(2.90)	(33.26)	(100.00)

(The percentages are given in parentheses)

of the retired people feel that their income is more than they require. This table also shows that 54.66 per cent of those who have income less than they require, have to take help from their financially independent sons to meet their expenditure. While 29.19 per cent of them have to cut down their expenditure to manage with less income, 16.15 per cent of them have to withdraw from their savings. The table reveals that but for the 32.35 per cent of the respondents, the rest have to depend on their own resources rather than on group resources. This is a new phenomenon in the modern Indian society.

The distribution of the Jabalpur respondents according to the adequacy of the income and the ways of handling the situation if the income is inadequate (Table 2.6-B) reveals that a great majority of the respondents, i.e. 66.74 per cent, feel that their monthly income is less than required for expenditure. While 27.00 per cent of them feel that their income is sufficient to meet the expenditure, only 6.26 per cent of the Jabalpur respondents' income is more than they require. This table also shows that a great majority, i.e. 62.21 per cent, of those who have income less than they require have to cut down their expenditure to manage with less income. While 26.75 per cent of the respondents having in adequate income get help from their sons, only 5.70 per cent of them have some saving to withdraw money at the time of financial crisis. The data on Jabalpur respondents also demonstrates the fact that the aged person has to depend on his own resources in the present society.

While looking at the information about the adequacy of income and the ways of handling the situation of financial crisis of the Chandigarh and Jabalpur respondents we find both, some expected and unexpected differences. In Chandigarh the percentage of the respondents having income less than the requirement is lower than the Jabalpur respondents coming in this category. In the same way the percentage of those having income more than the requirement is considerably more in Chandigarh than the Jabalpur respondents coming in this category. These differences may reasonably be expected by considering the different socio-economic backgrounds of these two groups of the respondents.

It can reasonably be expected that in the society like Jabalpur having symptoms of traditionalism in it, more old people will get financial help from their grown up sons than in the society like Chandigarh having symptoms of modernism. Contrary to this expectation we find that in Jabalpur quite a smaller number of the respondents, having income less than the requirement, are getting financial help from their sons and majority of them have to cut down their expenditure. Whereas in Chandigarh majority of the respondents having income less than requirement are getting financial help from their sons. This may be so, because of their better socio-economic background, the Chandigarh respondents could afford to provide good education and occupation to their sons and therefore, their sons are in the position to help their old parents financially. Whereas probably most of the Jabalpur respondents, due to the shortage of resources could not provide higher social status to their children, hence their sons are not able to lead comfortable life themselves. And in this situation of deprivation it is not possible for them to help their parents financially even if they want. In this situation as Chowdhry (1981 : 55) has noted they acquire negative attitudes towards the aged people. It is generally observed that with the emergence of modern values and norms and consequently the individualistic and materialistic attitudes of people in the society advancing towards the modernism, a person wants to satisfy all types of his own needs first, and after this, when he has some extra resources left, then he thinks of giving something to others. He does not want to sacrifice his own comforts for the pleasure of others. Since Jabalpur is in the transitional stage between traditionalism and modernism, due to shortage of resources sons are not helping to their parents and although Chandigarh is modern city, but the sons of Chandigarh respondents have plenty of resources, hence they are helping their parents without being suffering from the discomforts themselves.

To examine the association between the monthly income of both the groups of respondents and their adjustment, their monthly income has been divided into five hierarchical categories ranging from Rs. 200 and below to above Rs. 800. These five categories of income have been cross-tabulated with the five levels of adjustment. The distribution of the Chandigarh respondents according to their monthly income and the level of adjustment (Table 2.7-A) reveals that the high degree of positive association exists between these two factors. The majority of the retirees having a monthly income of Rs. 200 and below are very poorly adjusted while a relatively larger proportion of those having a monthly income of above Rs. 800 have achieved a good level of adjustment. The application of the test of association also shows that a statistically significant at .01 level, positive association exists between these two variables, (r,=.52, z=3.97) which shows that higher the income higher the level of adjustment.

The distribution of the Jubalpur respondents in table 2.7-B also reveals that the people having lower income are likely to achieve lower levels of adjustment, whereas the retirees having higher income have achieved higher levels of adjustment. On applying the test of association and testing the statistical significance of the value of it, it was found that a high degree of positive association, which is statistically significant at .01 level exists between the income and adjustment (r=.51, z=3.89). This finding also resembles with the finding of the study of Ramamurti (1968 : 78).

Palmore and Whittington (1973 : 424-425) have expressed the opinion that the per capita income seems to have greater importance than the total income while considering the financial condition of an individual. So for the purpose of knowing the per capita income of the respondents, their monthly income has been divided by the total number of dependents on that income including themselves. The monthly per capita income thus obtained, has been divided into five categories, ranging from Rs. 100 and below to above Rs. 400 and the association of these categories with the various levels of adjustment has been examined (Table 2.8). The association between these two variables has again been found in the positive direction revealing that higher the per capita income higher the score on the adjustment index.

As it can be seen from the table 2.8-A that a relatively higher proportion of the Chandigarh respondents having a per capita monthly income of Rs. 100 and below fall in the cate-

TABLE 2.7

Distribution of the Respondents of Chandigarh and Jabalpur According to the Income and the Level of Adjustment

Level of Adjustment	(A) Chandigarh Monthly Income						(B) Jabalpur Monthly Income					
	Rs. 200- and below	Rs. 201-400	Rs. 401-600	Rs. 601-800	Above Rs. 800	Total	Rs. 200- and below	Rs. 201-400	Rs. 401-600	Rs. 601-800	Above Rs. 800	Total
Vera poor	25	13	5	1	2	46	93	59	20	6	2	180
Poor	8	22	14	4	2	50	5	43	4	4	1	77
Average	11	9	21	9	19	69	10	13	8	3	4	38
Good	4	22	21	16	26	89	17	25	15	3	3	63
Very good	2	1	6	2	7	18	5	23	20	23	19	90
Total	50	67	67	32	56	272	150	163	67	39	29	448

(r=.52, z=3.97) (r=.51, z=3.89)

TABLE 2.8

Distribution of the Respondents of Chandigarh and Jabalpur According to the Per Capita Monthly Income and the Level of Adjustment

Level of Adjustment	(A) Chandigarh Per Capita Monthly Income						(B) Jabalpur Per Capita Monthly Income					
	Rs. 100 and blow	Rs. 101-200	Rs. 201-300	Rs. 301-400	Above Rs. 400	Total	Rs. 100 and below	Rs. 101-200	Rs. 201-300	Rs. 301-400	Above Rs. 400	Total
Very poor	29	13	1	1	9	46	120	50	4	5	1	180
Poor	19	19	8	2	2	50	19	40	12	4	2	77
Average	19	20	15	4	11	69	2	5	20	6	5	38
Good	12	33	17	13	14	89	5	4	31	15	8	63
Very good	1	6	6	1	4	18	7	18	30	20	15	90
Total	80	91	47	21	33	272	143	117	97	50	31	448

(r=.43, z=2.99) (r=.68, z=4.31)

gory of very poor adjustment while a larger section of the retirees with a per capita income of Rs. 400 and above have achieved a good level of adjustment. The value of the test of association (r= .43, z=2.99) also shows that higher degree of positive association, which is statistically significant at .01 level, exists between these two veriables. However, the degree of association with the adjustment is slightly smaller in case of per capita income then in the case of absolute income.

The distribution of the Jabalpur respondents according to the per capita monthly income and the level of adjustment (Table 2.8-B) shows a very high degree of positive association between these two factors. It can be seen in this table that the overwhelming majority of the pensioners having a per capita monthly income of Rs. 100 and below fall in the category of very poor adjustment while a larger section of the retirees with a per capita income of Rs. 400 and above have achieved a very good level of adjustment. The value of the test of association (r=.68, z=4.31) also shows that a very high degree of positive association, which is statistically significant at ·01 level, exists between the Jabalpur respondents per capita monthly income and their level of adjustment. This is probably so, because in the lower income groups, per capita income is more important to satisfy variety of needs, than in higher income groups, where after reaching at certain point, the utility of money starts decreasing. As we have seen, most of our Jabalpur respondents are very poor and they cannot satisfy even their basic needs of family members, hence poorly adjusted.

Because of the significance of the individual's own feelings of economic deprivation or his own appraisal of the adequacy of his income, it is important to examine the association between the felt adequacy of income and adjustment. For this purpose, three categories of respondents having a monthly income less, same or more than their requirements have been cross tabulated within five different levels of adjustment (Table 2.9). Once again the association between the felt adequacy of income and adjustment has come out in the positive direction. A large section of the Chandigarh retirees having less income than their required expenditure are very poorly adjusted, a

TABLE 2.9

Distribution of the Respondents of Chandigarh and Jabalpur According to the Felt Adequacy of Income and the Level of Adjustment

Level of Adjustment	(A) Chandigarh Felt Adequacy of Income				(B) Jabalpur Felt Adequacy of Income			
	Income less than the required expenditure	Income same as the required expenditure	Income more than the required expenditure	Total	Income less than the required expenditure	Income same as the required expenditure	Income more than the required expenditure	Total
Very poor	42	3	1	47	156	24	0	180
Poor	36	11	3	50	55	20	2	77
Average	35	16	18	69	28	7	3	38
Good	41	26	22	89	34	20	9	63
Very Good	7	6	5	18	26	50	14	90
Total	161	62	49	272	299	121	28	448

(r=.44, z=2.64) (r=.61, z=3.87)

larger section of those having income more than their expenditure have achieved a good level of adjustment. A statistically significant at .01 level, positive association of high degree, between these two variables has been shown by the value of the test of association (r=.44, z=2.64). It means that an aged individuals' own feeling about the adequacy of his income is also very important in adjustment.

In the case of Jabalpur respondents the felt adequacy of income and the level of adjustment are found to be more closely related positively. As the table 2.9-B shows that majority of the pensioners having income less than the requirement have achieved very poor level of adjustment whereas those having income more than the required expenditure are likely to achieve very good level of adjustment. On applying the test of association between these two variables it was found that a very high degree of positive association which is statistically significant at .01 level exists between them(r=.61, z=3.87).

It is said that the man never gets satisfied with the income, whatever it may be, and always wants more. Although this statement is true to a large extent but in the case of our Jabalpur respondents we have found that the large number of them are really having very little income which is not sufficient enough to provide them even two square meals every day satisfactorily. Therefore, their feelings about inadequacy of their income has become more effective and contributing regarding their maladjustment. In this way from all the angles financial condition of the Indian aged people has emerged out as to be a basic and very important variable regarding their adjustment.

Health Condition and Age

Apart from wealth, health is also a very important factor in adjustment in old age. It determine the resources of an aged individual to lead a satisfying life. Health may be considered that state of being, existing in the absence of disease, when all the reserve capacities of the organism are at their maximum (Stieglitz, 1957 : 43-62). A sick person cannot lead a harmonious life even if he has plenty of money. Therefore, it is important to examine the relationship between the respondents' health condition and age on one hand and the level of adjustment on the other.

For knowing the health condition of the respondents, information has been collected regarding their perception of their health condition, their physical ailments, the degree of seriousness of their suffering from the ailments and the time spent in bed due to illness during the last one year before the interview.

The distribution of Chandigarh respondents according to the number of ailments and the self-evaluated degree of seriousness of their suffering from the ailments on the whole (Table 2.10-A) shows that 27.68 per cent of the respondents are not suffering from any physical ailments or diseases. A larger section, i.e. 47.43 per cent of the retirees of Chandigarh have only one or two physical ailments. It has been found that 31.25 per cent of them are suffering very mildly and 26.47 per-cent mildly from physical ailments. Comparatively a smaller section, i.e. 11.76 per cent, are suffering seriously and 2.94 per cent are suffering very seriously from physical ailments. This shows that most of our Chandigarh respondents have satisfactory health by considering the lower age groups and nutritious food consumed by Chandigarh respondents this finding seems to be quite reasonable and the expected one.

The distribution of Jabalpur respondents according to the number of ailments and the self-evaluated degree of seriousness of their suffering from the ailments on the whole (Table 2.10-B) shows that 21.65 per cent of the pensioners are not suffering from any physical ailments or diseases. A larger section, i.e. 47.43 per cent, of the retirees have only one or two physical ailments. It has been found that 37.50 per cent of them are suffering very mildly and 27.00 per cent mildly from physical ailments. Comparatively a smaller section, i.e. 9.15 per cent and 4.70 per cent, are suffering seriously and very seriously from physical ailments respectively. This distribution of Jabalpur respondents also shows that majority of them are enjoying satisfactory health. This finding seems to be quite surprising and the unexpected one due to the higher age group, mal-nutritious and insufficient food available to most of the

TABLE 2.10

Distribution of the Respondents of Chandigarh and Jabalpur According to the Number of Ailments and the Degree of Seriousness of the Suffering from Ailments

(A) Chandigarh

Seriousness of Suffering	Number of Ailments					
	Nil	1—2	3—4	5—6	6+	Total
Not applicable	75 (100.00)	—	—	—	--	75 (100.00)
Very mild	—	73 (56.69)	6 (15.00)	0	6 (100.00)	85 (31.25)
Mild	—	25 (19.38)	25 (62.50)	22 (100.00)	0	72 (26.47)
Serious	—	23 (17.83)	9 (22.50)	0	0	32 (11.76)
Very serious	—	8 (6.20)	0	0	0	8 (2.94)
Total	75 (100.00)	129 (100.00)	40 (100.00)	22 (100.00)	6 (100.00)	272 (100.00)

(The percentages are given in parentheses)

(B) Jabalpur

Seriousness of Suffering	Number of Ailments: Nil	1—2	3—4	5—6	6+	Total
Not applicable	97 (100.00)	—	—	—	—	97 (21.65)
Very mild	—	131 (69.28)	20 (20.83)	10 (43.48)	7 (63.63)	168 (37.50)
Mild	—	49 (22.18)	55 (57.29)	13 (56.52)	4 (37.37)	191 (27.00)
Serious	—	21 (9.50)	20 (20.83)	0	0	41 (9.15)
Very serious	—	20 (9.04)	1 (1.04)	0	0	21 (4.70)
Total	97 (100.00)	221 (100.00)	96 (100.00)	23 (100.00)	11 (100.00)	448 (100.00)

(The percentages are given in parentheses)

Jabalpur respondents. Probably, it may be so that due to the hard working life before retirement the Jabalpur respondents specially those retired from class IV services must have developed the resistance power in their bodies to fight against the diseases. Then it is also possible that they may not be taking the ailments associated with the old age seriously.

While comparing the data on the issue of health of both the groups, we find that the number of respondents having no ailments is little less and the number of respondents suffering from the ailments very seriously, is little more in Jabalpur than Chandigarh, which is quite obvious and understandable considering the difference in their age groups and socio-economic status.

This fact is demonstrated by another table showing the distribution of the Chandigarh respondents according to their self-evaluation of health condition and the days spent in bed due to illness during the last one year before the interview (Table 2.11-A). This table reveals that a relatively higher percentage of Chandigarh respondents, i.e. 44.85 per cent, and about one-fifth of the retirees have evaluated their health condition as good and very good, respectively. Only 13.23 per cent and 8.10 per cent of them have felt that their health condition is bad and very bad respectively. When we look at the time spent in bed due to illness, it has again been found that a large section, i.e. 47.05 per cent, of the Chandigarh retirees have spent less than one week in bed and 25.73 per cent have not spent even a single day during the last one year. As cited by Bhatia (1976 : 234) in a study of pensioners conducted by Bharat Pensioner's Samaj also it was found that only 22 per cent of the pensioners were suffering from chronic diseases and infirmity.

The table also reveals an association between the time spent in bed due to illness and the self evaluation of health condition. The respondents, who have spent more time in bed, have reported their health condition as bad or very bad, whereas those who have spent comparatively less time have evaluated their health as good or very good.

While looking at the distribution of the Jabalpur respondents according to self evaluation of health and the time

TABLE 2.11

Distribution of the Respondents of Chandigarh and Jabalpur According to the Self-Evaluation of Health Condition and the Time Spent in Bed due to Illness During the Last One Year

(A) Chandigarh

Self evaluation of Health Condition	Time Spent in Bed due to Illness: Nil	Below one week	1 week to 15 days	15 days to one month	More than 1 month	Total
Very good	20 (28.57)	28 (21.87)	6 (17.64)	0	0	54 (19.85)
Good	38 (54.28)	56 (43.75)	20 (58.82)	6 (27.27)	2 (11.13)	122 (44.85)
Moderate	7 (10.00)	24 (18.75)	5 (14.72)	1 (4.54)	1 (4.54)	38 (13.97)
Bad	2 (2.86)	17 (13.29)	2 (5,88)	10 (45.45)	5 (27.77)	36 (13.23)
Very bad	3 (4.29)	3 (2.34)	1 (2.94)	5 (22.74)	10 (55.55)	22 (8.10)
Total	70 (100.00) (25.74)	128 (100.00) (47.06)	34 (100.00) (12.50)	22 (100.00) (8.10)	18 (100.00) (6.01)	272 (100.00) (100.00)

(The percentages are given in parentheses)

(B) Jabalpur

Self evaluation of Health Condition	Time Spent in Bed due to Illness: Nil	Below one week	1 week to 15 days	15 days to one month	More than 1 month	Total
Very good	50 (45.88)	29 (16.95)	11 (13.41)	0	0	90 (20.09)
Good	35 (32.11)	34 (19.89)	12 (14.63)	6 (12.00)	2 (5.55)	168 (36.50)
Moderate	18 (16.51)	99 (57.89)	40 (48.79)	10 (20.00)	1 (2.79)	89 (19.87)
Bad	5 (4.59)	8 (4.68)	15 (18.30)	29 (58.00)	21 (33.33)	69 (15.40)
Very bad	1 (.91)	1 (.59)	4 (4.87)	5 (10.00)	21 (58.33)	32 (7.14)
Total	109 (100.00)	171 (100.00)	82 (100.00)	50 (100.00)	36 (100.00)	448 (100.00)
	(24.33)	(39.15)	(18.30)	(4.16)	(8.03)	(100.00)

(The percentages are given in parentheses)

spent on bed in illness (Table 2.11-A) we find that a considerable number of them, i.e. 38.16 per cent, have spent below one week on bed due to illness and 24.33 per cent have not spent even a single day. This table also reveals that a considerable proportion of the retirees, i.e. 37.50 per cent and a little more than one-fifth of them have evaluated their health condition as good and very good, respectively. Only 15.40 per cent and 7.14 per cent of them have felt that their health condition is bad and very bad, respectively. Here also we find an association between the time spent in bed due to illness and the self evaluation of health condition. The respondents who have spent more time in bed, have reported their health condition as bad or very bad, whereas those who have spent comparatively less time, have evaluated their health as good or very good.

In this way we find that the health condition of majority of the respondents of Chandigarh and Jabalpur is fairly good, although the percentage of retirees enjoying good health is little less in Jabalpur than the pensioners in Chandigarh.

Now attention can be focussed on the relationship between the health condition and the level of adjustment of the retirees. For evaluating the health condition of the respondents on the whole, a crude index has been prepared on the basis of the respondents' evaluation of their health condition, number of ailments they are suffering from, seriousness of suffering from ailments on the whole and the time spent in bed due to illness. The information on the four items has been divided separately into five categories and scored. The score of each item ranges from one to five indicating from bad to good health condition, respectively so that total score of all the four items adds to 20. The range of total scores that one can achieve, i.e. four to 20, has been divided into three equal parts. Then, the respondents have been divided into three categories as having bad, fair and good health, if their score is between four to nine, ten to 15 and 16 to 20, respectively.

The distribution of the Chandigarh respondents on the basis of their health condition and the level of adjustment (Table 2.12-A) reveals that the majority of the respondents are enjoying good health. It also shows that those having

TABLE 2.12

Distribution of the Respondents of Chandigarh and Jabalpur According to the Health Condition and the Level of Adjustment

Level of Adjustment	(A) Chandigarh Health Condition: Bad Health Condition	Fair Health Condition	Good Health Condition	Total	(B) Jabalpur Health Condition: Bad Health Condition	Fair Health Condition	Good Health Condition	Total
Very poor	15	23	8	46	81	78	21	180
Poor	14	19	17	50	20	47	10	77
Average	11	18	40	69	7	11	20	38
Good	1	23	65	89	5	13	45	63
Very good	2	4	12	18	8	23	59	90
Total	43	87	142	262	121	172	155	448
	(r=.51, z=3.38)				(r=.58, z=3.84)			

good health have achieved a good level of adjustment also, whereas the retirees having bad health have a tendency to be concentrated in the categories of very poor and poor levels of adjustment.

The application of the test of association shows that a higher degree of positive association, which is statistically significant at .01 level, exists between these two variables, (r=.51, z=3.38), showing better the health condition higher the level of adjustment.

These two variables were found to have association among Jabalpur respondents also. The distribution of the Jabalpur respondents according to the health condition and the level of adjustment (Table 2.12-B) shows that a considerable number of them are enjoying good health, whereas relatively a larger number of them are having fair health condition. It also shows that among the Jabalpur pensioners, those having good health, have achieved a very good level of adjustment also, whereas the retirees having bad health, have a tendency to be concentrated in the two categories of very poor levels of adjustment. The application of the test of association shows that a high degree of positive association which is statistically significant at .01 level, exists between the health and adjustment (r=.58, z=3.84), showing better the health higher the level of adjustment. In the case of Jabalpur the value of 'r' is little higher than Chandigarh, though this difference is very little and negligible, hence does not need explanation.

Finally, it is important to examine the relationship that exists between the chronological age and the level of adjustment of the respondents. To some extent the resources of an individual are determined by his age itself and normally it is observed that the resources for satisfying the various needs decrease with advancing age. For this purpose, all the respondents have been divided into three age groups as 60 years and below, between 61 and 65 years and above 65 years. The distribution of the Chandigarh respondents into these categories (Table 2.13-A) shows that most of the respondents are aged 65 years and below.

These categories have been cross tabulated with the different levels of adjustment to find out whether these two variables

TABLE 2.13

Distribution of the Respondents of Chandigarh and Jabalpur According to the Age Group and the Level of Adjustment

Level of Adjustment	(A) Chandigarh Age Group				(B) Jabalpur Age Group			
	60 Years and below	61 to 65 Years	Above 65 Years	Total	60 Years and below	61 to 65 Years	Above 65 Years	Total
Very poor	11	20	15	46	5	34	141	180
Poor	11	21	18	50	3	20	54	77
Average	22	31	16	69	7	16	15	38
Good	19	51	19	89	14	19	30	63
Very good	7	5	6	18	17	27	46	90
Total	70	128	74	272	46	116	286	448

(r=.12, z=—.82) (r=—.39, z=2.47)

have inverse relationship. Table 3.13-A reveals some interesting rather surprising facts about Chandigarh sample. A larger proportion of the Chandigarh respondents aged 60 years and below have achieved the average level of adjustment whereas a larger section coming in the range of 61-65 years of age fall in the category of good level of adjustment. When we look at the respondents aged above 65 years according to their level of adjustment it has been found that more or less the same number of retirees have attained the poor as well as the good level of adjustment.

When we applied the test of association to these variables it has been found that age has no significant negative association with the adjustment in old age (r=.12, z=−.82). This finding indicates that health condition is more important and not the age itself for successful adjustment in old age.

But when we look at the distribution of the Jabalpur respondents according to the age groups and the level of adjustment (Table 2.13-B) we find that a larger proportion of the respondents aged above 65 years have achieved a very poor level of adjustment whereas relatively higher proportions of those aged below 60 years have achieved good and very good levels of adjustment. In the middle category of age we do not find a marked difference between poor and good level of adjustment.

On applying the test of association to these two variables it was found that in the case of Jabalpur age has statistically significant moderate negative association with the adjustment in old age (r=—.39, z=2.47), showing higher the age lower the level of adjustment.

On comparing the data on age and adjustment in old age, we find that while in Chandigarh age has no significant negative association with the adjustment of the respondents, in Jabalpur this association exists between these two variables. This difference in the state of affairs can easily be understood by keeping in mind the fact that Chandigarh respondents are comparatively younger than the Jabalpur respondents. This characteristic of the two groups of samples has already been discussed in Chapter I, which shows that quite a few Jabalpur respondents have crossed 70 years of age. Upto a certain age probably advancement in age does not really results in the noticeable deterioration of physical and mental facultics. As it is observed it is only after the age of 70 years one feels that he has become old and week to carry out the activities of middle age. This realization of old age comes later in the life of people of advanced and developed societies than in the life of members of poor and backward societies due to pre-mature aging as consequence of malnutrition and insufficient food on one hand and the hard work on the other.

In this way our data about the situational factors and adjustment in old age shows that education, pre-retirement occupational status, financial condition and health condition, all are positively associated with the adjustment in old age in both the groups. The chronological age itself has no significant negative association with this variable in the case of relatively younger group of Chandigarh respondents whereas it has significant negative association with adjustment of the comparatively older respondents of Jabalpur. The findings thus point towards the great importance of situational factors which determine the resources of an aged individual to satisfy his various needs by himself. From these findings we may conclude if a retired person is more resourceful he is likely to face less problems and hence it is easier for him to achieve a higher level of adjustment even in the developing section of Indian society like Jabalpur. It may also be pointed out that the findings about the association between the situational factors like socio-economic status and the health condition of the aged on the one hand and the adjustment on the other resemble the findings of most of the other similar studies conducted in the Western countries. This shows that with the advancing industrialization of Indian society the value of achieved properties like education, occupational status and income is also increasing more and the ascribed properties like age or seniority are losing their importance, which is very much unlike in the pre-industrial society. Therefore, the retired people from the upper strata of society with achieved properties are more likely to lead a harmonious and satisfying life in old age than those from the lower strata.

We are in the position now to comment that the social problem of old age has started emerging even in the developing regions, rather more severely there, producing a large number of the aged, needing social assistance to solve their problems.

3

ATTITUDINAL FACTORS AND ADJUSTMENT

In this chapter we will deal with the attitudes of the aged people towards various factors such as various social changes, non-interference in the personal affairs of the grown-up children and popular religious beliefs. The attitudes of the aged persons towards the changing social conditions in which they are placed, are very significant for their adjustment in this period of life. The Indian society is advancing towards modernization and passing through a transitional period at present. Changes in the social values and norms are causing the gradual transformation of social structure and are creating various problems for the senior members of society. The aging becomes more troublesome in a changing society because it becomes difficult for the aged people to depart from the traditional values and norms of the pre-industrial society and to adopt modern values and norms of the industrial society. But the changes in the functions of society as well as in the social structure keep on taking place and the old people have to change their traditional attitudes and develop positive attitudes towards these changes for leading a satisfying life. It is generally observed that the aged people, less resistant to the social changes approve the activities of the young people and do not have many complaints against their modern attitudes. So there are less conflicts between the two generations. The parents having non-interfering attitudes do not impose their own desires and decisions on their grown-up children and allow them to manage their own affairs independently. As Chowdhry (1981 : 54) has also noted the younger generation specially the married sons and daughter-in-laws do not like interference by the parents. Therefore, the non-interfering parents get more respect and affection from the younger generation than the conservative ones.

The religious beliefs may also play an important role in better adjustment in old age. Religiosity in terms cf belief in life after death gives a sense of 'ongoingness' and as Sharma and Jain (1969 : 113) have found, makes the old people less afraid of impending death. It releases them from the tension and worries of worldly affairs and gives mental peace and satisfaction. Moreover, it provides various activities to pass their leisure time, which becomes a problem in old age. Religiosity seems to have a special significance for adjustment in old age in view of the fact that the present society does not give important roles and opportunities of social participation to its senior-members. In this situation the aged people can divert their attention from the worldly matters to spiritual matters and draw some satisfaction and happiness from their religious activities.

Considering all this it is thought useful to find out the relationship that exists between the attitudes towards various social changes, non-interference in the personal affairs of the grown-up children and religious beliefs on the one hand and the level of adjustment on the other.

Attitudes towards Social Changes

Social change refers to the modification which occurs in the life patterns of people caused by a multitude of factors, either internal or external, in character (Koeing, 1963 : 279). Some small studies on the Indian aged people (Jagjit Singh, 1962 : 45-51; Indra, 1963 : 62-68 ; Gurusheran Kaur, 1964 : 66-71 ; Narang, 1968 : 90-98) have shown that the majority of the aged people are quite resistant to social changes. In the present study to find out the respondents' attitudes towards the social changes they have been asked whether they have favourable, indifferent or unfavourable attitudes towards the nuclear family system, inter-caste and inter-community marriages, abolition of the Pardah system (veiling of women), provision of equal rights to women, widow remarriage and divorce.

The distribution of the Chandigarh respondents according to their attitudes towards the nuclear family system and inter-caste or inter-community marriages (Table 3.1-A) shows that the majority, i.e. 63.40 per cent, of the retired people do not favour the emerging nuclear family system. Only 27.95 per cent favour the breaking up of the joint families in the present society.

As far as the inter-caste or inter-community marriages are concerned, more or less the same proportion, i.e. 43.75 per cent and 46.32 per cent, have shown unfavourable and favourable attitudes, respectively. This table indicates that quite a few of the Chandigarh respondents want the abolition of the caste system but they do not like the change in the joint family system, which gives financial and physical security to them. This shows that even the educated class of the society is in favour of joint family system. The table also shows the trend of a positive association between these two variables. The larger proportions of those having unfavourable and favourable attitudes towards the nuclear family system, are having unfavourable and favourable attitudes towards the abolition of the caste system also.

The distribution of the Jabalpur respondents according to their attitudes towards the nuclear family system and inter-caste or inter-community marriages (Table 3.1-B) also shows that a great majority, i.e. 66.74 per cent, of them do not favour the breaking up of the joint family system in Indian society. Only 24.33 per cent of the Jabalpur respondents favour the emerging nuclear family system. Regarding the inter-caste or inter-community marriages we find that 71.65 per cent of the Jabalpur respondents are having unfavourable attitudes and only 20.10 per cent of them have shown favourable attitudes towards this trend in the present society.

TABLE 3.1

Distribution of the Respondents of Chandigarh and Jabalpur According to the Attitudes Towards Nuclear Family System and Inter-Caste or Inter-Community Marriages

Attitude towards Inter-caste, and Inter-community Marriages	(A) Chandigarh Attitude towards Nuclear Family System				(B) Jabalpur Attitude towards Nuclear Family System			
	Unfavourable	Indifferent	Favourable	Total	Unfavourable	Indifferent	Favourable	Total
Unfavourable	86 (49.71)	6 (26.09)	27 (35.53)	119 (43.75)	281 (93.98)	19 (47.50)	21 (19.26)	321 (71.25)
Indifferent	16 (9.25)	4 (17.39)	7 (9.21)	27 (9.93)	10 (3.34)	12 (30.00)	15 (13.76)	37 (8.25)
Favourable	71 (41.04)	13 (56 52)	42 (55.26)	126 (46.32)	8 (2.68)	9 (22.50)	73 (66.98)	90 (20.10)
Total	173 (100.00) (63.60)	23 (100.00) (8.45)	76 (100.00) (27.95)	272 (100.00) (100.00)	299 (100.00) (66.74)	40 (100.00) (8.93)	109 (100.00) (24.33)	448 (100.00)

(The percentages are given in parentheses)

Among the Jabalpur respondents also these two variables have appeared to be positively associated. An overwhelming majority of those having unfavourable and favourable attitudes towards nuclear family system are having unfavourable and favourable attitudes towards the abolition of the caste system also.

While comparing the data on these two variables between Chandigarh and Jabalpur respondents we find that more or less same proportion of both these groups are not in favour of nuclear family system. But regarding the inter-caste marriages we find that quite a few of the Chandigarh respondents are quite liberal in this respect, whereas a great majority of Jabalpur respondents do not favour it. It shows that caste system is strictly followed in Jabalpur than in Chandigarh which can easily be observed in these two places. This difference of attitudes towards caste system easily be understood by considering the rural background of Jabalpur respondents and backwardness of this region of the country where Jabalpur is located.

This distribution of the Chandigarh respondents according to their attitudes towards the abolition of the Purdah system and provision of equal rights to women (Table 3.2-A) shows that the majority, i.e. 68.01 per cent, of the respondents are in favour of the abolition of the purdah system while 79.41 per cent favour equal rights to women. The cross tabulation of both these factors does not show a clear trend of positive association between them. The great majority, i.e. 72.60 per cent, of those having an unfavourable attitude towards the abolition of the purdah system have a favourable attitude towards equal rights to women. It shows that some people want that women should pay respect to their elders by covering their heads, although they do not mind their going out for education or occupation. But in the case of those having a favourable attitude towards the abolition of the purdah system, the majority have a favourable attitude towards equal rights to women also. On the whole most of the Chandigarh respondents feel that women should be given status, equal to men, which is a new phenomenon in the present society.

The distribution of Jabalpur respondents according to the

TABLE 3.2

Distribution of the Respondents of Chandigarh and Jabalpur According to Attitudes Towards the Abolition of Purdah System and the Provision of Equal Right to Women

Attitudes towards the provision of Equal Rights to Women	(A) Chandigarh Attitudes Towards the Abolition of Purdah System				(B) Jabalpur Attitudes Towards the Abolition of Purdah System			
	Unfavourable	Indifferent	Favourable	Total	Unfavourable	Indifferent	Favourable	Total
Unfavourable	9 (12.33)	2 (14.28)	16 (8.65)	27 (9.93)	88 (88.89)	5 (16.66)	64 (20.06)	1 57 (35.06)
Indifferent	11 (15.07)	6 (42.86)	12 (6.49)	29 (10.66)	6 (6.06)	21 (70.00)	13 (4.07)	40 (8.92)
Favourable	53 (72.60)	6 (42.86)	157 (84.86)	226 (79.41)	5 (5.05)	4 (13.24)	242 (75.86)	251 (56.08)
Total	73 (100.00) (26.84)	14 (100.00) (5.15)	185 (100.00) (68.01)	272 (100.00) (100.00)	99 (100.00)	30 (100.00)	319 (100.00)	448 (100.00)

(The percentages are given in parentheses)

attitudes towards abolition of purdah system and provision of equal rights to women shows that the majority, i.e. 71.20 per cent of them are in favour of abolition of purdah system while relatively smaller proportion, i.e. 56.02 per cent, want that equal status should be given to women. The table shows that quite a few Jabalpur respondents do not want any disturbance in the traditional pattern of the division of duties and rights between male and female members. This fact can easily be explained by the rural background and the low socio-economic status of the Jabalpur respondents. The cross tabulation of both these factors shows a clear trend of positive association between them. The overwhelming majority, i.e. 88.89 per cent of those, having an unfavourable attitude towards the abolition of purdah system have a unfavourable attitude towards equal rights to women. And in the case of those, having favourable attitude towards the abolition of purdah system, a great majority, i.e. 75.86 per cent, of them have unfavourable attitude towards equal rights to women also.

While comparing the data on these issues between both the groups of sample we find that majority of both the groups favour upliftment of the status of women in the society although the proportion of Jabalpur respondents favouring equal rights to women is relatively smaller than Chandigarh, which can be understood by keeping in mind the social characteristics of both these groups.

The distribution of the Chandigarh respondents according to their attitudes towards widow remarriage and divorce (Table 3.3-A) reveals that the majority, i.e 76.47 per cent, are in favour of widow remarriage. In the case of divorce also 61.40 per cent have favourable attitude: The cross tabulation of both the variables shows a clear trend of positive association between them. About 30.70 per cent of those having an unfavourable attitude towards widow remarriage have an unfavourable attitude towards divorce and 75.00 per cent, having a positive attitude towards widow remarriage, have a positive attitude towards divorce also.

The distribution of Jabalpur respondents according to the

TABLE 3.3

Distribution of the Respondents of Chandigarh and Jabalpur According to the Attitude Towards the Widow Remarriage and Divorce

Attitude Towards Divorce	(A) Chandigarh Attitude Towards Widow Remarriage				(B) Jabalpur Attitude Towards Widow Remarriage			
	Unfavourable	Indifferent	Favourable	Total	Unfavourable	Indifferent	Favourable	Total
Unfavourable	30 (90.70)	6 (28.57)	11 (5.29)	56 (20.59)	189 (93.10)	6 (25.00)	122 (55.20)	317 (70.75)
Indifferent	1 (2.32)	7 (33.33)	41 (19.71)	49 (18.01)	8 (3.94)	13 (54.16)	9 (4.07)	30 (6.69)
Favourable	3 (6.98)	8 (38.10)	156 (75.00)	167 (61.40)	6 (2.96)	5 (20.84)	90 (40.22)	101 (23.56)
Total	43 (100.00)	21 (100.00)	208 (100.00)	272 (100.00)	203 (100.00)	24 (100.00)	221 (100.00)	448 (100.00)
	(15.81)	(7.72)	(76.47)	(100.00)	(45.31)	(5.35)	(49.34)	(100.00)

(The percen.ages are given in parentheses)

attitudes towards the widow remarriage and divorce (Table 3.3-B) reveals that the great majority, i.e. 70.75 per cent, of them do not favour divorce. Regarding the widow remarriage we find that more or less same proportion, i.e. 49.34 per cent and 45.31 per cent, of them having favourable and unfavourable attitudes. Cross tabulation of both the variables among Jabalpur respondents does not show a very clear trend of positive association between them. The majority, i.e. 55.20 per cent, of those having favourable attitude towards widow remarriage have unfavourable attitudes towards divorce. But in the case of those having unfavourable attitude towards widow remarriage, an overwhelming majority, i.e. 93.10 per cent, have unfavourable attitude towards divorce also.

While comparing the data on these issues between the two groups of our respondents we find that most of the Chandigarh respondents are in favour of widow remarriage and divorce, whereas a great majority of Jabalpur respondents are not in favour of divorce and almost half of them do not like the widow remarriages also. This difference in attitudes of Chandigarh and Jabalpur respondents may reasonably be expected due to the fact that the former group has urban background and higher socio-economic status whereas the latter group has rural background and the lower-socio-economic status.

On the whole, the information about the respondents attitudes towards various social changes shows that except the nuclear family system, most of the Chandigarh respondents are in favour of the abolition of the caste system and purdah system, equal rights to women, widow remarriage and divorce, whereas most of the Jabalpur respondents are not in favour of nuclear family system and divorce specifically and the percentage of those having favourable attitudes towards other social changes is also smaller than Chandigarh. The simple reason for the difference is that the most of the Chandigarh respondents are educated above matriculation. Education develops better reasoning power and logical thinking, broadens the outlook and makes the individual modern. It becomes easier for the educated people to adopt the modern values and norms. A considerable proportion of Jabalpur respondents as we have seen earlier are illiterate and a large number of them have studied upto 4th class only, hence the traditional attitudes may obviously be expected from them towards social changes.

Now we will examine whether the overall type of attitudes towards the social changes has any association with adjustment in old age. For the purpose of finding out the over all type of attitudes towards the social changes, information regarding the respondents attitudes towards six social changes, i.e. nuclear family system, inter-caste marriages, abolition of the purdah system, provision of equal rights to women, widow remarriage and divorce has been scored. The respondents having unfavourable, indifferent and favourable attitudes towards each change have been given one, two and three scores respectively. The range of total scores one can obtain on this index, that is six to 18, has been divided into three equal parts The respondents achieving six to 10, 14 to 11 and 15 to 18 scores have been considered as having negative, neutral and positive attitudes towards social changes respectively.

The distribution of the Chandigarh respondents according to the overall type of attitudes towards social changes and the level of adjustment (Table 3.4-A) shows that a smaller proportion of them negative attitudes and more or less equal proportion have neutral and positive attitudes. The cross tabulation of these categories with the five levels of adjustment reveals a positive association between these two variables. The majority of those having negative attitudes towards the social changes are poorly adjusted while a larger proportion of those having positive attitudes have achieved a good level of adjustment. When we applied the test of association between these two variables it has been found that a high degree of positive association, which is statistically significant at .01 level, exists between them (r=.41, z=2.63).

The distribution of the Jabalpur respondents according to the overall type of attitudes towards social changes and the level of adjustment (Table 3.4-B) shows that majority of the Jabalpur respondents have negative attitudes, a considerable proportion has neutral attitudes and comparatively small proportion of them have positive attitudes towards the social changes. The

TABLE 3.4

Distribution of Respondents of Chandigarh and Jabalpur According to the Overall Type of Attitudes Towards Social Changes and the Level of Adjustment

Level of Adjustment	(A) Chandigarh Overall Type of Attitudes Towards Social Changes				(B) Jabalpur Overall Type of Attitudes Towards Social Changes			
	Nagative	Neutral	Positive	Total	Nagative	Neutral	Positive	Total
Very poor	30	12	4	46	172	6	2	180
Poor	9	19	22	50	61	9	7	77
Average	7	29	33	69	18	15	5	38
Good	10	36	43	89	25	20	18	63
Very good	0	8	10	18	13	47	30	90
Total	56	104	112	272	289	97	62	448

(r=.41, z=2.63) (r=.77, z=4.88)

cross tabulation of these categories with the five levels of adjustment reveals a very high positive association between these two variables. The great majority of those having negative attitudes towards social changes have achieved a very poor level of adjustment, whereas majority of those having positive attitudes towards social changes, are more likely to achieve very good level of adjustment. On application of the test of association between these two variables it has been found that a very high degree of positive association, which is statistically significant at .01 level, exists between them ($r=.77$, $z=4.88$).

The reason for relatively a higher degree of association in the case of Jabalpur than Chandigarh may be that a very large number of respondents are having negative attitudes towards social changes.

Attitudes Towards the Non-interference in the Personal Affairs of the Grown-up Children

In this respect the respondents' opinions have been asked about the proper degree of parents non-interference in the personal affairs of the grown-up children. They have been asked what should the grown-up children do while taking important decisions ? Whether they should take the parents' permission, take the parents' advice or inform the parents about the decision ? They have also been asked what should the grown-up children do while going out in the evening. Whether they should take the parents' permission, inform the parents before going out or they may go without informing the parents ?

The distribution of the Chandigarh respondents according to their response to these two questions (Table 3.5-A) reveals some interesting facts. Regarding the important decision, relatively a higher proportion, i.e. 38.60 percent, of the respondents think that the grown-up children should manage their own affairs. Only 28.31 per cent feel that the parents' permission should be taken by the children before taking any important decision. But as far as their going out in the evening is concerned, 51.10 per cent of the Chandigarh respondents feel that the children should inform the parents before going out, while a smaller section has mentioned that the parents'

TABLE 3.5

Distribution of the Respondents of Chandigarh and Jabalpur According to the Attitudes Towards the Duties of Grown-up Children While taking Important Decision and While Going Out in the Evening

Attitude Towards the Children's Duty While Going Out in the Evening	(A) Chandigarh Attitude Towards the Grown-up Children's Duty While Taking Important Decision				(B) Jabalpur Attitude Towards the Grown-up Children's Duty While Taking Important Decision			
	They should take parents permission	They should take parents advice	They should manage their own affairs	Total	They should take parents permission	They should take parents advice	They should mange their own affairs	Total
They should take Parents permission	53 (68.83)	4 (4.44)	7 (6.67)	64 (23.53)	95 (37.84)	24 (16.78)	6 (11.11)	125 (27.90)
They should inform the parents	21 (27.27)	72 (80.00)	46 (43.81)	139 (51.10)	148 (58.96)	06 (74.12)	19 (35.19)	273 (60.93)
They may go without informing the parents	3 (3.90)	14 (16.56)	52 (49.52)	69 (25.37)	8 (3.20)	13 (9.10)	29 (53.70)	50 (11.17)
Total	77 (100.00) (28.30)	90 (100.00) (33.08)	105 (100.00) (38.60)	272 (100.00) (100.00)	251 (100.00) (56.02)	143 (100.00) (31.91)	54 (100.00) (12.05)	448 (100.00) (100.00)

(The percentages are given in parentheses)

permission should be taken before going out. The cross tabulation of both the factors shows the trend of a positive association between them. The majority, i.e. 68.83 per cent, of those who think that the parents' permission should be taken by the children before taking any important decision, feel that the children should take parents' permission before going out in the evening. In the same way, relatively a higher proportion, i.e. 49.52 per cent, of these who think that the grown-up children should manage their own affairs, feel that the children may go out without informing the parents.

The determination of the Jabalpur respondents according to the attitudes towards the duties of grown-up children while taking important decision and while going out in the evening (Table 3.5-B) shows that regarding the important decision, i.e. 56.02 per cent, of them think that the grown-up children should take the parents' permission before taking any important decision. Only 12.05 per cent feel that the grown-up children should manage their own affairs. But as far as their going out in the evening is concerned, 60.93 per cent, of the Jabalpur respondents feel that the children should inform the parents before going out, while a smaller section has mentioned that the children should take the parents' permission before going out.

The cross tabulation of both the factors does not show a clear trend of a positive association between them. The majority, i.e. 58.96 per cent, of those who think that the parents' permission should be taken before taking any important decision, feel that the children should inform the parents before going out in the evening. But majority i.e, 53.70 per cent, of those who think that the grown-up children should manage their own affairs, feel that the children go out in the evening without informing the parents.

While comparing the data on these issues between the two groups of respondents, we find that the Chandigarh respondents are more liberal and have non-interfering attitudes regarding the personal affair of the grown-up children than the Jabalpur respondents. The reason for this difference simply is, the advancement and backwardness of these regions of country respectively. Due to the difference in educational background also most of the Chandigarh respondents are having modern outlook and the Jabalpur respondents are having traditional outlook regarding the affairs of younger generation.

Then the respondents have been asked whether the parents should go out with their grown-up children for entertainment, most of the time, sometimes or rarely. They have also been asked whether they should sit in the drawing-room with the friends of their grown-up children most of the time, sometimes or rarely?

The distribution of the Chandigarh respondents according to their response to both these questions (Table 3.6-A,) reveals that a considerable proportion, i.e. 44.48 per cent and majority i.e. 51.11 per cent, of the respondents think that the parents should rarely go out for entertainment with their grown-up children and should rarely sit in the drawing room with the friends of the children, respectively. The cross tabulation of both the variables shows a very clear positive association between them. An overwhelming majority, i.e. 84.44 per cent, of those who think that the parents should go out with their grown-up children for entertainment most of the time, think that parents should sit most of the time in the drawing-room with the friends of the grown-up children. In the same way 72.16 per cent of those, saying that the parents should rarely go out with the children for entertainment, also feel they should rarely sit in the drawing-room with the friends of the children.

The distribution of the Jabalpur respondents according to their response about the duties of parents about going out for entertainment with grown-up children, and sitting in the drawing-room with children's friends (Table 3.6-B) shows that the majority, i.e. 55.80 per cent and a considerable proportion i,e. 43.75 per cent, of the Jabalpur respondents think that the parents should sometimes go out for entertainment with their grown-up children and should sit in the drawing-room with the friends of the grown-up children. The cross tabulation of both the variables shows a very clear trend of positive association between them among Jabalpur respondents also. The great majority, i.e. 75.70 per cent, of those who think that the parents should go out most of the time with their

TABLE 3.6

Distribution of Respondents of Chandigarh and Jabalpur According to the Attitudes Towards the Duties of Parents about Going for Entertainment with Grown-up Children and Sitting in the Drawing-room with Children's Friends

Attitude Towards Sitting in the Drawing-room with the Friends of Grow-up Children	(A) Chandigarh Attitude Towards Going-out with Grown-up Children for Entertainment				(B) Jabalpur Attitudes Towards Going-out with Grown-up Children for Entertainment			
	Most of the time	Some-times	Rarely	Total	Most of the time	Some-times	Rarely	Total
Most of time	38 (84.44)	13 (14.89)	13 (9.28)	64 (23.83)	81 (75.70)	65 (25.00)	21 (23.07)	167 (37.27)
Sometimes	3 (6.67)	58 (65.91)	36 (18.56)	87 (31.99)	16 (14.95)	154 (61.60)	26 (28.57)	196 (43.75)
Rarely	4 (8.89)	17 (19.30)	101 (72.16)	122 (44.48)	10 (9.26)	31 (12.40)	44 (28.67)	85 (18.98)
Total	45 (100,00) (16.54)	83 (100.00) (32.35)	140 (100.00) (51.11)	272 (100.00) (100.00)	107 (100.00) (23.88)	250 (100.00) (55.80)	91 (100.00) (70.31)	448 (100.00) (100.00)

(The percentages are given in parentheses)

grown-up children for entertainment, feel that the parents should sit most of the time in the drawing-room among the friends of grown-up children. In the same way larger proportion of those who think that the parents should rarely go out with their grown-up children for the purpose of entertainment, think that their parents should rarely sit in the drawing room with the friends of the grown-up children.

On the whole the data regarding the non-interference issue shows that while a larger proportion of the Chandigarh respondents have liberal and non-interfering attitudes whereas a large proportion of Jabalpur respondents have traditional and interfering attitudes in the personal affairs of the younger generation. This difference in the outlook of two groups of people once again shows the importance of education in adopting the new values and norms of modern society. Since most of the Jabalpur respondents are not very educated, the traditional attitude may reasonably be expected from them.

Now let us examine whether the overall degree of non-interfering attitudes of the retired people has any association with the level of adjustment. To find out the overall degree of non-interfering attitudes, the answers of the respondents to the four questions regarding the duties of the children while taking important decision and going out in the evening, and the parents' duties about going out with the grown-up children for entertainment and sitting among the friends of the children have been scored. The range of the total possible scores, i.e. four to 12, has been divided into three equal parts and the respondents have been divided into three categories, as having low, medium and high degree of non-interfering attitudes. A higher score of an individual on this crude index shows a higher degree of non-interfering attitude.

The distribution of the Chandigarh respondents according to the overall degree of non-interfering attitudes (Table 3.7-A) shows that a larger section of them have got the higher degree of non-interfering attitudes. Only a little more than one-fifth of the retirees have the low degree of non-interfering attitudes. The cross tabulation of these three categories with the five levels of adjustment shows that a positive association exists between these two variables. The majority of the respondents

TABLE 3.7

Distribution of the Respondents of Chandigarh and Jabalpur According to the Overall Degree of Non-interfering Attitudes and the Level of Adjustment

Level of Adjustment	(A) Chandigarh Degree of Non-interfering Atttitude				(B) Jabalpur Degree of Non-interfering Attitude			
	Low	Medium	High	Total	Low	Medium	High	Total
Very poor	21	21	4	45	145	32	3	180
Poor	20	16	14	50	41	25	11	77
Average	12	26	31	69	10	16	12	38
Good	7	26	56	89	14	39	10	63
Very good	4	7	7	18	1	48	41	90
Total	64	96	112	272	211	160	77	448
	(r=.45, z=2.98)				(r=.38, z=2.41)			

having the low degree of non-interfering attitudes have very poor and poor levels of adjustment, whereas the majority of those having the high degree of non-interfering attitudes have achieved average and good levels of adjustment. The application of the test of association also shows that a high degree of positive association, which is statistically significant of .01 level, exists between these two variables showing higher the degree of non-interfering attitudes better the adjustment (r=.45, z=2.98).

The distribution of the Jabalpur respondents according to the overall degree of non-interfering attitudes and the level of adjustment (Table 3.7-B) shows that a larger section of them have got the lower degree of non-interfering attitudes. Relatively a smaller section of the retirees at Jabalpur have high degree of non-interfering attitudes. The cross tabulation of these three categories with the five levels of adjustment shows that a positive association exists between these two variables. A great majority of the respondents having the low degree of non-interfering attitudes have very poor level of adjustment, whereas the majority of those having the high degree of non-interfering attitudes have achieved average and good level of adjustment. The application of the test of association also shows that a moderate degree of positive association, which is statistically significant at .01 level, exists between these two variables (r=.38, z=2.41).

While comparing the value of positive association between non-interfering attitudes and the level of adjustment between the two groups of individuals, we find that while in Chandigarh higher degree of positive association exists, in Jabalpur moderate degree of positive association exists between these two variables. The possible reason for this difference although it is not significant, seems that in the society, having symptoms of traditionalism, the younger generation does not disapprove much the interference by the parents in their affairs. But in the modern society as it is observed, it is disapproved and taken seriously by the younger generation.

Attitudes Towards Religious Beliefs

In this respect the respondents have been asked four

questions to find out how strongly they believe in the existence of gods and goddesses, in the concepts of 'Punya' (grace) and 'Pap' (Sin), 'Karma' (The result of the action of past life) and rebirth, and hell and heaven. The distribution of the Chandigarh respondents according to the strength of their belief in the existence of gods and goddesses and concept of 'Pap' and 'Punya' (Table 3.8-A) reveals very interesting facts. It is normally said that in old age people become more religious-minded. But the data about Chandigarh respondents show that the majority, i.e. 51.84 per cent, of them have only moderate belief in the existence of gods and goddesses. Relatively a larger section, i.e. 45.22 per cent, of the respondents moderately believe in the concept of 'Pap' and 'Punya'. The cross tabulation of both the variables shows clearly that a positive association exists between them. The larger proportions of those having weak, moderate and strong belief in the existence of gods and goddesses respectively, have weak, moderate, and strong belief in the concept of 'Punya' and 'Pap' also.

The distribution of the Jabalpur respondents according to the strength of their belief in the 'Pap' and 'Punya' (Table 3.8-B) reveals that great majority, i.e. 67.20 per cent, of them have strong belief in the existence of gods and goddesses. In the same way 62.50 per cent of the Jabalpur respondents believe strongly in the concept of 'Pap' and 'Punya'. The cross tabulation of both the variables shows clearly that a positive association exists between them. The majority of these having weak, moderate and strong belief in the existence of gods and goddesses, respectively have weak, moderate and strong belief in the concept of 'Punya' and 'Pap' also.

Comparison between the two groups of respondents on the religious belief, concerned with the existence of gods and goddesses and 'Pap' and 'Punya' shows that Jabalpur respondents are more religious minded than the Chandigarh respondents. This difference seems quite obvious and reasonable by considering the difference in socio-economic background and educational levels of these two groups.

In the same way, the information about the strength of belief in the concept of 'Karma' and 'rebirth' and hell and

TABLE 3.8

Distribution of the Respondents of Chandigarh and Jabalpur According to the Strength of Belief in the Existence of Gods and Goddesses and in the Concept of 'Punya' and 'Pap'

Belief in the Concept of 'Pap' and 'Punya'	(A) Chandigarh Belief in the Existence of Gods and Goddesses				(B) Jabalpur Belief in the Existence of Gods and Goddesses			
	Weak	Moderate	Strong	Total	Weak	Moderate	Strong	Total
Weak	21 (95.46)	10 (7.09)	12 (11.01)	43 (15.81)	25 (62.50)	2 (1.87)	2 (.68)	29 (6.47)
Moderate	1 (4.54)	87 (61.70)	35 (32.11)	123 (45.22)	7 (17.50)	97 (90.65)	35 (11.67)	139 (31.02)
Strong	—	44 (31.21)	62 (56.88)	106 (38.97)	8 (20.00)	8 (7.48)	264 (87.70)	280 (62.50)
Total	22 (100.00)	141 (100.00)	109 (100.00)	272 (100.00)	40 (100.00)	107 (100.00)	301 (100.00)	448 (100.00)
	(8.09)	(51.84)	(40.07)	(100.00)	(8.92)	(23.88)	(57.20)	(100.00)

(The percentages are given in parentheses)

heaven (Table 3.9) also demonstrates the same findings. The majority, i.e. 56.62 per cent, of the Chandigarh respondents have only moderate belief in the concept of 'Karma' and rebirth. Comparatively a larger section, i.e. 40.81 per cent, of the respondents believe only moderately in the concept of hell and heaven. The cross tabulation of both the variables shows quite a strong positive association between them. Most of the people having weak, moderate and strong belief in the concept of 'Karma' and rebirth are also having weak, maderate and strong belief in the concept of hell and heaven, respectively.

The distribution of the Jabalpur respondents according to the strength of belief in the concepts of 'Karma' and rebirth, and hell and heaven (Table 3.9-B) reveals that majority, i.e. 66.74 per cent and 64.97 per cent, of them have strong belief in the concepts of 'Karma' and rebirth, and the hell and heaven respectively. Only 9.15 per cent and 8.70 per cent of the Jabalpur respondents have weak belief in these concepts respectively. The cross tabulation of both the variables shows quite a clear trend of high degree of positive association between them. Most of the people having weak, moderate and strong belief in the concept of 'Karma' and rebirth have respectively the weak, moderate and strong belief in the concept of hell and heaven also. It is said that fear of death brings the aged people nearer to religion (Hazan, 1984 : 137) and it seems quite true specially in the case of our Jabalpur respondents since quite a large number of them have strong religious beliefs.

On the whole the data shows that a larger section of the Chandigarh respondents have moderate religious beliefs whereas a larger section of the Jabalpur respondents have strong religious belief. The reason for this difference may be that most of the respondents are quite educated and do not have blind faith in the spiritual sayings. But most of the Jabalpur respondents are very little educated, hence do not apply the reasoning power or any logic to understand the spiritual sayings and blindly believe in them. The attitudes of contentment, peace and tranquillity are values which are deep rooted in Indian society. In Lucknow survey of aged also it was found

TABLE 3.9

Distribution of the Respondents of Chandigarh and Jabalpur According to the Strength of Belief in the Concepts of 'Karma' and Rebirth and Hell and Heaven

Belief in the Concept of Hell and Heaven	(A) Chandigarh Belief in the Concepts of 'Karma' and Rebirth				(B) Jabalpur Belief in the Concepts of 'Karma' and Rebirth			
	Weak	Moderate	Strong	Total	Weak	Moderate	Strong	Total
Weak	23	48	12	83	27	7	5	39
	(95.83)	(31.17)	(12.77)	(30.51)	(65.85)	(6.49)	(1.68)	(8.70)
Moderate	1	106	4	111	6	99	13	118
	(4.17)	(68.83)	(5.13)	(40.81)	(14.63)	(91.66)	(4.34)	(26.35)
Strong	—	—	78	76	8	2	281	291
			(82.10)	(28.68)	(19.52)	(1.85)	(93.98)	(64.97)
Total	24	154	94	272	41	108	299	448
	(100.00)	(100.00)	(100.00)	(100.00)	(100.00)	(100.00)	(100.00)	(100.00)
	(8.82)	(56.62)	(36.65)	(100.00)	(9.15)	(24.10)	(66.74)	(100.00)

(The percentages are given in parentheses)

as cited by Bose (1982 : 17), that overwhelming majority of them have faith in religious prayers.

Now we will examine the relationship between the overall strength of religious beliefs and the level of adjustment. To find out the overall strength of religious beliefs, a crude index has been developed on the basis of the respondents' answer to the four questions regarding the existence of gods and goddesses, the concept of 'Punya' and 'Pap', 'Karma' and rebirth and hell and heaven. All the answers to these questions have been scored. The range of total possible scores, i.e. four to 12, has been divided into three equal parts and the respondents have been divided into three categories as having low, moderate and high strength of religious beliefs.

The distribution of the Chandigarh respondents according to the strength of religious beliefs and the level of adjustment (Table 3.10-A) shows that a comparatively larger section of the respondents are having moderate strength of religious beliefs. The cross tabulation of both these variables does not show any association between them, neither in the positive nor in the negative direction. Quite a few of those having a low strength of religious beliefs have achieved the average level of adjustment. Comparatively, larger proportion of both having moderate as well as high strength of religious beliefs have achieved the good level of adjustment. The value of the test of association between these two variables also shows that no association neither positive nor negative, exists between these variables, showing that both of them are independent of each other (r=.061).

The distribution of the Jabalpur respondents according to the overall strength of religious beliefs and the level of adjustment (Table 3.10-B) reveals that majority of the Jabalpur respondents are having high strength of religious beliefs. But the cross tabulation of both these variables among Jabalpur respondents shows that the strength of religious beliefs and the level of adjustment are moderately associated in the negative direction, showing higher the strength of religious beliefs, lower the level of adjustment. As it can be seen from the table 3.10-B, quite a considerable proportions, of the respondents, having moderate and high strength of religious

TABLE 3.10

Distribution of the Respondents of Chandigarh and Jabalpur According to the Overall Strength of Religious Beliefs and the Level of Adjustment

Level of Adjustment	(A) Chandigarh Overall Strength of Religious Beliefs				(B) Jabalpur Overall Strength of Religious Beliefs			
	Low	Moderate	High	Total	Low	Moderate	High	Total
Very poor	7	26	13	46	5	82	93	180
Poor	11	23	16	50	3	23	51	77
Average	22	30	17	69	7	18	13	38
Good	14	38	37	89	12	23	28	63
Very good	1	9	8	18	15	29	46	90
Total	55	126	91	272	42	175	231	448
	(r=.061)				(r=−.34, z=−2.15)			

beliefs, have achieved very poor level of adjustment, whereas the respondents having law strength of religious beliefs are more likely to fall in the category of good and very good level of adjustment. The value of the test of association between these two variables also shows that a moderate degree of negative association, which is statistically significant at .05 level exists between them (r=—.34. z=—2.15).

The finding shows that religiosity has no role to play regarding the adjustment of the highly educated people in old age, and it plays a negative role regarding the adjustment of the less educated people in old age. Probably the highly educated people do not find the solution to their problems in religion and they draw satisfaction from worldly affairs. Religiosity goes with the traditionalism and it helps the people to withdraw from the worldly affairs. But at the same time all their basic needs specifically, have to be fulfilled appropriately, in which religiosity does not help. Probably the religious minded people have a tendency to depend on others for the satisfaction of their needs, whereas one has to depend upon his own resources for this purpose in today's society. Most of our Jabalpur respondents are facing the problem of poverty and it seems quite ridiculous to think that higher dagree of religiosity will help them to take their economic problem lightly and draw satisfaction of their worldly needs such as hunger from the spiritual thinking and beliefs.

On the whole, the findings about the relationship between the attitudinal factors on the one hand and adjustment on the other show, that while the positive attitudes towards the soeial changes and the parents' non-interference in the affairs of the grown-up-children certainly facilitate better adjustment in later years of life of all sorts of people, religiosity does not play any role in the case of highly educated people and it plays a negative role in the case of less educated people in this respect. Thus the link between religion and aging remains unclear. Our findings on this issue support the statement of Russell (1979 : 265) that older people express a variety of religious beliefs and consider religion an important part of their lives but there is no clear evidence that religion itself contributes to the *psychological* well-being of the aged.

4

BEHAVIOURAL FACTORS AND ADJUSTMENT

An attempt has been made to study those factors in this chapter which are concerned with the behaviour and activities of the retired people. These factors include relationship and interaction with the family members living in the same household and children living separately, with the relatives, with the groups of friends and neighbours and the members of voluntary organisations, involvement in occupational activities, hobbies and religious activities overall activenesss and social interaction.

As it has been discussed earlier, unlike the pre-industrial society, the present industrial society does not offer such roles to the aged people which give them opportunities for remaining occupied in various activities, enjoying higher status in the family and society, social participation and association with various groups of people. On the contrary the 'terminal sick role' is imposed on them mainly through retirement. Moreover, the functions performed by the aged people in the joint families of the pre-industrial society have been transferred to various social institutions on the emergence of the nuclear family system in the present industrial society.

The aged people today are left on their own resources or

capacities to satisfy their socio-psychological needs. Many aged people cannot cope with the situation and become the victims of idleness, loneliness, boredom and frustration. This problem is more acute in India than in other countries, where there is no organised recreation even for the normal population (Chowdhry, 1981 : 54). Hence the study of the factors like relationship and interaction with various groups of people and involvement in various other activities through which the socio-psychological needs can be met, becomes important regarding the adjustment in old age. It is generally observed that the aged people, who keep themselves occupied in various activities and interact with various groups of people, remain satisfied and lead a harmonious life.

Almost in all the studies the relationship of these factors has been examined with the adjustment of the aged people and, except a few, in most of them a positive association has been found between these factors and the level of adjustment. So much so that, as cited by Rosow (1967 : 106), on the basis of these behavioural factors association with adjustment, the gerontologists have tried to develop two opposite theories of successful aging. They are the activity theory and the disengagement theory. While the former one suggests high activity and high interaction, the latter one emphasizes on the desirability of low activity and low interaction for leading a satisfactory life in old age. Although as cited by Russell (1979 : 20), Maddox and Wiley (1976) have noted that systematic theory development has been 'Strikingly absent' in gerontology. About both the theories mentioned above, it is said that they offer an over-simplified view of aging and its effects on the individual. According to the latest thinking on the issue, a development approach is preferable, since it recognises both, stability and change. Individuals want to maintain previous patterns of living but aging places constraints on the ability to maintain continuity. Each individual develops his own style of aging in light of his personal history and current context. As cited by Russell (1979 : 105) some empirical investigations indicate a number of patterns of aging and apparently several ways to age 'successfully'. Rose (1964) as cited by Cheit (1968 : 194), had also concluded that both the theories are inadequate and require modification. Successful aging seems to depend on a large extent on a flexible combination of disengagement and engagement. The limitation of both the theories become even more apparent on their application in primitive or traditional societies, because the two theories have been evolved from the research in industrial socieities. Hence there is a need for a wide ranging and rigorous comparative analysis by keeping in mind the cultural differences.

Considering the immense significance and the difference of opinion among the gerontologists about the desirable type of life style, i.e. 'active' or 'disengaged' and the new developmental approach towards it, it will be useful to find out the type of relationship that exists between these behavioural factors on the one hand and the adjustment on the other. Though direct testing of the theories of successful aging through controlled observation has not been intended here but still it may be found out tentatively that which type of life style is more desirable for better adjustment in later years of life. Apart from this it may also be known to us that what are the other patterns or styles of aging successfully and the aged with what characteristics develop different patterns of adjustment.

Family Relationship

Family is considered to be the most important social unit and it has a special significance for the aged people (Russell : 1979 : 307). Thompson and Streib (1962:905-912) have stated that people live their lives through social relationships and family relationships are among the most important relationships. The most frequent forms of interaction take place in the family and high frequency of interaction in the family is important for the retired people.

After retirement the aged people have to depend on their family members for the satisfaction of various needs. With the advancement of industrialisation and urbanisation the traditional joint families of Indian society are breaking up. Owing to the mobility of children to their places of work and changing attitudes of youngsters towards the aged, the joint families are yielding place to nuclear families. Moreover, in the pre-industrial society it was considered a moral duty of the younger generation to make the elder's life a peaceful one. But in the present society it is often observed, especially in urban areas, that the older people are neglected by the younger ones and left to their own resources for the satisfaction of their needs. Even about the rural Indian society it has been reported by Bose and Saxena (1969 : 33-39) that only 50 per cent of the aged enjoy the status of either the head of the household or the wife of the head of the household. These changes creat many problems for the aged and many of them get overwhelmed by the situation. Hence good relationship with the family members is very important for the adjustment in old age. Before examining the association between the familial relationship and the level of adjustment it will be better to study the living arrangement, types of respondents' relationship and interaction with the family members living with them and with the children living separately.

Living Arrangement and the Type of Family Relationship

With a view to find out the quality of the respondents' relationship with the family members according to their living arrangements, the living arrangements have been classified into five types viz., self only or self and wife, self or self and wife with unmarried childern, self or self and wife with married children, self or self and wife with married and unmarried children and self or self and wife having miscellaneous living arrangements. The types of familial relationship as per the respondents' self-evaluation on an average, have been named as unsatisfactory, satisfactory and very satisfactory.* The living arrangements and the types of familial relationship have been cross-tabulated in Table 4.1. The table reveals firstly that relatively a high percentage (44.85%) of the respondents are

* Although the self-evaluated quality of respondents relationship with the family members, living with them in the same household discussed here and with the children living away, discussed later, cannot be considered behavioural factor but they are considered in this category of factors because they are based to a greater extent on an aging individual's behaviour, activities and interaction with the people of these groups.

TABLE 4.1

Distribution of the Respondents of Chandigarh and Jabalpur According to the Living Arrangement and the Quality of Relationship With the Family Members Living with Them

Quality of Family Relationship	(A) Chandigarh Living Arrangement					
	Self only or Self & Wife	Self only or Self and Wife with unmarried Children	Self only or Self and Wife with Married Children	Self only or Self and wife with unmarried and married Children	Self only or Self and Wife with Miscellaneous living arrangements	Total
Unsatisfactory	9 (11.84)	28 (22.95)	23 (51.11)	6 (33.33)	4 (36.36)	70 (25.73)
Satisfactory	50 (65.79)	32 (67.21)	18 (40.00)	11 (61.11)	7 (64.64)	168 (61.76)
Very satisfactory	11 (14.48)	12 (2.84)	4 (8.89)	1 (5.56)	—	28 (10.29)
Not applicable	6* (7.89)	—	—	—	—	6* (2.20)
Total	76 (100.00) (27.94)	122 (100.00) (44.86)	45 (100.00) (16.54)	18 (100.00) (6.61)	11 (100.00) (4.06)	272 (100.00) (100.00)

(B) Jabalpur

Quality of Family Relationship	Living Arrangement					
	Self only or Self & Wife	Self only or Self and Wife with Unmarried Children	Self only or Self and Wife with Married Children	Self only or Self and Wife with Unmarried and Children	Self only or Self and Wife with Miscellaneous living arrangements	Total
Unsatisfactory	11 (12.94)	64 (42.38)	67 (66.33)	56 (60.87)	10 (52.63)	208 (46.42)
Satisfactory	43 (50.58)	51 (33.78)	23 (22.77)	24 (26.09)	8 (42.10)	149 (33.25)
Very Satisfactory	28 (21.18)	36 (23.84)	11 (10.90)	2 (13.04)	1 (5.27)	78 (17.41)
Not applicable	13* (15.30)	—	—	—	—	13 (2.92)
Total	85 (100.00) (19.97)	15 (100.00) (33.70)	101 (100.00) (22.54)	92 (100.00) (20.53)	9 (100.00) (4.26)	448 (100.00) (100.00)

(The percentages are given in the parentheses)

* These Six Chandigarh respondents and 13 Jabalpur respondents are living alone, therefore, this question is not applicable to them.

living with their unmarried children and secondly that the majority, i.e. 61.76 per cent, of the retired people have evaluated their relationship with the family members living with them, as satisfactory.

But the point worth noting is that a considerable number, i.e. 25.73 per cent, of the respondents have evaluated their relationship with the family members as unsatisfactory while only 10.29 per cent have considered their relationship as very satisfactory. In the case of all the living arrangements, except self or self and wife with married children, the majority of the respondents have evaluated their relationship with the family members as satisfactory while the majority of those, who are living with their married children with or without spouses, have evaluated their relationship as unsatisfactory. It shows to some extent, as also stated by Russell (1979 : 308), that they are living with their married childern only due to some compulsion but they do not get proper treatment and respect from their children.

The distribution of the Jabalpur respondents according to the living arrangements and the quality of relationship with the family members living with them (Table 4.1-B) reveals that a considerable number of the respondents, i.e. 33.70 per cent, living with their unmarried children. But the point worth noting is that 22.54 per cent and 20.53 per cent of the Jabalpur respondents are living with married children and with both married and unmarried respectively, in all 43.07 per cent of them are having living arrangement with their married children. About the quality of family relationship this table shows that the larger proportion, i.e. 46.42 per cent, of them have evaluated their relationship with the family members as unsatisfactory. While 33.25 per cent of the respondents have considered their relationship as satisfactory, only 17.41 per cent have evaluated it as very satisfactory.

Although in the case of Jabalpur respondents, in all the living arrangements except self only or self and wife, the proportion of those having unsatisfactory relationship with family members is larger than those having satisfactory and very satisfactory relationships, but it is much higher in the case of those having living arrangement either with married children only or with both married and unmarried children with or without spouses. It shows probably that living with married children creates conflicts in the family. They are living with their married children due to some compulsion but they do not get proper respect and threatment from their children.

While comparing the data on living arrangement and quality of family relationship between the Chandigarh and Jabalpur respondents we find a striking difference. In Chandigarh we find that larger proportion of the retired people are living with their unmarried children, whereas in Jabalpur we find that higher percentage of them are living with their married sons. While majority of the Chandigarh respondents are enjoying satisfactory relationship with their family members larger proportion of Jabalpur respondents are suffering from unsatisfactory relationships with the family members. The percentage of aged people living alone or with spouses only is also considerably higher in Chandigarh than Jabalpur. The difference about living arrangements of both the groups of retirees shows once again that while Chandigarh is a modern city Jabalpur is a city having symptoms of traditional society. But the finding, that most of the Chandigarh respondents are enjoying satisfactory relationships with family members whereas most of Jabalpur respondents are suffering from bad relationship with family members, compels us to think that although in Jabalpur aged people live with their married sons they do not enjoy the higher status and powerful position of Head of the family which is the typical characteristic of changing society. Considering the lower socio-economic status of Jabalpur respondents it seems possible as Russell (1979 : 308) has stated that poor health, low income or widowhood might have led them to live with their married children, whereas our Chandigarh respondents are in the position, financially and physically both, to live independently and manage their own affairs by themselves.

Frequency of Conflicts and the Main Reason for Confiicts.

Apart from the respondents' own evaluation about their relationship with their family members, the frequency of their conflicts with the family members is also important to find out the quality of their relationship. For this purpose, the respondents have been asked to mention the frequency of their conflicts as quite often, sometimes or rarely and also the main reason for the conflicts. All the reasons given by them have been divided into four categories as financial problem, difference of opinion, indiscipline and miscellaneous.

Table 4.2-A shows the distribution of the Chandigarh respondents according to the information. The table shows that the larger proportion, i.e. 44.11per cent, of the respondents have conflicts with the family members sometimes and a most prominent reason for conflicts is difference of opinion. The cross tabulation of both the variables shows that the majority, i.e. 53.33 per cent, of those, who quite often have conflicts with the family members, have mentioned financial problem as the main reason. The largest section, i.e. 47.50 per cent, of the respondents having conflicts sometimes have conflicts due to difference of opinion, whereas most of those who have conflicts rarely, mentioned disrespect and disobedience by their family members as the main reason of conflicts. These reasons also point towards the financial problem of the retirees, the generation gap between the aged and young people and the changing attitudes of the younger generation towards the aged.

The distribution of the Jabalpur respondents according to the frequency of conflicts with family members and the main reason for the conflicts (Table 4.2-B) shows that majority. i.e. 50.90 per cent, of them have conflicts with the family members quite often and in the case of larger proportion, i.e. 48.00 per-cent, of the respondents, the main reason of conflicts is the financial problem. The cross tabulation of both the variables reveals that an overwhelming majority, that is, 78.50 per cent of those, who quite often have conflicts with the family members, have mentioned financial problem as the main reason. The majority, i.e. 55.89 per cent, of the respondents having conflicts sometimes have conflicts due to difference of opinion, whereas most of these who have conflicts rarely, mentioned disrespect and disobedience by the family members as the main reason of conflicts. This data shows most of the Jabalpur respondents are suffering from financial hardships which creates conflicting situation among the family members.

TABLE 4.2

Distribution of the Respondents of Chandigarh and Jabalpur According to the Frequency of Conflicts with Family Members and the Main Reason for Conflicts

(A) Chandigarh

Main Reason for Conflicts	Frequency of Conflicts: Quite often	Sometimes	Rarely	Not applicable	Total
Financial problem	24 (53.83)	31 (25.83)	22 (24.79)	—	77 (28.31)
Difference of Opinion	5 (11.11)	57 (47.50)	33 (32.67)	—	95 (34.93)
Indiscipline	8 (17,76)	17 (14,13)	37 (26.63)	—	62
Miscellaneous	8 (17.78)	15 (12.50)	9 (8.91)	—	32 (11.76)
Not applicable	—	—	—	6 (100.00)	6 (2.20)
Total	45 (100.00) (16.54)	120 (100.00) (44.11)	104 (100.00) (38.25)	6 (100.00) (2.20)	272 (100.00) (100.00)

(B) Jabalpur

Main Reason for Conflicts	Frequency of Conflicts				
	Quite often	Sametimes	Rarely	Not applicable	Total
Financial problem	179 (78.59)	29 (21.38)	7 (9.85)	—	215 (48.00)
Difference of opinion	21 (9.21)	76 (55.89)	23 (31.40)	—	120 (26.78)
Indiscipline	18 (7.99)	27 (19.85)	39 (54.53)	—	84 (18.75)
Miscellaneous	10 (4.39)	4 (2.94)	2 (2.32)	—	16 (3.75)
Not applicable	—	—	—	13 (100.00)	13 (2.90)
Total	228 (100.00) (50.90)	136 (100.00) (30.36)	71 (100.00) (15.84)	13 (100.00) (2.90)	44 (100.00) (100.00)

(The percentages are given in parentheses)

It also reveals that the attitude of younger generation are changing and only age or seniority itself is not sufficient to command respect in the family.

The comparison between the two groups of the respondents on the frequency of conflicts and the main reason of conflicts reveals some important facts. While in Chandigarh majority of the respondents, sometimes have conflicts with their family members and the main reason of conflict in most of the cases is difference of opinion on various issues, the majority of the Jabalpur respondents have the conflicts with their family members quite often and the financial problem is most prominent reason of conflicts among family members in Jabalpur. This data reveals the difference of socio-economic status of the respondents of both these groups. By considering the characteristics of both the samples of Chandigarh and Jabalpur, this difference seems quite obvious. It again shows that although majority of the retirees of Jabalpur are staying with their grown-up children, they are not commanding the powerful position in the family due to the shortage of their own financial resources, whereas majority of the Chandigarh respondents are financially well off, living independently and only sometimes they have conflicts due to difference of opinion with the family members. In the case of insufficiency of income in the household, every family member wants his own needs to be satisfied first, creating higher frequency of conflicting situations among them. If all the needs of all the members get satisfied easily then everyone remains satisfied.

Interaction with the Family Members Living in the Same Household and the Type of Household

One more factor, that is, face to face interaction with the family members, is also very important in adjustment. Interaction with the family mainly shows an individual's association with them but it also shows the quality of his relationship with them. For this purpoes, the respondents have been askcd that on an average how much time, quarter, half or most of the day, they spend in face to face interaction with their family members. To find out whether the type of household makes any difference in the time spent in interaction, all the living arrangements have been divided into three types of household. Since the husband and wife normally form the core of the family, we have called the households having no married couple, one married couple, and more than one married couple as quasinuclear family, nuclear family and joint family, respectively.

Table 4.3 shows the distribution of the respondents according to the interaction with the family members and the household types. It reveals that more or less or same percentages, i.e. 34.92, 30.14 and 32.72 of the Chandigarh respondents spend quarter, half and most of the day respectively, in the interaction with the family members. An overwhelming majority, i.e. 74.63 per cent, of the retirees are living, in the nuclear families and only 20.96 per cent are living in the households consisting of more than one couple. This shows, as Kapadia (1959 : 244-281) has said and Bose and Saxena (1964 : 33-39) have found out, that the joint families are disappearing and nuclear families are emerging in the Indian society. A very small percentage of the respondents have households consisting of no married couple. Regarding the respondents' interaction with the family members, according to their family types, it has been found that 50.88 per cent of those respondents, who are living in the joint families, interact with the family members half of the day and considerable member of them interact most of the day. In case of the nuclear families, a relatively higher percentage of the retirees interact with the family members for a quarter of the day. This fact may be understood by keeping in mind the large number of the family members and the presence of grand children in joint families. In the nuclear families unmarried children go to their educational institutions and the retirees themselves are required to take up some occupational activity to fulfil their responsibilities towards the children. So they find little time to interact with the family members. Normally after completing the liabilities the old people live with their married children. They spend more time with the family members because they cannot exert much in outdoor activities.

The distribution of the Jabalpur respondents to the amount of interaction with family members and the type of household (Table 4.3-B) shows that a great majority, i.e. 70.09 per cent

TABLE 4.3

Distribution of the Respondents of Chandigarh and Jabalpur According to the Amount of Interaction with the Family Members Living in the same Household and the Household Types

Amount of Interaction	(A) Chandigarh Household type				(B) Jabalpur Household type			
	Joint Family	Nuclear Family	Quasi-Nuclear Family	Total	Joint Family	Nuclear Family	Quasi-Nuclear Family	Total
Quarter of the day	4 (7.02)	88 (43.34)	3 (25.00)	95 (94.92)	27 (17.20)	38 (15.20)	8 (19.51)	78 (6.30)
Half of the day	29 (50.88)	50 (24.54)	3 (25.00)	82 (30.16)	19 (12.10)	23 (9.20)	6 (14.64)	48 (10.31
Most of the day	24 (42.10)	65 (32.02)	—	89 (32.72)	111 (70.70)	189 (25.60)	14 (34.15)	314 (70.09)
Not applicable	—	—	6 (50.00)	6 (2.20)	—	—	13 (31.70)	13 (2.90)
Total	57 (100.00) (20.56)	203 (100.00) (74.63)	12 (100.00) (4.41)	272 (100.00) (100.00)	157 (100.00) (35.04)	250 (100.00) (55.80)	41 (100.00) (9.16)	448 (100.00) (100.00)

(The percentages are given in parentheses)

of the respondents spend most of the day in the interaction with the family members. It also shows that although majority, i.e. 55.80 per cent, of them are living in the nuclear families a considerable proportion of the Jabalpur respondents are living in the households consisting of more than one couple, that is, joint family. Cross tabulation of both the variables reveals that the type of family does not make difference as far as the amount of their interaction with the family members is concerned. Great majority, i.e. 70.70 per cent and 75.60 per cent of the respondents living respectively in the joint family and nuclear family spend most of the day in the interaction with the family members. The possible reasons for this fact may be firstly, the larger number of the family members even in the case of nuclear families and secondly, most of Jabalpur respondents are uneducated and cannot spend time on hobbies like reading or indoor games. As it is, the people of this class of society do not have hobbies to spend leisure time. Moreover they are quite aged and cannot take up any occupational activity or go out to interact with other groups of people. Under these circumstances the dependence of an individual of family for the interaction increases. Their rural background also seems to have some role behind their interaction with family members. Because as noted by Wonger (1982 : 219) the availability of and contact with family members including grand children and the satisfaction derived out of it, is comparatively more in rural context than the urban communities. It is observed also that the sons of lower class of people rarely go to very far places for their occupation and try to find out some job in the same city, hence they remain available for their parents.

As far as the Chandigarh respondents are concerned, most of them are educated and financially well off, have very many sources to spend time. Quite a few might have taken up occupational activity and most of them may be spending more time in reading newspapers and books. Comparatively they are younger and physically fit to go out of house for interaction with various groups of people.

Interaction and Relationship with the Children Living Separately

The relationship of the old people with their children living separately is also very important. The children may live separately due to some compulsion but if their relationship with the parents is good, they can solve the problems of the old people and make them happy. To find out the type of respondents' relationship with the children living separately, they have again been asked to evaluate their relationship as unsatisfactory, satisfactory or very satisfactory. The frequency of their meetings with the children on an average in a year was also inquired at the same time. The frequency of meetings with the children indicates the parents' relationship as well as their interaction with the children. The old people may not feel so isolated and neglected if they meet their children frequently

The distribution of the retired people according to the information about the quality of their relationship and the frequency of meetings with the children living away from them is given in table 4.4. About Chandigarh respondents the Table 4.4-A shows that a large section of those having children away from them have evaluated their relationship with them as satisfactory. It also reveals that a larger section meet their children more than once in a year and more or less the same number of them meet their children atleast once in a year.

The cross tabulation of both the variables shows that a majority, i.e. 65.22 per cent, of those who meet their children once in more than a year, have evaluated their relationship as unsatisfactory, while an overwhelming majority, i.e. 75.79 per cent, of those who meet their children more than once in a year, evaluated the relationship as satisfactory. It shows a positive association between these variables.

The distribution of the Jabalpur respondents according to the quality of relationship and the frequency of meetings with the children living separately (Table 4.4-B) shows that a considerable population, i.e. 37.50 per cent, of those having children away from them have evaluated their relationship with them as unsatisfactory whereas only 14.33 per cent have very satisfactory relations with their children living separately.

TABLE 4.4

Distribution of the Respondents of Chandigarh and Jabalpur According to the Quality of Relationship and the Frequency of Meeting on an Average with the Children Living Separately

(A) Chandigarh

Quality of Relationship with the Children living Separately	Frequency of Meeting with Children: Less than once in a year	Once in a year	More than once in a year	Not applicable	Total
Unsatisfactory	15 (65.22)	39 (43.33)	9 (9.47)	—	63 (23.17)
Satisfactory	8 (34.78)	45 (50.00)	72 (75.79)	—	125 (45.95)
Very satisfactory	—	6 (6.67)	14 (14.74)	—	20 (7.35)
Not applicable	—	—	—	64* (100.00)	64 (100.00)
Total	23 (100.00) (8.46)	90 (100.00) (33.08)	95 (100.00) (34.93)	64 (100.00) (23.53)	72 (100.00) (100.00)

(B) Jabalpur

Quality of Relationship with the Children Living Separately	Frequency of Meeting with Children				
	Less than once in a year	Once in a year	More than once in a year	Not applicable	Total
Unsatisfactory	14 (48.28)	75 (2.44)	79 (41.38)	—	168 (37.50)
Satisfactory	13 (44.82)	43 (30.06)	73 (38.21)	—	129 (28.79)
Very satisfactory	2 (6.90)	25 (17.50)	39 (20.41)	—	66 (14.73)
Not applicable	—	—	—	85* (100.00)	85* (100,00)
Total	29 (100.00) (6.48)	143 (100.00) (31.91)	191 (100·00) (42.63)	85 (100.00) (18.93)	448 (100.00) (100.00)

(The percentages are given in parentheses)

* 64 Chandigarh respondents and 85 Jabalpur respondents do not have any children living separately. Therefore, the question is not applicable to them.

This table also reveals that a larger section meet their children more than once in a year and comparatively smaller number of them meet their children once in a year.

The cross tabulation of both the variables does not shows a trend of association between them. Relatively higher proportions of those meeting with their children less than once in a year, once in a year, more than once in a year and comparatively smaller proportions of respondents in these categories have evaluated their relationship with their children living separately as unsatisfactory and satisfactory, respectively.

While comparing the data on the issue between Chandigarh and Jabalpur respondents we find that while in Chandigarh larger proportion of the retirees are enjoying good relationships with the children living separately, in Jabalpur larger proportion of them are suffering from the bad relationship with their children living away. The reason behind this difference between the two groups seems to be the higher socio-economic status of both, the aged parents and their children in Chandigarh and the lower socio-economic status of both the aged parents and their children in Jabalpur. In Chandigarh most of the Pensioners do not need financial help from their sons and even if they want their sons are in the position to support them comfortably. It is not so in the case of Jabalpur respondents. Most of the Jabalpur respondents look towards their sons for the financial help whereas sons are not in a position to help them even if they want. The unfulfilled expectations from the children create frustration in the minds of aged people and consequently the conflicting situations arise between the two generations. Apart from this, it is also possible that due to their modern attitudes and thinking Chandigarh respondents may not have many expectations from their sons whereas due to traditional outlook and attitudes, Jabalpur respondents may be expecting too much from their sons. But in both the cases respondents are meeting with their children more than once in a year.

On the whole our findings regarding the living arrangements of the respondents, their relationship and interaction with the family members, living with them and the children living separately, resemble with the findings of the study of the family life of the old people in East London. The study has reported that a very few people are isolated from all their children. They get help from their relatives and normally do not live alone (Townsond, 1961 : 170), so the wide spread belief, especially in America, that a large proportion of older people are isolated from their families and relatives is not strongly supported by our findings, although the status of the aged having very little income of their own, has gone down in the families of present Indian society but still they are living among their near and dear ones.

We will now examine the association that exists between the respondents self-evaluated quality of relationship, the frequency of conflicts and interaction with the family members living with them, and the quality of relationship and the frequency of meetings or interaction with the children living separately on one hand and the level of adjustment on the other.

To examine the association between respondents' self-evaluated quality of relationship with the family members living with them and their adjustment, three categories of relationship i.e. unsatisfactory, satisfactory and very satisfactory have been cross tabulated with the level of adjustment (Table 4.5). The cross tabulation of the two factors among the Chandigarh respondents shows that better the relationship with the family members higher the level of adjustment. Most of the respondents evaluating their relationship as unsatisfactory have achieved very poor and poor levels whereas most of those having very satisfactory relationship have achieved a good level of adjustment. The result of the test of association also shows that a higher degree of positive association, which is statistically significant at .01 level, exist between these two variables ($r=.61$, $z=4.09$).

The distribution of the Jabalpur respondents according to their self-evaluated quality of relationship with their family members and the level of adjustment, the cross tabulation of these two variables (Table 4.5-B) shows that better the relationship with the family members, higher the level of adjustment. Most of them, evaluating their relationship as unsatisfactory, have achieved very poor level of adjustment,

TABLE 4.5

Distribution of the Respondents of Chandigarh and Jabalpur According to the Quality of Relationship with the Family Members living in the Same Household and the Level of Adjustment

Level of Adjustment	(A) Chandigarh Quality of Relationship with the Family Members Living in the Same Household					
	Unsatisfactory	Satisfactory	Very srtisfactory	Total	N/A	Grand Total
Very poor	25	17	0	42	4	46
Poor	24	21	4	49	1	50
Average	11	55	2	68	1	69
Good	10	64	15	89	0	89
Very good	0	11	7	18	0	18
Total	70	163	28	266*	6	272

(r=.61, z=4.09)

(B) Jabalpur

Level of Adjustment	Quality of Relationship with the Family Members Living in the Same Household					
	Unsatisfactory	Satisfactory	Very Satisfactory	Total	N/A	Grand Total
Very poor	121	47	4	172	8	180
Poor	64	7	3	74	3	77
Average	4	26	7	37	1	38
Good	4	34	41	90	0	90
Very good	15	34	41	90	0	90
Total	208	149	78	425*	13	498

(r=.83, z=5.27)

* The statistical analysis has been done in these tables for only those respondents who are not living alone.

whereas the aged people, evaluating their relationship with family members as very satisfactory, are more likely to achieve good and very good level of adjustment. On the application of the test of association it was found that a very high degree of positive association, which is statistically significant at .01 level exists between these two variables ($r=.83$, $z=5.27$). This finding shows the importance of good family relations for the happiness of the aged people.

Along with the subjective measure of the quality of relationship, that is self-evaluation by the respondents, the objective measure, which is the frequency of conflicts with the family members, is also important to examine the association between the quality of relationship and the level of adjustment. Three categories of respondents having conflicts quite often sometimes and rarely, have been cross tabulated with the five levels of adjustment.

The distribution of the Chandigarh respondents according to the frequency of conflicts and the level of adjustment (Table 4.6-A) clearly shows the negative association between these two variables. As the frequency of conflicts increases the level of adjustment decreases. Excluding the six retirees, living alone, a larger section of the respondents having conflicts, rarely, have achieved a good level of adjustment whereas the large number of those, having conflicts quite often are very poorly adjusted. When we applied the test of association between these two variables it has been found that a moderate degree of negative association, which is statistically significant at .01 level exists between them ($r=-.37$, $z=-2.70$).

The distribution of Jabalpur respondents according to the frequency of conflicts with the family members living in the same household and the level of adjustment (4.6-B) clearly shows that a very high degree of negative association exists between these variables. As the frequency of conflicts increases, the level of adjustment decreases. Excluding the 13 retirees, living alone, the majority of those having conflicts rarely, have achieved a very good level of adjustment, whereas majority of those having conflicts quite often, are very poorly adjusted. When we applied the test of association between these two variables among the Jabalpur respondents, it

TABLE 4.6

Distribution of the Respondents of Chandigarh and Jabalpur According to the Frequency of conflicts with the Family Members Living in the Same Household and the Level of Adjustment

Level of Adjustment	(A) Chandigarh Frequency of Conflicts with Family Members living in the same Household					
	Rarely	Sometimes	Quite often	Total	N/A	Grand Total
Very poor	7	14	21	42	4	46
Poor	16	26	7	49	1	50
Average	27	35	6	68	1	69
Good	44	36	9	89	0	89
Very good	10	6	2	18	0	18
Total	104	117	45	266*	6	272

$(r=-.37, z=-2.70)$

(B) Jabalpur

Level of Adjustment	Frequency of Conflicts with Family Members living in the Same Household					
	Rarely	Sometimes	Quite often	Total	N/A	Grand Total
Very poor	2	45	126	172	8	180
Poor	3	5	66	74	3	77
Average	4	28	5	37	1	38
Good	19	30	13	62	1	63
Very good	41	30	19	90	0	90
Total	71	136	228	235*	13	448

$(r=-.80,\ z=-5.08)$

* The statistical analysis has been done in this table for only those respondents who are not living alone.

was found that a very high degree of negative association, which is statistically significant at .01 level, exists between them (r=—.80, z=−5.08).

While comparing the association between these two variables in Chandigarh and Jabalpur, we find that while among the Chandigarh respondents, a moderate degree of negative association exists among the Jabalpur respondents, a very high degree of negative association exists between these two variables. This difference in the degree of association may be due to the fact, as we have discussed earlier that majority of the Jabalpur respondents have conflicts quite often with their family members due to the financial problem mainly.

How we will examine the relationship that exists between the time spent in interaction with the family members living in the same household and the level of adjustment. For this purpose, the three categories of respondents spending quarter, half and most of the day in face to face interaction with their family members, have been cross tabulated with the five levels of adjustment (Table 4.7).

The distribution of the Chandigarh respondents according to this information reveals that a positive association exists between these two variables. The Table 4.7-A clearly shows that a larger section of those respondents, who spend quarter of the day in interaction with the family members, fall in the category of very poor level of adjustment, whereas majority of these spending most of the day in interaction have achieved a good level of adjustment. The application of the test of association also shows that a higher degree of positive association, which is statistically significant at .01 level, exists between these two variables (r=.57, z=4.10). Ramamurti (1968 : 78) has also concluded that the individuals, having spouse alive and living in joint family are better adjusted.

The distribution of the Jabalpur respondents according to the time spent in interaction with the family members and the level of adjustment (Table 4.7-B) shows that a negative association exists between these two variables. This table clearly shows that most of the Jabalpur respondents spend most of the day in interaction with the family members and a larger proportion of them are very poorly adjusted. The appli-

TABLE 4.7

Distribution of the Respondents of Chandigarh and Jabalpur According to the Time Spent in Interaction with the Family Members and the Level of Adjustment

(A) Chandigarh

Level of Adjustment	Time Spent in interaction with the Family Members: Quarter of the day	Half of the day	Most of the day	Total	N/A	Grand Total
Very poor	35	4	3	42	4	46
Poor	27	16	6	49	1	50
Average	19	26	23	68	1	69
Good	9	30	50	89	0	89
Very good	5	6	7	18	0	18
Total	95	82	89	266*	6	272

(r=.57, z=4.10)

(B) Jabalpur

Level of Adjustment	Time Spent in Interaction with the Family Members					
	Quarter of the day	Half of the day	Most of the day	Total	N/A	Grand Total
Very poor	21	1	150	171	8	180
Poor	19	3	52	74	3	77
Average	12	5	20	37	1	38
Good	11	14	37	62	1	63
Very good	10	25	55	90	0	90
Total	73	48	314	435*	13	448

(r= -.27, z=—1.71)

* The statistical analysis has been done in this table for only those respondents who are not living alone.

cation of the test of association also shows that a weaker degree of negative association, which is not statistically significant even at .05 level, exists between these two variables ($r=-.27$, $z=-1.71$).

While comparing the findings about association between the amount of interaction with family members and level of adjustment between Chandigarh and Jabalpur respondents, we find the opposite facts. While in Chandigarh these variables are positively associated, in Jabalpur they are negatively associated. This finding points at the fact that in Chandigarh more interaction with the family members is the voluntary and chosen one by the respondents whereas in Jabalpur it is a compulsion and forced one in the absence of other alternatives.

While voluntary interaction with family members improves the good relations with them, the forced interaction creates conflicting situations among them. As we have seem earlier, most of our Jabalpur respondents are quite aged, they are not involved in occupational activities and they are not in position, physically and financially, to go away from their houses for the interaction with various other groups of people. They are not educated hence cannot spend time in reading books, due to the shortage of space in their houses they have to share room with others and spend most of the day in face to face interaction with family members. This is not so in the case of Chandigarh respondents. Most of them are not very aged, they have involved themselves in occupational activities, they are physically and financially in a position to go away from the house to interact with other groups of people. They are educated and due to availability of many rooms in the residence they got privacy and they can spend time in the hobbies like reading or listening music while relaxing in their own rooms. Considering all these different states of affairs between the two groups of sample, the opposite finding regarding the association of interaction with family members and the level of adjustment seems quite reasonable.

Here it also seems useful to find out what type of relationship exists between the respondents' living arrangement with their children and their adjustment. Living with children may create some conflicts in the family due to financial problem, difference of opinion or any other reasons. But it certainly provides financial and physical security and opportunity of interaction with the near and dear ones to the aged people which is very necessary in this period of life. For the purpose, excluding those having miscellaneous living arrangements, all the respondents have been divided into two groups, i.e. not living with their children and living with their children.

Table 4.8 shows the distribution of the respondents according to their living arrangement with or without children and the level of adjustment. The distribution of Chandigarh respondents accordingly and the cross tabulation of both these variables show that the aged people living with their children have a tendency to achieve higher levels of adjustment, whereas a larger section of those, who are not living with their children, are concentrated in the categories showing very poor and poor levels of adjustment. The value of the test of association also shows that these two variables are considerably associated in the positive direction though this association is not statistically significant even at .05 level, ($r=.23$, $z=1.63$). The insignificance of the positive association between these two variables may reasonably be understood by keeping in mind the findings discussed earlier about the respondents frequent conflicts with the family members due to financial problem and difference of opinion. But the association between the two factors certainly indicates the fact that old people get satisfaction while living with children.

The distribution of the Jabalpur respondents according to the living arrangement with or without children and the level of adjustment (Table 4.8-B) shows that there is no association, either positive or negative, between these two variables and they are independent from each other. Relatively higher proportions and smaller proportions of those having both types of living arrangements have achieved respectively, a very poor and a very good level of adjustment. On application of test of association also it was found that no association exists between them ($r=-.04$, $z=0$). It shows that in both type of living arrangement the aged people have different type of problems. While living without children brings loneliness, isolation and boredom, and living with children creates the problem

TABLE 4.8

Distribution of the Respondents of Chandigarh and Jabalpur According to the Living Arrangement with or without Children and the Level of Adjustment

Level of Adjustment	(A) Chandigarh Living Arrangement with or without Children					(B) Jabalpur Living Arrangement with or without Children				
	Not Living with Children	Living with Children	Total	N/A	Grand Total	Not Living with Children	Living with Children	Total	N/A	Grand Total
Very poor	20	21	41	5	46	28	143	171	9	180
Poor	20	26	46	4	50	21	51	72	5	77
Average	16	52	68	1	69	8	29	37	1	38
Good	12	76	88	1	89	11	49	60	3	63
Very good	8	10	18	0	18	17	72	89	1	90
Total	76	185	261*	11	272	85	344	429*	19	448

(r=.33, z=1.63) (r=—.04, z=0)

* For the statistical analysis in the table respondents having miscellaneous living arrangements have been excluded.

of adjustment with them. Apart from them in the case of Jabalpur rerpondents quite a considerable number of them are having unmarried and unsettled children with them who are the additional liabilities in this period of life, creating worries and tensions in the minds of the retirees.

While comparing the finding about association of these two variables among respondents in Jabalpur with the respondents in Chandigarh we find that in Chandigarh these variables are positively associated though not very significantly. The reason for this may be that when the financial condition of the respondents remain comfortable, the aged people command respect in the family and living with children can be enjoyed even if some responsibilities have to be fulfilled, whereas the poor aged do not get higher status of the Head of the family in the present family set up and financial crisis creates conflicts in the household.

We may now study the quality of relationship with the grown-up children living separately and its association with the level of adjustment of the retired people. For this purpose, by excluding respondents having no children living separately, all others, on the basis of self-evaluation of the quality of relationship, have been divided into three categories as having unsatisfactory, satisfactory and very satisfactory relationship with the grown-up children living separately. Then to examine whether the quality of relationship is linked with the level of adjustment, these two variables have been cross tabulated (Table 4.9).

The distribution of the Chandigarh respondents according to the quality of relationship with the children living separately and the level of adjustment (Table 4.9-A) shows that the retired people having satisfactory and very satisfactory relationship with the children living away are more likely to achieve good level of adjustment than those having unsatisfactory relationship. The value of the test of association also supports the existence of a positive association of higher degree, which is statistically significant at .01 level ($r = .50$, $z = 2.70$), showing that better the relationship with the grown-up children higher the level of adjustment.

TABLE 4.9

Distribution of the Respondents of Chandigarh and Jabalpur According to the Quality of Relationship with the Children Living Separately and the Level of Adjustment

(A) Chandigarh

Level of Adjustment	Quality of Relationship with Children Living Separately: Unsatisfactory	Satisfactory	Very Satisfactory	Total	N/A	Grand Total
Very poor	15	10	0	25	21	46
Poor	15	15	3	33	17	50
Average	20	39	3	62	7	69
Good	12	50	9	71	18	89
Very good	1	11	5	17	1	18
Total	63	125	20	208*	64	272

(r=.50, z=2.70)

* The statistical analysis has been done in this table only for those respondents whose children are living separately.

(B) Jabalpur

Level of Adjustment	Quality of Relationship with Children Living Separately					Grand Total
	Unsatis-factory	Satis-factory	Very Satisfactory	Total	N/A	
Very poor	98	51	3	152	28	180
Poor	42	20	2	64	13	77
Average	11	19	3	33	5	38
Good	8	13	23	44	19	63
Very good	9	26	35	70	20	90
Total	168	129	66	363*	35	448

(r=.62, z=3.93)

The distribution of the Jabalpur respondents according to the quality of relationship with the children living separately and the level of adjustment (Table 4.9-B) shows that the majority of those retired people of Jabalpur who are having very satisfactory relationship with their children living separately, have achieved a very good level of adjustment. In the same way majority of those having unsatisfactory relations with their grown-up children are very poorly adjusted. Thus cross tabulation of both the variables shows that a positive association exists between these variables. The value of the test of association also reveals that positive association of a high degree, which is statistically significant at .01 level, is existing between the relationship with grown-up children and the level of adjustment. In this regard our findings are same among the respondents of Chandigarh and Jabalpur.

Apart from the self-evaluation, an indirect way of finding out the quality of relationship with the grown-up children as well as the interaction with them, that is, frequency of meetings with them, on an average, is also important to see its association with the level of adjustment. By excluding the respondents, having no children living away from them, all others have been divided into three categories, as having meetings with children once in more then a year, once in a year and more than once in a year. Then those categories have been cross tabulated with the five levels of adjustment (Table 4.10).

The distribution of Chandigarh respondents in Table 4.10-A shows that more the frequency of meetings with the children, higher the level of adjustment. The majority of the respondents, meeting their children after one year are very poorly adjusted, whereas those, meeting their children more than once in a year, have achieved a good level of adjustment. The value of the test of association between these two variables also shows that a moderate degree of positive association which is statistically significant at .05 level, exists between these two variables ($r=.40$, $z=2.13$). From this finding we may infer that good relationship and high interaction with the grown-up children have an important role to play in adjustment in old age.

Our findings resemble with the findings or studies conducted in the western countries showing that better the relationship with the wife and children higher the level of adjustment. It can be said that since in old age people have to depend more on their family members for the satisfaction of their physical as well as socio-psychological needs, family relationship play a very important role in adjustment in old age. If the relationship is good the old people can be looked after and helped by the children to lead a happy life in old age.

But the distribution of the Jabalpur respondents according to the frequency of meetings with the grown-up children living away and the level of adjustment (Table 4.10-B) shows quite a different fact. It shows that both these variables are not associated, neither positively nor negatively with each other. It is clear, from the table that majority of those, meeting more than once in a year with their children living away from them are very poorly adjusted. In the same way relatively higher section of the respondents, meeting with children once in a year or less than once in a year are also more likely to achieve poor and very poor level of adjustment. On application of the test of association it was found that no association exists between these variables and they are independent from each other ($r=0$, $z=0$).

In this regard we find quite a different fact in both the groups of our sample. While in Chandigarh frequency of meeting with grown-up children is positively associated with the level of adjustment, it is not related, neither in negative nor in positive direction, in the case of Jabalpur respondents. It reveals that frequent meetings with the children does not mean that good relations exist between the respondents and the children atleast in the case of Jabalpur respondents, majority of whom are suffering from the financial problem. The grown-up children of most of the Jabalpur respondents are living in Jabalpur itself. As we have seen while discussing the reasons for not settling down in their home towns after retirement, a considerable number of respondents have mentioned the reason of the service of the son in Jabalpur Atleast one son of quite a few of the respondents has taken up the job in the same factory, where the respondent was working before retirement. But while living in the same city, quite a

TABLE 4.10

Distribution of the Respondents of Chandigarh and Jabalpur According to the Frequency of Meetings with the Children Living Separately and the Level of Adjustment

(A)
Chandigarh

Level of Adjustment	Frequency of Meeting with the Children Living Separately					
	Less than once in a year	Once in a year	More than once in a year	Total	N/A	Grand Total
Very poor	10	15	0	25	21	46
Poor	4	11	18	33	17	50
Average	4	34	24	62	7	69
Good	3	25	43	71	18	89
Very good	2	5	10	17	1	18
Total	23	90	95	208*	64	272

($r=.40$, $z=2.13$)

(B)

Jabalpur

Level of Adjustment	Frequency of Meetings with the Children Living Separately					
	Less than once in a year	Once in a year	More than once in a year	Total	N A	Grand Total
Very poor	17	39	96	152	28	180
Poor	6	36	22	64	13	77
Average	1	21	11	33	5	38
Good	2	19	23	44	19	63
Very good	3	28	39	70	20	90
Total	29	143	191	363*	85	448

(r=0, z=0)

* The statistical analysis has been done in this table only for those respondents whose children are living away from them.

few married sons are living separately. Therefore, it is possible for them to meet quite often even if they are not having very good relations with them. Due to the lower socio-economic status of the children also, they are not in position to fulfill the expectations of their parents. In this situation, meeting with the children brings unhappiness. As expressed by the respondents during interviews, more interaction with the children living away creates conflicting situation most of the time, because they do not give them financial help. It seems quite reasonable also by considering the poor economic condition of a large section of Jabalpur respondents and their traditional attitude towards the duty of sons to look after the parents in old age.

While in the case of Chandigarh respondents due to their modern outlook, most of them do not expect much from their grown-up children. They themselves and their sons are financially well off. In the case of needy people, their sons are in the comfortable position to support them financially. In this situation meeting with the children brings pleasure and happiness.

It means meetings between the grown-up children and the aged parents bring happiness either in the absence of mutual expectations or in the fulfillment of mutual expectations. Unfulfillment of the expectations creates conflicting situations during the meetings.

On the whole our findings show that good family relationship is very important for the happiness of the aged people. If the relationship is good the aged people can easily and smoothly pass through this period of life otherwise the life becomes miserable.

Social life

Man is a social being by nature and he wants to associate himself and share his feelings, experiences, worries and jobs with others. Hochschild (1973 : 18-25) has said that the main problem of the older people is isolation from family, work and young people outside family due to the decline in work, age stratification and weakening of kinship ties. The present industrial society does not provide much opportunity for social participation to the aged people. Pre-retirement occupational activity gives opportunities for social contacts throughout the day and a sudden fall in the contacts due to retirement may create a feeling of isolation and loneliness in them. The emerging smaller size of the family also deprives them of the opportunities for meeting and interacting with many people. In this situation substitute activities of contacts with other people such as interaction with friends, neighbours, relatives and members of voluntary organisations may give them the feelings of belongingness, recognition and usefulness. Membership of social groups or organizations provides a sense of belonging, pleasure of sociability, satisfaction of activity and a routine of attendance at events (Russell, 1979 : 264). Therefore, the importance of interaction with friends, neighbours, relatives and the members of voluntary organizations etc. regarding adjustment has been established by quite a few gerontologists, as has been discussed earlier while reviewing the literature on adjustment in old age.

To examine the relationship between the interaction with friends, neighbours, relatives and other members of voluntary organizations on one hand and the adjustment on the other, information has been collected regarding the number of the retirees' intimate friends in the city, the frequency of mutual visits between them and their friends, the number of families of neighbours they meet, the frequency of mutual visits between them and their neighbours, number of families of relatives in the city, the frequency of mutual visits between them and relatives, number of voluntary organizations located in the city, of whose membership they are holding and the frequency of their attendance at the meetings of these organizations.

The distribution of the Chandigarh respondents according to the number of their intimate friends, families of relatives in the city and families of neighbours they meet and the voluntary organizations of whose membership they are holding at present (Table 4.11-A) reveals some interesting facts. Relatively a larger section, i.e. 36.77 per cent, of the respondents do not have any intimate friend in Chandigarh. This fact shows probably the loss of friends after retirement. But among those having friends, a substantial section have more than four

TABLE 4.11

Distribution of the Respondents of Chandigarh and Jabalpur According to the Number of Intimate Friends, Neighbours, Relatives and the Voluntary Organizations of whose Membership They are Holding

Name of Group	(A) Chandigarh Number of Friends, Neighbours, Relatives and Voluntary Organizations					(B) Jabalpur Number of Friends, Neighbours, Relatives and Voluntary Origanizations				
	Nil	1-2	3-4	Above 4	Total	Nil	1-2	3-4	Above 4	Total
Friends	100	60	41	71	272	91	168	107	92	448
	(35.77)	(22.05)	(15.08)	(26.10)	(100.00)	(20.31)	(35.27)	(35.27)	(20.53)	(100.00)
Neighbours	18	111	81	62	272	11	96	131	210	448
	(5.62)	(40.82)	(29.77)	(22.79)	(100.00)	(2.45)	(21.42)	(21.42)	(46.89)	(100.00)
Relatives	28	132	83	29	272	31	84	149	184	448
	(10.29)	(48.50)	(1.10)	(10.66)	(100.00)	(6.91)	(18.75)	(13.25)	(41.09)	(100.00)
Voluntary Organizations	195	52	22	3	272	349	71	26	0	448
	(71 69)	(19.12)	(8.09)	(1.10)	(100.00)	(77.90)	(15.84)	(6.26)		(100.00)

(The percentages are given in parentheses)

friends with whom they can share their feeling and experiences. In the case of neighbours only a very small number of the retirees are not meeting their neighbours. It is because they have recently shifted to the newly built houses in the expanding areas of the city and they do not have any next-door neighbour. But the point worth noting is that a larger section, i.e. 40.53 per cent, of the retirees are meeting only with one or two families living in their neighbourhood. This is a special feature of Chandigarh. Being a newly-built city the neighbourhood relations have not yet developed extensively. It is the special character of modern cities. Sometimes people do not even know the identity of people living in their neighbourhood. A small number of the respondents do not have any relative in Chandigarh, 48.53 per cent of them are having one or two and 30.51 per cent have three or four families of relatives. It may be because, that Chandigarh being a new city, people belonging to the nearby areas have migrated to this city and after retirement everyone wants to settle down among his relatives. An overwhelming majority, i.e. 71.69 per cent, of the respondents are not members of any voluntary organization. And among those who are the members, most of them are members of only one or two organizations. The reasons for this lack of interest in voluntary organizations may be that in India the social life of the Indian aged people mostly moves around their family members and other near and dear ones, and they do not have to depend on organizations to feel the sense of belonging, unity and security. It substantiates the hypothesis derived by Rose (1960 : 666-697) that voluntary organizations for the benefit of aged, tend to develop and establish in those societies in which the family has partially ceased to maintain and help the aged and participation of the aged in voluntary organization is greater when the older people lose their family roles.

The distribution of the Jabalpur respondents according to the number of intimate friends, neighbours they meet, relatives and the voluntary organizations of whose membership they are holding is given in the Table 4.11-B. This table reveals that a considerable proportion of them, i.e. 35.27 per cent, are having one or two friends. Relatively smaller proportion, that is, 23.89 per cent of them, are having three or four friends. Almost same proportion, i.e. a little more than one-fifth of the respondents either do not have any friends or more than four friends. In all, a little less than 80 per cent of Jabalpur respondents claimed to have intimate friends, with whom they can share their feelings and experiences. In the case of neighbours a larger section, i.e. 46.80 per cent, of the Jabalpur respondents are meeting with more than four neighbours, while 29.24 per cent and 21.42 per cent of them are meeting with three to four and one to two neighbours respectively. A negligible proportion, i.e. 2.45 per cent, of Jabalpur respondents is not meeting with any neighbour. This shows that neighbourhood relations are maintained in Jabalpur which is a symptom of traditional society. This symptom in the interest of aged people is good because in old age the local neighbourhood and surrounding community assumes greater importance in the fulfillment of the personal needs (Russell, 1979 : 308).

As far as the relatives are concerned, 41.09 per cent and 33.25 per cent of the Jabalpur respondents have above four and three to four families of relatives in Jabalpur, while 21.42 per cent have one or two relatives, only 6.91 per cent of them have no relatives in this city. The existence of relatives in Jabalpur seems quite reasonable by considering the migration of people of the surrounding rural areas to this city. The presence of some relatives in the city attracts as well as facilitates the migration of their relatives also. Because the residential place to stay for some time in the initial stage and the guidance for seeking the job becomes readily available to them in the city. And after retirement specially everyone wants to settle down among his own relatives. In the case of Jabalpur respondents also an overwhelming majority, i.e. 71.69 per cent, of the respondents are not members of any voluntary organization and among those who are the members, most of them are members of only one or two organizations. The reason for this lack of interest again shows that the life of Indian aged people moves around the family members and they do not depend upon any organization for the interaction.

While comparing the data on the number of friends, neighbours, relatives and voluntary organization in the two groups

TABLE 4.12

Distribution of the Respondents of Chandigarh and Jabalpur According to the Frequency of Visits Between Them and Friends, Neighbours and Relatives and Meetings of Voluntary Organizations Attended by Them

Name of the Group	(A) Chandigarh Frequency of Visits Between Respondents and Various Groups of People and the Meetings of Voluntary Organizations Attended by them					(B) Jabalpur Frequency of Visits Between Respondents and Various Groups of People and the Meetings of Voluntary Organizations Attended by them.				
	N/A	Rarely	Some-times	Quite often	Total	N/A	Rarely	Some-times	Quite often	Total
Friends	100	28	83	56	272	91	23	35	299	448
	(36.77)	(10.29)	(32.35)	(20.59)	(100.00)	(20.31)	(5.13)	(7.81)	(66.75)	(100.00)
Neighbours	18	115	92	47	272	11	13	114	310	448
	(6.62)	(42.27)	(33.82)	(17.28)	(100.00)	(2.45)	(2.90)	(25.45)	(69.20)	(100.00)
Relatives	28	89	113	42	272	31	20	278	119	448
	(10.29)	(32.72)	(41.54)	(15.44)	(100.00)	(6.91)	(4.47)	(62.05)	(26.57)	(100.00)
Voluntary Organiza-tions	195	52	3	22	272	34	60	29	10	448
	(71.69)	(19.12)	(1.10)	(8.08)	(100.00)	(77.99)	(13 40)	(6.47)	(2.33)	(100.00)

(The percentages are given in parentheses)

of sample, we find that the interaction of Jabalpur respondents with friends, neighbours and relatives is more than the Chandigarh respondents. This difference seems to have its base in the rural background of Jabalpur respondents and urban background of Chandigarh respondents in most of the cases. The importance of neighbours and the interaction with neighbours is more in the case of rural aged people than their counterpart in urban community because they choose their friends from their neighbourhood (Wenger, 1982 : 221). In the case of voluntary organizations the state of affairs is same in both the cities. This difference of interaction may be due to the difference of educational and financial level of both the groups of respondents. The Chandigarh pensioners by the virtue of being quite educated and financially well off, can spend their leisure time in reading, gardening and music listening etc. Quite a few of them have involved themselves in occupational activity again after retirement. Whereas most of the Jabalpur respondents pass their leisure by gossiping because they have nothing else to do in this phase of life.

The number of friends, neighbours, relatives and voluntary organizations are not sufficient to indicate the interaction of the respondents with these groups of people. The frequency of mutual visits between the retirees and their friends, neighbours, and relatives and, frequency of the meetings of the organizations attended by them seems to be more appropriate in this respect. The interaction with these groups of people also shows the type of the respondents' relationship with them. Table 4.12-A shows the distribution of the Chandigarh respondents according to the frequency of meeting with various groups of people and attendance at the meetings of the voluntary organizations. About 36.77 per cent of respondents do not have any intimate friends. Therefore, the question of mutual visits does not arise in their case. Among those who have friends a larger section of the retirees visit their friends sometimes and vice versa. In the case of neighbours, relatively a larger proportion, i.e. 42.27 per cent, rarely visit their neighbours and vice versa. It again shows the lack of neighbourly relations of the respondents. But 41.54 per cent of the respondents sometimes visit their relatives and vice versa. Regarding voluntary organizations, 71.69 per cent of the retirees are not the member of any organization and the question of attendance at the meetings of those organizations does not arise in their case. Among those who are members of any organization, a larger number of them rarely attend the meetings. This indicates the respondent's lack of interest in voluntary organizations.

The distribution of the Jabalpur respondents according to the frequency of visits between them and friends, neighbours and relatives and the meetings of voluntary organizations attended by them (Table 4.12-B) shows that a great majority, i.e. 66.75 per cent, of the respondents visit their friends quite often and vice versa, Same in the case regarding the mutual visits with neighbours, 69.20 per cent of them visit their neighbours quite often and vice versa. It again shows that respondents are having good neighbourly relations. But regarding the relatives this table shows that 62.05 per cent of them sometimes visit their relatives and vice versa. 77.90 per cent of retirees are not the members of any voluntary organization and among those who are the member of one or two voluntary organizations, majority of them very rarely attend the meeting of those organizations. As a matter of fact they do not require it as they get the company in neighbourhood itself. D'Souza (1982 : 60) has also found out that on the whole aged people in India are integrated in the society.

On comparing the data on the frequency of mutual visits between various groups of people and the respondents of Chandigarh and Jabalpur, we again find that the Jabalpur respondents are meeting with their friends and neighbours more often than the Chandigarh respondents, whereas in the case of relatives majority of both the groups are meeting sometimes and the meetings of voluntary organizations are very rarely attended by both the groups. The reason for the difference in interaction with neighbours and friends in both the groups of sample is, as also stated by Rusell (1979 : 344) that the aged, especially those in the working class, are dependent on their local residential settings for the provision of peers to interact with. They select friends from their neighbourhood, whereas the Chandigarh respondents might have selected their friends from the distant places in the city.

Therefore, quite frequent visits between friends do not take place. And in the neighbourhood if they do not find the people of their own liking they prefer to stay in their own houses than to gossip with neighbours.

Now we will examine the relationship between the respondents' interaction with various groups of people mentioned above on the one hand and the level of adjustment on the other. For the purpose, the frequency of the respondents' meeting with any group of people has been cross tabulated with their adjustment. Regarding their interaction with the friends, all the respondents of both the groups have been divided into four categories as having nil, low, moderate and high interaction on the basis of the frequency of mutual visits between them and the friends as never, rarely, sometimes and quite often, respectively. The respondents having no friends in the city have been included in the category of those having no visits at all. These four categories have been cross tabulated with the five levels of adjustment. The distribution of the Chandigarh respondents according to this information (Table 4.13-A) shows that a larger proportion of the respondents having no interaction with the friends, have achieved a poor level of adjustment, whereas most of the respondents having moderate and high interaction with the friends, have achieved a good level of adjustment. On application of the test of association between these two variables it was found that a positive association of a higher degree, which is statistically significant at .01 level, exists between them (r= .53, z=3.88).

The distribution of the Jabalpur respondents according to the amount of interaction with friends and the level of adjustment (Table 4.13-B) shows quite a different state of affair among them than the Chandigarh respondents. The table very clearly shows that a larger proportion of those, having high interaction with friends, have achieved very poor level of adjustment, although it is the same in the case of the respondents having no interaction with the friends. Regarding the low and moderate interaction no clear difference is observed in various levels of adjustment. On application of test of ssociation also it was found that there is a very weak positive

TABLE 4.13

Distribution of the Respondents of Chandigarh and Jabalpur According to the Amount of Interaction with Friends and the Level of Adjustment

Level of Adjustment	(A) Chandigarh Amount of Interaction with Friends					(B) Jabalpur Amount of Intercation with Friends				
	No interaction	Low interaction	Moderate interaction	High interaction	Total	No interaction	Low interaction	Moderate intreaction	High interaction	Total
Very poor	35	6	5	0	46	41	7	6	126	180
Poor	23	8	16	4	50	39	7	4	27	77
Average	27	7	26	11	69	4	2	6	26	38
Good	12	6	39	32	89	3	2	8	50	63
Very good	3	1	45	9	18	4	5	11	70	90
Total	100	28	88	56	272	91	23	35	299	448

(r= .53 z= 3.88) (r= .17, z= 1.07)

assaciotion, which is not statistically significant at .05 level, exists between these two variables (r=.17, z=1.07).

While comparing the data on interaction with friends and the adjustment between two groups of present study we find that while in the case of Chandigarh higher interaction with friends facilitates to achieve higher level of adjustment, in the case of Jabalpur respondents very weak and statistically insignificant positive association exists between them. By considering the lower socio-economic status of Jabalpur respondents it seems reasonable. The interaction with friends may solve the problem of isolation or loneliness. By sharing the sorrows or worries with friends one can feel light hearted for some time but it can not provide relief from the problem, specially those connected with the fulfillment of basic needs. But in the case of Chandigarh respondents whose basic needs are being fulfilled satisfactorily, the interaction with friends certainly removes boredom and loneliness from their life and add to their happiness.

Regarding the interaction with the neighbours also the respondents have been divided into four categories as having nil, low, moderate and high degree of interaction on the basis of the frequency of mutual visits between them and the neighbours as never, rarely, sometimes and quite often respectively. The distribution of the Chandigarh respondents according to above mentioned categories of interaction and the level of adjustment (Table 4.14-A) shows a positive association between these variables. Relatively a larger proportion of the respondents having low interaction with the neighbours are very poorly adjusted, whereas those having high interaction with the neighbours are more likely to achieve a good level of adjustment. On application of the test of association it has been found that quite a moderate degree of positive association, which is statistically significant at .01 level, exists between these two variables (r= .40, z=2.64).

The distribution of the Jabalpur respondents according to the amount of interaction with neighbours and the level of adjustment (Table 4.14-B) shows that there is a very weak positive association between these two variables. As it can be seen from the table, relatively a larger and quite considerable

TABLE 4.14

Distribution of the Respondents of Chandigarh and Jabalpur According to the Amount of Interaction with Neighbours and the Level of Adjustment

Level of Adjustment	(A) Chandigarh Amount of Interaction with Neighbours					(B) Jabalpur Amount of Interaction with Neighbours				
	No Interaction	Low Interaction	Moderate Interaction	High Interaction	Total	No Interaction	Low Interaction	Moderate Interaction	High Interaction	Total
Very poor	4	32	9	1	46	7	8	17	147	180
Poor	5	23	16	6	50	2	1	24	50	77
Average	6	28	27	8	69	1	2	16	19	38
Good	3	26	35	25	89	1	1	18	33	63
Very good	0	6	5	7	18	0	0	29	61	90
Total	18	115	92	47	272	11	13	114	310	448

(r= .40, z = 2.64) (r=.13, z = .82)

number of those having high interation with neighbours have achieved a very poor level of adjustment. Whereas the proportion of those respondents, having lower degree of interaction is not very prominent in the lower levels of adjustment. Application of the test of association between these variables also shows that a very weak positive association which is not statistically significant at .05 level, exists between them (r= .13, z= .82). On the comparison of the data of both the groups on the interaction with neighbours and the level of adjustment, again we find that while in Chandigarh interaction with neighbours is facilitating the respondents in achieving the higher level of adjustment, it is not at all helpful in the case of Jabalpur respondents. The reason for this finding again lies in the difference of socio-economic status between the Chandigarh and Jabalpur respondents. As we have seen while discussing the special characteristics of both the samples, most of our Jabalpur respondents are suffering from the poverty whereas most of the Chandigarh respondents are in the comfortable financial position. The finding regarding the association between the two variables, discussed above, among the Chandigarh and Jabalpur respondents, shows that social interaction can provide satisfaction and happiness in life only when the basic needs get fulfilled sufficiently.

The distribution of the Chandigarh respondents according to the amount of interaction with the relatives living in Chandigarh and the level of adjustment (Table 4.15-A) also reveals the positive association between these two variables. Comparatively a larger section of the respondents, who have low interaction with their relatives, have achieved a poor level of adjustment. But most of those having high interaction with the relatives have achieved a good level of adjustment. The value of the test of association also shows that a higher degree of positive association, which is statistically significant at ·01 level, exists between these two variables (r=.45,z=3.01)

The distribution of the Jabalpur respondents according to the amount of interaction with relatives and the level of adjustment (Table 4.15-B) shows that there is a very weak positive association between these variables. Relatively quite a larger proportion of those having moderate interaction with relatives

TABLE 4.15

Distribution of the Respondents of Chandigarh and Jabalpur According to the Amount of Interaction with Relatives and the Level of Adjustment

Level of Adjustment	(A) Chandigarh Amount of Interaction with the Relatives					(B) Jabalpur Amount of Interaction with the Relatives				
	No interaction	Low interaction	Moderate interaction	High interaction	Total	No interaction	Low interaction	Moderate interaction	High interaction	Total
Very poor	3	30	7	1	46	11	10	140	19	180
Poor	4	23	19	4	50	7	4	53	13	77
Average	7	22	33	7	69	2	1	27	8	38
Good	7	12	43	27	89	6	3	22	32	63
Very good	2	2	11	3	18	5	2	36	47	90
Total	28	89	113	42	272	31	20	278	119	448

(r= ,45, z=3.01) (r = .15,z=0.95)

have achieved a very poor level of adjustment. Although a considerable section of those having high interaction have achieved a good level of adjustment. but it does not seem to be very significant by considering the number of respondents in this category. The value of the test of association also shows that a very weak positive association, which is not statistically significant, exists between these variables (r=.15, z=0.95).

A comparison on this issue between both the groups of respondents again shows that while in Chandigarh interaction with relatives' facilities the respondents in the process of adjustment, it does not help to the respondents of Jabalpur in doing so. We can conclude from this finding that meeting with the relatives brings happiness and pleasure in the real sense only to those who are financially well off. As it is observed it becomes very difficult for the retired people with limited means to ful the expectations of the relatives. Therefore, probably majority of the Jabalpur respondents have moderate interaction with the relatives. Whereas in the case of well-to-do Chandigarh respondents meeting with the relatives brings satisfaction of life to them.

Interaction with the Members of Voluntary Organizations

As far as the interaction with the members of voluntary organizations is concerned, as discussed earlier, most of the respondents of Chandigarh and Jabalpur both, have not taken the membership of any organization. Table 4.16-A shows the cross tabulation between the four categories of Chandigarh respondents' interaction with the members of voluntary organization, prepared on the basis of the frequency of attendance in the meetings of the organizations, and the various levels of adjustment. It reveals that most of the retired people having high interaction with other members of the voluntary organization due to their quite frequent attendance at the meetings, have achieved a good level of adjustment. A larger proportion of even those having low interaction have achieved a good level of adjustment, whereas relatively a larger section, that is a little more than one-fourth of the respondents, having no interaction with the members of the organizations have

TABLE 4.16

Distribution of the Respondents of Chandigarh and Jabalpur According to the Amount of the Interaction with the Members of the Voluntary Organizations and the Level of Adjustment

Level of Adjustment	(A) Chandigarh Amount of Interaction with the Members of Voluntary Organizations					(B) Jabalpur Amount of Interaction with the Members of Voluntary Organizations				
	No interaction	Low interaction	Moderate interaction	High interaction	Total	No interaction	Low interaction	Moderate interaction	High interaction	Total
Very poor	42	3	0	1	46	167	12	1	0	180
Poor	39	10	1	0	50	61	13	2	1	77
Average	53	12	1	3	69	33	3	1	1	38
Good	49	24	1	15	89	40	13	8	2	63
Very good	12	3	0	3	18	48	19	17	6	90
Total	195	52	3	22	272	349	60	29	10	448

(r=.42, z=2.20) (r=.58, z=3.68)

achieved only an average level of adjustment. This positive association of higher degree has also been found to be statistically significant at .05 levels (r=.42, z=2.20).

The distribution of the Jabalpur respondents according to the amount of interaction with the members of the voluntary organizations (Table 4.16-B) shows that a very large proportion of the respondents having no interaction are very poorly adjusted whereas the respondents having low, moderate and high interaction have a tendency to achieve good or very good level of adjustment. On application of the test of association between these two variables, it was found that a higher degree of positive association which is statistically significant at .01 level, exists between them (r=.58, z=3.68). In this way in both the groups of respondents we find that whosoever has taken membership of voluntary organizations and attending the meetings of those organizations is better adjusted than others who are not the members of any such organizations. This finding is different than the finding regarding interaction with friends, neighbours and relatives in the case of Jabalpur respondents. The reason for this is that only the financially well off people have become the members of voluntary organizations.

The general findings regarding both the groups of respondents' family relationship and other social relationship resemble with the conclusions derived by Shanas et al. (1968:425) on the basis of the studies of three industrial societies of Denmark, Britain and the United States, that most of the aged people are fairly integrated and securely knitted in the social structure of the industrial society through the maintenance of informal primary relationship with the family and local community. And the findings regarding the relationship between the interaction with the friends, neighbours, relatives and the members of the voluntary organizations on the one hand and the adjustment on the other shows that the interaction with the people other than the family members is desired and enjoyed by the aged people. It aids to raise their morale provided their life is physically and financially comfortable. It gives the feeling of integration in society, belongingness, usefulness and recognition to the aged people. Thus one can lead a more harmonious and satisfying life in old age if he keeps himself associated with others.

Occupational Activities

After retirement one has plenty of time at his disposal and there is not much pressure to use it for socially prescribed purposes. The old people react to this situation in various ways. Some people reduce their activities, withdraw from the outside world and spend more time in meditation or sheer inaction. Others utilise the time in various activities and continue without much reduction of action. It is often observed that quite a few people again engage themselves, in occupational activities after retirement. Because the job gives them an income, regulates the pattern of activity, determines the status, provides associates and gives purpose to life (Hunter, 1968 : 10; Havighurst, 1954: 2-6; Wormal and Gelbaum, 1945: 16-21). By emphasizing the importance of creative activity in old age, Lawton (1951:113-130) has said that it carried with it the extraordinary potentialities for emotional adjustment. He has further suggested that even the physically handicapped people should work according to their ability because employment is nature's best physician and essential to human happiness (Lawton 1951: 266).

Considering the importance of occupation it is useful to find out what kind of relationship exists between the involvement in occupational activity in the post-retirement period and the adjustment of the retired people. To find out the occupational activity of the respondents they have been asked whether they have any occupation at present, and if they have, what type of occupation, service, business, private practice, farming or any other, they have.

Table 4.17-A shows the distribution of the Chandigarh respondents according to above mentioned information. This table shows that the majority, i.e. 63.90 per cent, of the respondents are leading a complete retired life. But it is not worthy that a considerable numbers, i.e. 36.40 per cent, have again taken up some occupation as a source of income. A larger proportion of those who have taken up some occupation are doing service in private establishments and rest of them have either started their business or private practice of their profession or doing farming.

TABLE 4.17

Distribution of the Respondents of Chandigarh and Jabalpur According to the Present Occupation

Present Occupation	(A) Chandigarh Frequency	Percentage	(B) Jabalpur Frequency	Percentage
Completely retired	173	63.60	314	70.09
Service	61	22.43	43	9.60
Private practice of the profession	14	5.15	26	5.80
Business	16	5.88	27	6.02
Farming	8	2.94	38	8.49
Total	272	100.00	448	100.00

The distribution of the Jabalpur respondents according to their present occupation (Table 4.17-B) shows that a great majority, i.e. 70.09 per cent, of them are leading a complete retired life. Among the rest of the 29.91 per cent of the Jabalpur respondents, more or less same proportions of them have involved themselves either in service, private practice of the profession, business or farming.

In this way in both the groups of sample we find that a great majority of them have not involved themselves in the occupational activity again after retirement. But the difference between the state of affairs of these two groups of respondents is that while the Chandigarh retirees do not need it for earning money, the Jabalpur retirees can not do it due to the shortage of resources, poor health and non-availability of services.

To find out the degree of involvement in occupational activity, information regarding the time spent on occupational activity everyday has been taken into account.* It has been

* To find out the respondents involvement in various activities they have been asked to report about their routine activities and the approximate time they spend on those activities excluding compulsory activities like taking bath, dressing, eating etc.

found that whatsoever has taken up some occupation, he is spending about six hours everyday on it. In the absence of any variation regarding the time spent on occupational activity the respondents have been divided only into two categories, that is, not involved and involved in occupational activity. Those who spend no time, came in the first category and those who spend about six hours on occupational activity, come in the second category.

When in the case of Chandigarh respondents these two categories of involvement in occupational activity were cross tabulated with the five levels of adjustment (Table 4.18-A), it has been found that a positive association exists between these two variables. This table shows that a larger proportion of the respondents involved in occupational activity have achieved a good level of adjustment and very few of them are very poorly or poorly adjusted. Whereas among those respondents, leading completely retired life, this pattern has not been found. More or less the equal proportions of them fall in the categories of very poor, poor, average and good levels of adjustment and there are very few respondents who have achieved a very good level of adjustment. The value of the test of association also shows a very high degree of positive association, which is statistically significant at .01 level, exists between these variables (r=.62, z=3.92).

Same is the finding among the Jabalpur respondents also. The distribution of them according to the degree of involvement in occupational activity and the level of adjustment (Table 4.18-B) shows that relatively a higher proportion of these who have involved themselves in the occupational activity have achieved a very good level of adjustment and relatively smaller proportions of them have achieved lower levels of adjustment whereas majority of those who have not involved themselves in the occupational activity are very poorly adjusted and comparatively smaller proportion of them have achieved good level of adjustment. Application of the test of association between these variables also shows that a higher degree of positive association, which is statistically significant at .01 level, exists between them (r=.65, z=4.12).

TABLE 4.18

Distribution of the Respondents of Chandigarh and Jabalpur According to the Degree of Involvement in Occupational Activity and the Level of Adjustment

Level of Adjustment	(A) Chandigarh Degree of Involvement in Occupational Activity			(B) Jabalpur Degree of Involvement in Occupational Activity		
	Not Involved	Involved	Total	Not Involved	Involved	Total
Very poor	40	6	46	161	19	180
Poor	43	7	50	62	15	77
Average	46	23	69	25	13	38
Good	41	48	89	35	28	63
Very good	3	15	18	31	59	90
Total	173	99	272	314	134	448
	(r=.62, z=3.92)			(r=.65, z=4.12)		

Hobbies

Aging presents critical challenges to the use of time in modern societies (Russell, 1979 : 235). To pass the leisure time in satisfying ways is an important issue and a big problem, the retirees of present society are confronted with. With advancing age participation in voluntary organizations declines, informal relations reduce and the aged spent most of the day in doing nothing (International Encyclopedia of the Social Sciences, Vol. I, P. 192, 1968). The gerontologists have emphasized the importance of hobbies for this purpose. They facilitate a better adjustment in old age. Howell (1953 : 58-73) says that successful retirement is to possess a variety of interests and activities which can take the place of former occupation. By emphasizing importance of cultivation of flexibility of roles for old age, Havighurst (1954 : 309-311) has said that the satisfaction of new experience, creativity and status which one gets from his work in middle age, he may get in old age from hobbies. In the same way Lawton (1951 : 113-130) has pointed out that these self-realization and the expression of self are possible even in old age through creative hobbies like arts and crafts. When retirement is inevitable, substitute activities may, to some extent take the place of job. Therefore, the individual should find some way which can give him the feeling that he is still a part of society (Wermal and Gelbaum, 1945 : 16-21 ; Hunter, 1968 : 10). Many studies have also established the association between hobbies and adjustment of the aged people as discussed earlier while reviewing the literature on adjustment in old age.

Considering the immense importance of hobbies or special interests for adjustment in old age, it is useful to focus attention on the special interests of the respondents. The respondents have been asked whether they have any hobbies or special interests in any activities, if they have, what are their special interests?. To find out the degree of involvement in hobbies, the time they spend daily on those activities, which they have mentioned as their hobbies, is taken into consideration. For analysis all hobbies have been divided into two broad categories. The first category includes that are less likely to involve interaction with other people, like reading, gardening, walking, painting, listening to radio, etc. The second category includes hobbies that are more likely to involve interaction with others, such as indoor games and outdoor games, social visits, social services, etc.

The distribution of the Chandigarh respondents according to the time spent on all hobbies and then on both type of hobbies separately (4.19-A) reveals some interesting facts. It shows that quite a considerable number, i.e. 28.31 per cent, of the respondents do not devote any time to hobbies since they do not have any hobby. But among those, who have some hobbies, a higher proportion of them devote more than four hours daily to their hobbies. This table also shows that the percentage of the respondents, who have no such hobbies which involve interaction with others is much higher (54.05%) in comparison with the percentage of the retirees who have no such hobbies which do not involve interaction with other persons (30.51%). The reason for this difference may be that almost all of them are educated and for them hobbies like reading may be most convenient to maintain in old age. This table also reveals that the percentage of the retired people, spending more than four hours daily on hobbies, like reading, walking, gardening etc., is higher than the percentage of those spending same time on hobbies like indoor and outdoor games, social visits, social service, etc. It indicates that hobbies, which can be pursued alone, are more common than those where the company of others is needed.

The distribution of the Jabalpur respondents according to the time spent daily on all hobbies, hobbies involving interaction with others and hobbies not involving interaction with others (Table 4.19-B) shows that a great majority, i.e. 67.19 per cent, of the Jabalpur respondents do not devote any time to hobbies since they do not have any hobby. But among those, who have some hobbies, more or less same proportion of them devote upto two hours, two to four hours and above four hours daily to their hobbies. This table also shows that the percentage of the respondents, who have no such hobbies which involve interaction with others is more or less same (75.63%) as the percentage of the retirees who have no such

TABLE 4.19

Distribution of the Respondents of Chandigarh and Jabalpur According to the Time Spent on All Hobbies, Hobbies Involving Interaction with others and Hobbies not Involving Interaction with others Everyday

Type of Hobbies	(A) Chandigarh Time Spent on Hobbies Everyday					(B) Jabalpur Time Spent on Hobbies Everyday				
	None	Up to Two hrs.	Two to Four hrs.	Above Four hrs.	Total	None	Up to Two hrs.	Two to Four hrs.	Above Four hrs.	Total
All Hobbies	77 (28.31)	43 (15.81)	66 (24.26)	86 (31.62)	272 (100.00)	301 (67.19)	59 (13.17)	51 (11.39)	37 (8.25)	448 (100.00)
Hobbies not Involving Interaction with others.	83 (30.51)	81 (29.78)	58 (21.32)	50 (18.39)	272 (100.00)	339 (75.68)	49 (10.93)	41 (9.15)	19 (4.24)	448 (100.00)
Hobbies Involving Interaction with other.	147 (54.04)	107 (39.33)	13 (4.78)	5 (1.85)	272 (100.00)	347 (77.45)	67 (14.95)	23 (5.15)	11 (2.45)	448 (100.00)

(The percentages are given in parentheses)

hobbies which do not involve interaction with other persons (77.45%).

The reason for this similaritly may be that Jabalpur retirees along with the hobbies, involving no interaction with others, also giving importance to the hobbies involving interaction with others. The percentage of those spending up to two hours daily on their hobbies is little higher in the case of such hobbies which do not involve interaction whereas the percentages of those spending two to four hours and above four hours are higher in the case of such hobbies which involve interaction.

While comparing the data of time spent on hobbies by the Chandigarh and Jabalpur respondents we find a striking difference. While majority of the Chandigarh respondents are spending some time on hobbies, most of the Jabalpur respondents have no hobbies at all. While Chandigarh respondents are concentrating mostly on such hobbies which do not involve interaction with others, we do not find any such clear difference in Jabalpur. The reason for this may be that by the virtue of being highly educated the earlier group can devote more time to the hobbies like reading, whereas most of our Jabalpur respondents due to their illiteracy or very little education have to depend on such hobbies which involve interaction with other people. It is observed that a person who is fond of reading does not require anybody's company to gossip.

Now we will examine the relationship that exists between the degree of involvement in hobbies and the level of adjustment. To find out the degree of involvement in hobbies, the total time spent on both types of hobbies daily by the respondents has been divided into four categories as none, up to two hours, from two to four hours and above four hours. On the basis of these categories the respondents have been divided into four groups as having nil, low, moderate and high degree of involvement. Then these four categories of involvement were cross tabulated with the five levels of adjustment.

The distribution of the Chandigarh respondents according to the degree of involvement in hobbies and the level of adjustment (Table 4.20-A) reveals that with the increase in

TABLE 4.20

Distribution of the Respondents of Chandigarh and Jabalpur According to the Degree of Involvement in Hobbies and the Level of Adjustment

Level of Adjustment	(A) Chandigarh: Degree of Involvement in Hobbies					(B) Jabalpur: Degree of Involvement in Hobbies				
	No involvement	Low involvement	Moderate Involvement	High involvement	Total	No involvement	Low involvement	Moderate involvement	High involvement	Total
Very poor	34	6	4	2	46	166	13	1	0	180
Poor	26	7	10	7	50	57	15	3	2	77
Average	8	19	21	21	69	13	12	8	5	38
Good	8	10	25	47	89	28	9	15	11	63
Very good	1	1	6	10	18	37	10	24	19	90
Total	77	43	66	86	272	301	59	51	37	448

(r=.61, z=4.87) (r=.64, z=5.10)

involvement in hobbies the level of adjustment also increases. A larger section of the retirees who do not devote any time to hobbies, are poorly adjusted, whereas the majority of those, having high involvement in hobbies, have achieved a good level of adjustment. The application of the test of association has also supported the fact. A higher degree of positive association which is statistically significant at .01 level, exists between these two variables ($r=.61$, $z=4.87$). These findings resemble the findings of other studies conducted in the western countries showing the positive association between hobbies and adjustment in old age. So it can be concluded from this finding that the special interests or hobbies play a very important role in the adjustment of old people.

The distribution of the Jabalpur respondents according to the degree of involvement in hobbies and the level of adjustment (Table 4.20-B) shows that majority of those having no involvement in hobbies are very poorly adjusted whereas the respondents having moderate and high involvement in hobbies are more likely to achieve good and very good level of adjustment. On applying the test of association it was found that a higher degree of positive association which is statistically significant at .01 level, exists between these two variables ($r=.64$, $z=5.10$). The finding on this issue in both the groups of sample shows the importance of hobbies in life specially in old age.

Religious Activities

As we have noticed earlier while reviewing the literature on adjustment in old age, quite a few studies have found an association between religious activities like going to the Church and adjustment. Religious activities provide various ways of passing the leisure time which becomes a problem in old age. Thus, religious activities may also facilitate better adjustment in old age. In this study also it was thought useful to examine the relationship between religious involvement and adjustment. For this purpose the respondents have been asked about their religious activities and the time they spend on those activities everyday. For analysis all the religious activities have been divided into two broad categories. The first category includes the religious activities performed inside the home such as prayer, worship, meditation, reading religious literature, etc. The second category includes the religious activities performed outside the home such as going to the temple or any other religious institutions for worship, prayer or reading religious books.

The distribution of the Chandigarh respondents according to the time spent on all the religious activities and each type of religious activities separately (Table 4.21-A) reveals some surprising facts. This table shows that the majority, i.e. 54.04 per cent, of the respondents are spending only upto one hour everyday on religious activities while 22.80 per cent are not devoting any time to such activities. Regarding the two types of activities it has been found that the percentage of the respondents not having outdoor religious activities is much higher, (58.09), than the percentage of the retirees not devoting any time to the indoor religious activities (20.59). A higher proportion of the respondents are spending upto one hour on indoor religious activities while the majority of them do not devote any time to outdoor religious activities. On the whole, this table reveals the lack of interest among most of the Chandigarh respondents in religious activities.

The distribution of the Jabalpur respondents according to the time spent on all the religious activities, and each type of religious activities separately (Table 4.21-B) reveals that the majority, i.e. 56.02 per cent, of the respondents are spending above two hours everyday on religious activities while only 10.04 per cent are not devoting any time to such activities. Regarding the two types of activities it has been found that percentage of the respondents, not having outdoor religious activities, is much higher (60.26), than the percentage of the retirees, not devoting any time to the indoor religious activities (13.40). Relatively a higher proportion of the respondents are spending one to two hours on indoor religious activities whereas a little less than one-fifth of them are devoting more than the hours on indoor religious activities. Relatively smaller percentage of the Jabalpur respondents are spending more time on outdoor religious activities whereas majority is spending no time at all on such activities. On the whole it

TABLE 4.21

Distribution of the Respondents of Chandigarh and Jabalpur According to the Time Spent on all Religious Activities, Indoor Religious Activities and Outdoor Religious Activities Every Day

Type of Activities	(A) Chandigarh: Time Spent on Religious Activities Everyday					(B) Jabalpur: Time Spent on Religious Activities Everyday				
	None	Up to one hour	One to two hour	Above two hour	Total	None	Up to one hours	One to two hours	Above two hours	Total
All Religious Activities	62 (22.80)	147 (54.04)	46 (16.54)	18 (6.62)	272 (100.00)	45 (10.04)	32 (1.14)	180 (26.80)	251 (56.02)	448 (100.00)
Indoor Religious Activities	56 (20.59)	123 (45.22)	79 (29.04)	14 (5.15)	272 (100.00)	60 (13.60)	129 (28.80)	170 (37.94)	89 (19.06)	448 (100.00)
Out door Religious Activities.	158 (58.09)	83 (30.51)	27 (9.93)	4 (1.47)	272 (100.00)	270 (60.26)	26 (6.25)	81 (18.09)	69 (15.40)	448 (100.00)

(The percentages are given in parentheses)

shows that most of the Jabalpur respondents are devoting time to religious activities.

A comparative look on the issue between the two groups of sample of our study, reveals that a higher proportion of the Jabalpur respondents are spending more time whereas the higher proportion of the Chandigarh respondents are spending less time on religious activities. While in the case of indoor religious activities, Jabalpur respondents are devoting more time than the Chandigarh respondents, in the case of outdoor religious activities, majority of both the groups is not spending any time on them. Considering the old age of our respondents it seems quite obvious also. Indoor religious activities can conveniently be maintained. As far as the difference in the time spent on religious activities among both the groups is concerned, considering the background characteristics of respondents of both the cities it may also be the expected one. Most of the Chandigarh respondents are not very old, educated, have modern outlook, have some other more tangible and interesting activities even after retirement. Whereas most of Jabalpur respondents are quite aged, very little educated, have traditional outlook, and do not have much other activities like hobbies, to remain occupied at this period of life. Therefore, we find that while the Chandigarh retirees are not giving much importance to religious activities, the Jabalpur respondents are considering them a most important aspect of their life.

Now we will examine the association that exists between the degree of involvement in religious activities and the level of adjustment. For this purpose, the time spent on all religious activities everyday by the respondents has been divided into four categories. The respondents spending none, upto one hour, one to two hours and obove two hours have been categorized as having nil, low, moderate and high degree of involvement in religious activities, respectively. To find out the association between the involvement in religious activities and adjustment these four categories have been cross tabulated with the five levels of adjustment.

The distribution of the Chandigarh respondents according to the above mentioned information (Table 4.22-A) reveals that no association, neither positive nor negative exists between the degree of involvement in religious activities and the level of adjustment in old age. In the table we do not find any clear trend of either increasing or decreasing level of adjustment with the increasing degree of involvement in religious activities. This means both these variables are independent from each other. When the test of association has been applied between the two variables it has been found that no association exists between these variables (r=-035). This finding enables us to conclude that religious activities are not very important for the adjustment in old age.

The distribution of the Jabalpur respondents according to the degree of involvement in religious activities and the level of adjustment (Table 4.22-B) shows that a moderate degree of negative association, which is statistically significant at .05 level, exists between these two variables (r=—.36, z=—2.28). As it can be seen from the table, majority of those respondents who have high degree of involvcment in religious activities have achieved a very poor level of adjustment, whereas no such trend is seen in the categories of lower degree of religious involvement. It shows that religious involvement is not helpful in the better adjustment in old age. On the contrary it seems that probably the frustrated and unhappy aged people involve themselves in religious activities to find some solace somewhere but their religious involvement does not increase their morale. By considering the background characteristics of our Jabalpur respondents it is quite understandable that religious activities may keep the retired people busy for sometime but they cannot solve their problems concerned with the fulfillment of basic needs specially. Most of our Jabalpur respondents have traditional and rural background. As we have seen earlier they have a faith in all the religious beliefs and they devote much time on religious activities also, but due to their financial suffering, they are not being able to lead a satisfying and happy life. In the case of Chandigarh respondents also both of these factors have emerged as the independent variables. From this finding we can conclude as Russel (1979 : 264-265) has cited Stark (1968) that probably due to fear of death people in old age involve themselves in religious activities. The statement that religious

TABLE 4.22

Distribution of the Respondents of Chandigarh and Jabalpur According to the Degree of Involvement in Religious Activities and the Level of Adjustment

Level of Adjustment	(A) Chandigarh Degree of Religious Involvement					(B) Jabalpur Degree of Religious Involvement				
	Nil	Low	Moderate	High	Total	Nil	Low	Moderate	High	Total
Very poor	6	28	6	6	46	8	13	25	144	180
Poor	9	30	8	3	50	10	11	32	14	77
Average	24	32	12	1	69	3	2	20	13	38
Good	13	51	15	5	89	18	2	24	19	63
Very good	5	6	4	3	18	6	4	19	61	90
Total	62	147	45	18	272	45	32	120	251	448

(r=.035) (r=—.36, z=—2.28)

activities outside the home tend to decline but inside activities show some increase with age, but there is no clear evidence that religion itself contributes to the psychological well being of the aged and the link between religion and aging remains unclear (Russell, 1979 : 265) gets strongly supported by our finding.

Overall Activeness and Social Interaction

Lastly by considering the difference of opinion among gerontologists about the desirability of two opposite types of life style, i.e. 'active' and 'disengaged' for adjustment in old age, it seems quite useful to examine the association that exists between the degree of overall activeness and social interaction of the respondents on the one hand and the level of their adjustment on the other. Although direct testing of the two opposite theories of successful aging through controlled observation has not been intended here, but still it may be found out tentatively that which type of life style is more desirable for better adjustment in latter years of life. Apart from this by considering the criticism of both the theories for over simplification of the affairs and towards the importance given to the developmental approach towards it lately, it seems proper to find out what are the other patterns of styles of successful aging and the aged people with what characteristics have developed these different patterns of adjustment in their lives.

By considering the importance of usage of the 'Time-Budget Methodology to study the Age-related Behaviour' as stated by Little (1984 : 17), to find out the overall activeness and social interaction of the respondents, the time they spend daily on their routine activities from morning to night, excluding necessary activities like taking bath, dressing, eating, etc. has been taken into consideration. All the activities have been divided into two broad categories. The first type of activities are those which are more likely to involve interaction with people other than the family members living in the same household. This category mainly includes occupational activities, meeting with people other than the family members living in the same household, marketing and other odd jobs outside the house, visits to religious institutions, voluntary organizations, clubs, etc. The second type of activities are those which are less likely to involve interaction with people other than the family members living in the same household. These includes mainly reading, writing, listening to ratio, gardening, worship, walking, physical exercise at home, etc.

The distribution of the Chandigarh respondents according to the time spent on all activities and then on each type of activities separately (Table 4.23-A) reveals some interesting facts. The table shows that the majority, i.e. 53.07 per cent, of the respondents are very active and spend more than eight hours daily on various activities. A glance at the time spent on two type of activities, i.e. those involving and those not involving interaction with non-family members, separately shows that in the case of activities not involving interaction with non-family members, larger sections of the respondents, i.e. 29.23 per cent, are spending two to four hours everyday, whereas no such clear trend is seen in the case of activities involving interaction with non-family members. More or less same proportion of them are spending upto two, two to four and six to eight hours on such activities. The percentage of the respondents spending upto two hours on activities not involving interaction with the non-family members is higher (38.23) then the percentage of the respondents spending two to four hours in activities involving interaction with the non-family members (25.36). The table also reveals that the percentage of the respondents spending six to eight hours daily on the activities involving interaction with the non-family members is higher (23.19) than the percentage of the respondents spending four to six hours daily on the activities not involving interaction with outsiders (7.35). It shows that people who remain active for a longer time of the day, involve themselves considerably in the social interaction too.

The distribution of the Jabalpur respondents according to the time spent on all activities and then on each type of activities separately (Table 4.23-B) reveals that relatively a larger section, i.e. 34.38 per cent, of them are very active and spend more than eight hours daily on various activities. A glance at the time spent on two types of activities, i.e. those

TABLE 4.23

Distribution of the Respondents of Chandigarh and Jabalpur According to the Time Spent on All Activities. Activities Involving Interaction with the Non-Family Members and Activities not Involving Interaction with the Non-Family Members Everyday

Type of Activities	(A) Chandigarh Time Spent on Various Activities Everyday					
	Up to two hrs.	Two to Four hrs.	Four to Six hrs.	Six to Eight hrs.	Above Eight hrs.	Total
All Activities	0	35 (12.75)	40 (14.70)	53 (19.48)	144 (53.07)	272 (100.00)
Activities Involving Interaction with Non-Family Members	72 (26.47)	69 (25.36)	34 (12.50)	63 (23.17)	34 (12.50)	272 (100.00)
Activities Not Involving Interaction with Non-Family Members	87 (31.99)	104 (38.23)	53 (19.48)	20 (7.35)	20 (2.94)	272 (100.00)

(B) Jabalpur

Type of Activities	Time Spent on Various Activities Everyday					
	Up to two hrs.	Two to Four hrs.	Four to Six hrs.	Six to Eight hrs.	Above Eight hrs.	Total
All Activities	0	69 (15.40)	101 (22.54)	124 (37.68)	154 (34.38)	448 (100.00)
Activities Involving Interaction with Non-Family Members	112 (25.00)	80 (17.85)	110 (24.55)	107 (23.90)	39 (8.70)	448 (100,00)
Activities Not Involving Interaction with Non-Family Members	98 (21.88)	117 (39.50)	123 (27.45)	30 (6.70)	20 (4.47)	448 (100.00)

(The percentages are given in parentheses)

involving and those not involving interaction with non-family members, separately shows that while relatively a larger section, i.e. 39.50 per cent, of the Jabalpur respondents are spending two to four hours everyday on the activities not involving interaction with non-family members whereas no such clear trend is seen regarding the activities involving interaction with non-family members. More or less same proportion of them, are spending upto two, four to six and above six hours on such activities. The percentage of the respondents spending two to four hours on the activities not involving interaction with the non-family members is higher (39.50) than the percentage of the respondents spending two to four in activities involving interaction with the non-family members (17.85). The table also reveals that the percentage of the respondents spending six to eight hours daily in the activities involving interaction with the non-family members is higher (23.70) than the percentage of the respondents spending four to six hours daily on the activities not involving interaction with outsiders (6.70). It also shows that the people who remain active for a longer time of the day, involve themselves considerably in the social interaction too.

A comparative look at the routine activities of the two groups of the respondents makes it clear that on the whole a larger section of the Chandigarh respondents than the Jabalpur respondents are very active. While most of the Chandigarh respondents are spending their day in useful activities, most of the Jabalpur respondents are just idling down. This difference of affairs may be due to the physical weakness, lack of money, illiteracy, and ignorance of the Jabalpur respondents.

We will now examine the relationship that exists between the degree of activeness and the level of adjustment. For activeness the respondents who remain active upto four hours, four to eight hours and above eight hours daily on various activities, excluding the compulsory ones, have been considered as having low, moderate and high degree of activeness respectively. Then these three degrees of activeness have been cross tabulated with five levels of adjustment.

The distribution of the Chandigarh respondents according to this information (Table 4.24-A) shows that the retired

TABLE 4.24

Distribution of the Respondents of Chandigarh and Jabalpur According to the Degree of Activeness and the Level of Adjustment

Level of Adjustment	(A) Chandigarh Degree of Activeness				(B) Jabalpur Degree of Activeness			
	Low	Moderate	High	Total	Low	Moderate	High	Total
Very poor	12	16	18	46	33	133	14	180
Poor	13	21	16	50	23	42	12	77
Average	8	29	32	69	6	14	18	38
Good	2	24	63	89	5	17	41	63
Very good	0	3	15	18	2	19	69	90
Total	35	93	144	272	69	225	154	448

(A) Chandigarh: ($r=.46$, $z=2.90$) (B) Jabalpur: ($r=.76$, $z=4.82$)

people having low, moderate and high degree of activeness have achieved a poor, average and a good level of adjustment respectively. Thus the degree of activeness and the level of adjustment increase or decrease together in the same direction. The application of the test of association between these two variables has also shown the existence of a higher degree of positive association, which is statistically significant at .01 level, between them (r=.46, z=2.90) demonstrating more active a person is better adjusted he will be.

The distribution of the Jabalpur respondents according to the degree of activeness and the level of adjustment (Table 4.24-B) shows that while most of the retired people having low and moderate degree of activeness have achieved very poor and poor level of adjustment, a majority of those having high degree of activeness have a tendency to achieve a very good and good level of adjustment. On application of the test of association between these two variables it was found that a very high degree of positive association, which is statistically significant at .01 level, exists between them (r=.76, z=4.82) showing more active an aged person is better adjusted in life he will be. In this regard findings are same in both the groups of the sample.

For the purpose of examining the association between the social interaction and the adjustment the respondents spending upto two hours, two to four hours, four to six hours, six to eight hours and above eight hours in the activities involving interaction with non-family members have been considered as having very low, low, moderate, high and very high degree of social interaction respectively. Then the five degrees of social interaction have been cross tabulated with the five levels of adjustment.

The distribution of the Chandigarh respondents according to the degree of social interaction and the level of adjustment (Table 4.25-A) reveals that a positive association exists between these two variables which shows that higher the social interaction, better the adjustment. A majority of those having very high degree of social interaction have achieved a good level of adjustment, whereas in the case of those having a very low degree of interaction, the pattern is reverse. Almost equal

TABLE 4.25

Distribution of the Respondents of Chandigarh and Jabalpur According to the Degree of Social Interaction and the Level of Adjustment

(A) Chandigarh

Level of Adjustment	Degree of Social Interaction					
	Very low	Low	Moderate	High	Very high	Total
Very poor	20	10	4	9	3	46
Poor	19	12	5	9	5	50
Average	21	17	9	14	8	69
Good	11	26	11	24	17	89
Very good	1	4	5	7	1	18
Total	72	69	34	63	34	272

$(r=.32,\ z=2.11)$

(B) Jabalpur

Level of Adjustment	Degree of Social Interaction: Very low	Low	Moderate	High	Very high	Total
Very poor	65	31	67	14	3	180
Poor	34	19	11	9	4	77
Average	10	13	8	6	2	38
Good	3	5	10	33	12	63
Very good	0	13	14	45	18	90
Total	112	80	110	107	39	448

(r=.49, z=3.11)

number of such respondents fall in the categories of very poor, poor and average level of adjustment. The application of the test of association shows that a moderate degree of positive association, which is statistically significant at .05 level, exists between these two variables (r=.32, z=2.11).

The distribution of the Jabalpur respondents according to the degree of social interaction and the level of adjustment (Table 4.25-B) shows that the majority of those having very low and moderate degree of interaction and a larger proportion of those having low degree of interaction, have achieved a poor level of adjustment whereas the larger proportion of those having high and very high degree of interaction have achieved a very good level of adjustment. On applying the test of association between these two variables, it was found that a higher degree of positive association, which is statistically significant at .01 level, exists between them.

On comparing the data on social interaction and level of adjustment between the two groups of respondents we find that while among Chandigarh respondents a moderate degree, whereas among the Jabalpur respondents a higher degree of positive association exists between these two variables. The reason for this difference may be, that among those who are from the lower strata of the society, if the aged persons involve themselves, to a very high degree, in the activities, involving interaction with non-family members, mostly they do involve themselves in the occupational activity which along with the interaction provides money also. It is more satisfying since it solves their financial problem and makes them happy. But this phenomenon is not necessary in the case of those having higher educational, economical and pre-retirement occupational status. They can find various other activities for providing opportunities of social interaction.

Thus the data regarding the behavioural factors and the adjustment in old age reveals that in the case of Chandigarh respondents, except religious activities, all the behavioural factors i.e. relationship and interaction with the family members living in the same household and with the children living separately, association or interaction with the friends, neighbours, relatives and the members of voluntary organizations, involvement in occupational activities and hobbies, activeness and social interaction with people other than the family members, etc. are positively associated with the adjustment of the respondents. These findings seem to support the activity theory which status that the aged persons are better adjusted if they remain active and involved in interaction with other people. The explanation of this finding is that by being active and associated with people, a retired person can satisfy his physical as well as socio-psychological needs and lead a satisfying life. We did not find any association, either negative or positive between the involvement in religious activities and the adjustment among Chandigarh respondents. This fact also supports the activity theory because religiosity indicates to a great extent the withdıawal or disengagement of an individual from the worldly affairs. From these findings we may infer as Shanas et al. (1968 : 425-426) and Lipman and Sterne (1969 : 194-203) have pointed out that the aged people do not wish to disengage themselves from society, but it is society which wants to segregate them from the rest of the society and forces them to disengage by providing them the terminal 'sick role' of old age, specially through retirement. This creates frustration, tension and anxiety among them because they do not get opportunities for satisfying their needs. On the whole, our data regarding Chandigarh respondents demonstrates that the retirees, who are capable enough to engage themselves in various activities and interaction with other people, are leading a happy and satisfying life, whereas the retirees, having low degree of activeness and interaction with others find themselves unable to lead a harmonious life in this period of life. Thus, we can conclude that activity, interaction and good relations with others play very important roles in the adjustment of old people.

As far as the Jabalpur respondents are concerned, findings regarding the relationship between the behavioural factors and adjustment shows that while the relation with the family members living in the same household, relationship with the children living separately, interaction with the members of voluntary organizations, involvement in occupational activities and hobbies, activeness and social interaction with people other than the family members have strong positive association, interaction with friends, neighbours and relatives have weak positive association with the adjustment of the Jabalpur respondents. Among them while interaction with the family members living in the same household and involvement in the religious activities have negative association, living with the children, frequency of meetings with the children living separately have no association, neither positive nor negative with adjustment of the retired people living in Jabalpur.

The reasons for these discrepancies about the association between the various behavioural factors on one hand and the adjustment of the Jabalpur respondents on the other, may be to some extent the physical weekness and to great extent, the poverty in this period of life. As we have discussed earlier most of our Jabalpur respondents are suffering from very acute financial problems and although they may not be suffering from any disease, they are very weak physically. During the interviews the author come to know that quite a few of them cannot afford even one meal a day regularly during the whole month. Due to these sufferings and hardships, although our Jabalpur respondents are interacting more than the Chandigarh respondents, with the family members, grown-up children, friends, neighbours and relatives, which is a typical symptom of a traditional society, the interaction itself is not contributing to their psychological well being or higher morale. In the same way although the Jabalpur respondents are devoting more time than Chandigarh respondents in religious activities, it is not contributing to their happiness or satisfaction.

On the contrary in the case of Chandigarh respondents who are financially well off and physically strong, by excluding the religious involvement, the interaction with various groups of people discussed above is contributing to their psychological well being and higher morale.

From these findings we can conclude that the social interaction with various groups of people produce the desired effect, in the form of satisfaction or happiness in life, only in the situation when the basic needs of the aged people are fulfilled satisfactorily. Otherwise it may create conflicts specially with the family members living in the same household.

In this way our findings very strongly support the statement of Estreib and Thompson (1957 : 151) that there seems to be a fairly wide agreement in the gerontological literature that there are two very important variables related to adjustment in old age and they are socio-economic status and physical health. Therefore, they should be regarded as basic variables in any analysis.

The Developmental approach

The above mentioned statement, showing the immense importance of socio-economic status, and physical health for adjustment in old age gives us the clue to find out as suggested by the advocates of developmental approach in this matter, the characteristics of the respondents, adopting two opposite life styles, i.e. 'Active' and 'disengaged' or the middle path by the combination of both styles of successful aging. This will show, who are the people who adopt a particular life style after retirement willingly.

Although we have completed the objective of our study, that is, to find out the correlates of 'good adjustment' of the retired Government employees living in Chandigarh and Jabalpur, and as far as the life style is concerned our findings support the activity theory, though with some condition in Jabalpur, but at the same time we cannot neglect the disengaged well adjusted people. By considering the criticism of these theories and the suggestion of adopting a developmental approach towards this matter, it was thought useful to know about the characteristics of aged people, who have adopted opposite life styles or the mid-way to age successfully and what are their activities at this age. Although the existing theories have been criticized and recently the idea of developmental approach towards successful aging has been launched but as far as the knowledge of researcher goes, no one has done the empirical research work, atleast in India to find out possibility of applying it. Therefore, this effort will contribute certainly to the gerontological knowledge.*

For this purpose all the respondents of both the cities, who have achieved good and very good level of adjustment were combined together and considered as well adjusted retired people. They were divided into three categories, as having low, moderate and high degree of activeness on the basis of their routine activities. The respondents who remain active upto four hours, four to eight hours and above eight hours daily on verious activities, excluding the compulsory ones, have been considered as having low, moderate and high degree of activeness respectively.

By considering the immense importance given by the gerontologists to the two basic variables i.e. the socio-economic status and the health condition it was though proper to find out first about these variables in the case of well adjusted respondents having low, moderate and high degree of activeness separately. After this we will try to find out their involvement in various activities.

Table 4.26 shows the distribution of these well adjusted Chandigarh and Jabalpur respondents according to the degree of activeness on one hand and the other variables discussed above on the other. In the case of Chandigarh 2,27 and 78 and in the case of Jabalpur 7, 36, and 110 well adjusted respondents have come under the categories of low, moderate and high degree of activeness respectively.

First of all we will concentrate on the pre-retirement socio-economic status of these respondents. For this purpose pre-retirement class of service, which is associated with the educational qualification and the financial condition of an individual, as we have seen in chapter I also, was thought off as the best indicator of socio-economic status of the respondents. The distribution of the Chandigarh respondents according to the degree of activeness and the pre-retirement class of service in the same table (4.26-A) shows that the retirees from class IV

---

* This type of analysis was not done even by the researcher while studying the Chandigarh respondents for her Ph. D. thesis because at that time the idea of developmental approach was not familiar in the gerontological literature.

services are having a low degree of activeness, while the majority, i.e. 59.26 per cent, of the retirees having moderate degree of activeness have retired from class III services. The majority, i.e. 58.97 per cent and a considerable proportion i.e. 37.18 per cent, of those having high level of activity are having the background of class I and class II Government services respectively. The table reveals that the retirees having higher socio-economic status and high educational background are able to keep themselves engaged in variety of activities, whereas the retirees having lower socio-economic status and lower educational background remain contented with the lesser degree of activeness since they are not able to take up very many activities to remain busy after retirement. The class of a person gives us the idea about his financial position also. A person having sufficient money in hand can spend it in many ways including the present occupation to remain active whereas lack of money becomes a handicap of a person and he has to remain contented with few activities which can be performed without spending money.

As far as the present health condition is concerned, it was thought proper to take their health condition into consideration which has been determined through a crude index, prepared on the basis of the respondents' self evaluation, number of ailments, seriousness of suffering from the ailments and the number of days spent on bed in illness during last one year.* All the well adjusted retirees were divided into three categories having bad, fair and good health condition. Cross tabulation of these three categories of health condition with the three degrees of activeness (Table 4.26-A) shows that those coming under the category of low degree of activeness are having a bad health condition. In the case of moderate activeness we find that majority, i.e. 62.96 per cent, have fair health. But in the case of high degree of activeness the table shows that an overwhelming majority of the Chandigarh respondents, i.e. 87.18 per cent, are enjoying a good health. It shows that health condition plays a major role regarding the activities of the aged people. If their health permits and they feel physically

* The index for determining the health condition of the respondents has been discussed in detail in chapter II.

TABLE 4.26

Distribution of the Well-adjusted Respondents of Chandigarh and Jabalpur According to Their Degree of Activeness on one hand and Pre-retirement Socio-economic Status, Present Health Status and Daily Involvement in Various Activities on the their

(A)
Chandigarh

Degree of Activeness	Total No	Pre-retirement Occupational Status				Health Condition		
		IV	III	II	I	Bad	Fair	Good
Low	2 (100.00)	2 (100.00)	0	0	0	2 (100.00)	0	0
Moderate	27 (100.00)	0	16 (59.26)	7 (25.92)	4 (14.83)	1 (3.70)	17 (62.96)	9 (33.34)
High	78 (100.00)	0	3 (3.85)	29 (37.18)	46 (58.97)	0	10 (12.82)	68 (87.18)
Total	107 (100.00)	2 (1.89)	19 (17.75)	36 (33.64)	50 (46.72)	3 (2.80)	27 (25.24)	77 (71.96)

Occupational Activity at Present		Monthly Income			Sufficiency of Income		
Not-Invved	Involved	Rs. 400 and below	Rs. 401 to Rs. 800	Above Rs. 800	Less	Same	More
2 (100.00)	0	2 (100.00)	0	0	0	2 (100.00)	0
21 (77.77)	6 (22.23)	2 (7.41)	20 (74.07)	5 (18.51)	0	21 (77.77)	6 (22.23)
21 (35.92)	87 (73.08)	25 (38.05)	25 (32.05)	21 (35.90)	48 (61.54)	9 (11.54)	21 (26.92)
44 (41.12)	63 (58.88)	29 (27.10)	45 (42.05)	33 (30.84)	48 (44.86)	32 (29.91)	27 (25.23)

Degree of Activeness	Total No.	Involvement in Social Interaction		
		Low	Moderate	High
Low	2 (100.00)	2 (100.00)	0	0
Moderate	27 (100.00)	7 (25.92)	20 (74.08)	0
High	78 (100.00)	3 (3.86)	10 (12.88)	65 (83.33)
Total	107 (100.00)	12 (11.21)	30 (28.04)	65 (60.75)

Involvement In Hobbies			Involvement in Religious Activities		
Nil	Low	High	Nil	Low	High
2 (100.00)	0	0	2 (100.00)	0	0
4 (14.82)	23 (85.13)	0	1 (3.70)	1 (3.70)	25 (92.60)
3 (3.35)	19 [34.36]	56 [71,79]	56 (26.64]	56 (71.79]	2 (2.57)
9 (8.41)	42 (39.25)	56 (53.34)	23 (21.49)	57 (53.27)	27 (25.24)

(B)

Jabalpur

Degree of Activeness	Total No.	Pre-retirement Occupational Status			
		IV	III	II	I
Low	7 (100.00)	6 (85.71)	1 (14.29)	0	0
Moderate	36 (100.00)	6 (16.67)	18 (50.00)	7 (19.44)	5 (13.89)
High	110 (100.00)	22 (20.00)	20 (18.18)	47 (42.73)	21 (19.09)
Total	153 (100.00)	34 (22.32)	39 (25.49)	54 (36.29)	26 (16.99)

Health Condition			Occupational Activity at Present		Monthly Income		
Bad	Fair	Good	Not Involved	Involved	Rs. 400 and below	Rs. 401 to Rs. 800	Above Rs. 800
7 (100.00)	0	0	7 (100.00)	0	6 (85.71)	1 (14.29)	0
6 (16.67)	21 (58.33)	9 (25.10)	31 (86.11)	5 (13.89)	12 (33.33)	24 (66 67)	0
0	15 (13.64)	95 (86.36)	28 (26.45)	82 (74.54)	52 (47.27)	36 (32.72)	22 (20.00)
13 [8.50]	36 (23.53)	104 (67.97)	66 (43.13)	87 (56.87)	70 (45.75)	61 (39.87)	22 (14.38)

Degree of Activeness	Total No.	Sufficiency of Income			Involvement in Social Interaction		
		Less	Same	More	Low	Moderate	High
Low	7 (100.00)	0	7 (100.00)	0	3 (42.86)	4 (57.14)	0
Moderate	93 (100.00)	1 (2.78)	28 (77.78)	7 (19.44)	0	14 (38.89)	22 (61.11)
High	110 (100.00)	59 (53.63)	35 (31.82)	16 (14.54)	0	0	110 (100.00)
Total	153 (100.00)	50 (39.21)	70 (46.75)	23 (15.04)	3 (1.96)	18 (11.76)	132 (86.28)

Involvement in Hobbies			Involvement in Religious Activities		
Nil	Low	High	Nil	Low	High
7 (100.00)	0	0	7 (100.00)	0	0
11 (30.56)	25 (69.45)	0	3 (8.33)	6 (16.67)	27 (75.00)
47 (42.73)	33 (30.00)	30 (27.27)	14 (12.73)	0	96 (87.27)
65 (42.48)	58 (37.91)	30 (19.61)	24 (15.69)	6 (3.92)	123 (80.39)

(The percentages are given in parentheses)

strong and energetic, they take up various activities after retirement, otherwise they accept the 'terminal sick role' given by the society to them, quietly and willingly, and do not indulge in any new activities.

After having the information about the pre-retirement socio-economic status and present health condition of the well adjusted Chandigarh respondents now we can focus our attention towards the type of activities they are involved with daily. First of all we will consider the occupational activity, which is most important in the Indian society from the economic point of view apart from the provision of activity and social interaction.

The distribution of the well adjusted Chandigrah respondents according to their involvement in occupational activity and degree of activeness (Table 4.26-A) clearly shows that while most of the retirees having low and moderate degree of activeness are leading a completely retired life satisfactorily, the overwhelming majority, i.e. 73.08 percent, of retirees having high degree of activeness have involved themselves in the occupational activity again after retirement, which provides them both the money and the opportunity of interaction with the people other than the family members.

Now it will be proper to find out the present financial condition of the well adjusted Chandigarh respondents coming under the three categories of degree of activeness. The information about these variables in table 4.26-A shows that while both the respondents having low level of activeness have monthly income of Rs. 400/- and below, the majority of those having moderate degree of activeness (74.07%) are having their monthly income between Rs. 401 to 800. The point worth noting here is that relatively a larger proportion, i.e. 35.90 per cent, of the respondents having high level of activity get above Rs. 800/- every month as their income, although rest of them fall equally in both the lower income levels which is understandable by considering the capabilities of Chandigarh retirees. This shows that probably most of those who are very active have engaged themselves in occupational activity and therefore, they have been able to earn more and remain in a comfortable financial position even after retirement.

Regarding the financial condition, apart from the actual monthly income, the respondents feeling about the sufficiency of their income also seems to be useful rather more important. The distribution of the respondents according to the felt adequacy of the income and degree of activeness very clearly shows that both the retirees having low degree of activeness and majority of the respondents in the moderate degree of activeness (77.78%) are having the monthly income same as the required expenditure. The point worth noting here is that in the case of those, having high level of activeness, a considerable proportion, i.e. 26.92 per cent of the respondents are having monthly income more than their required expenditure and 11.54 percent have enough income to meet the expenditure, although majority of 61.54 per cent of them feel insufficiency of income, which seems quite reasonable considering the rising price level.

As far as the degree of involvement in social interaction is concerned, the table shows that while all the two retirees having low degree of activeness are having the low degree of social interaction, the majority of those having moderate degree of activeness (74.07%) and high degree of activeness (83.33%) have also involved themselves in the moderate level of interaction (2 to 4 hours) and high level of interaction (above 4 hours) respectively showing that activity and interaction go together in the same direction having positive association between them. Form the table it is revealed that those who takeup the occupational activity again after retirement get a chance of interaction with variety of people. Here it can very well be imagined that the retirees having moderate degree of interaction are leading a completely retired life but they are devoting some time in the interaction with neighbours, friends, relatives etc. during the mutual social visits. They also must be getting the chance of interaction with other people while performing the outdoor household jobs.

Now we will try to find out how much time, these well adjusted Chandigarh respondents, belonging to the three categories of activeness, devote towards the hobbies and the religious activities everyday. The distribution of the well adjusted Chandigarh respondents according to the degree of activeness and the involvement in hobbies in Table 4.26-A shows that while both the respondents having low degree of activeness have no hobbies, the majority, i.e. 85.18 per cent, of those having moderate degree of activeness have some hobbies and they devote upto two hours on them daily. The majority, i.e. 73.08 per cent, of those having high degree of activeness have high involvement (more than two hours) in the hobbies everyday. This finding once again shows the importance of habbies for remaining occupied and consequently leading a satisfying life through adjustment in the later years of life.

The distribution of the respondents according to the involvement in religious activities and the degree of activeness (Table 4.26-A) shows that both the two respondents having low degree of activeness have no involvement in religious activities. While majority of those having moderate degree of activeness (92 60%) have high religious involvement (more than one hour) and the majority of those having high degree of activeness (65.38%) have low (upto one hour) involvement in religious activities which is quite understandable by considering the complete retirement of the earlier group and the occupational engagement of the later one.

Now we will have a look at the Jabalpur respondents according to these variables. Regarding the pre-retirement socio-economic status of the Jabalpur respondents, the table (4.26-B) shows that most of the retirees from class IV services are having a low degree of activeness, while the majority, i.e. 50.00 per cent, of the retirees having moderate degree of activeness have retired from class III services. It also shows that quite a considerable amount of well-adjusted highly active Jabalpur respondents (42.73%) have retired from class II services, while 19.09 per cent of them were holding the class I designations before retirement. It shows the utility of higher socio-economic status of the aged people for leading an active life with satisfaction. From this information the conclusion, derived by Chiriboga (1982 : 7) that the generalization about the behaviour of all the aged people cannot be made and may be misleading, seems to be quite true. Because as he has expressed that the stressful life events have their influence on happiness and stability or change in behaviour in advancing age. It seems quite possible that the retirees from lower class of services must have got tired from hard work and feeling happy and relaxed from the restful retired life.

The distribution of the well-adjusted Jabalpur respondents according to the degree of activeness and the health condition (Table 4.26-B) shows that most of those coming under the category of low degree of activeness are having a bad health condition. In the case of moderate activeness we find that majority, i.e. 58.33 per cent, have fair health. But in the case of high degree of activeness, an overwhelming majority, i.e. 86.36 per cent, of the Jabalpur respondents are enjoying a good health, showing the importance of health in the adoption of active life style.

About the occupational activity of the Jabalpur respondents the table shows as we have stated earlier, that while most of the retirees having low and moderate degree of activeness are leading a completely retired life happily, the overwhelming majority, i.e. 81.82 per cent, of the retirees, having high degree of activeness, have involved themselves in the occupational activity again after retirement, which provides them both, the money as well as the opportunity of social interaction.

The information about the present financial condition of the well-adjusted Jabalpur retirees shows that while most of the respondents having low level of activeness, have monthly income of Rs. 400/- and below, the majority of those having moderate degree of activeness, i.e. 66.67 per cent, are having their monthly income between Rs. 401 to Rs. 800/-. Although relatively a larger proportion of highly active retirees (47.27%) have monthly income of Rs. 400/- and below, 32.73 per cent of them have fallen in the category of Rs. 401/- to Rs. 800/-. The point worth noting here is, that a considerable number, i.e. 20.00 per cent of the respondents, having high level of activity get above Rs. 800/- every month as their income. This reveals that probably most of those who are very active have engaged themselves in occupational activity.

About the felt adequacy of the income the table shows that all the seven retirees having low degree of activeness and majority of respondents in the category of moderately active,

(77.78%) are having sufficient income to meet their expenditure. As far as the highly active retirees are concerned though majority, i.e. 53.63 per cent of them are having insufficient income to meet their expenditure, which is quite understandable by considering the lower class of majority of Jabalpur respondents and the rising price level, a considerable proportion of them 31.82 per cent have enough money to meet the expenses whereas 14.55 per cent of them are having more money than they require. In all 46.37 per cent of the highly active respondents have no financial problems, which is worth noting.

As far as the degree of involvement in social interaction is concerned the table 4.26-B shows that more or less same number of retirees having low and moderate degree of activeness are having the low (0 to 2 hours) and moderate (2 to 4 hours) level of interaction. The majority of those having moderate and high degree of activeness have involved themselves in the high (above 4 hours) level of social interaction showing that those who are moderately active and very active have involved themselves enough in social interaction. It reveals that highly active people must be getting the chance of social interaction during the occupational activity while those leading a completely retired life must be interacting with various groups of people willingly during the social visits and while performing the outdoor household jobs. On the whole most of the Jabalpur well adjusted respondents have involved in social interaction highly which demonstrates its utility in good adjustment in old age.

The distribution of the well adjusted Jabalpur respondents according to the degree of activeness and the involvement in hobbies (Table 4.26-B) shows that while all the seven respondents having low degree of activeness have no hobbies. The majority, i.e. 69.44 per cent, of those having moderate degree of activeness have moderate involvement in hobbies. Although 42.73 per cent of those having high degree of activeness have no involvement which can easily be understood by their occupational engagement and lower social strata more or less same proportion of them, that is 30.00 per cent and 27.27 per cent, have low (upto 2 hours) and high (above 2 hours) involvement in hobbies. It shows the importance of hobbies for leading an active and happy life in old age.

The distribution of the respondents according to the involvement in religious activities and the degree of activeness (Table 4.26-B) shows that all the seven respondents having low degree of activeness have no involvement in religious activities. While mojority of those having moderate degree of activeness (75%) and the majority of those having high degree of activeness (87.27%) have high involvement in religious activities, In this way we find that those who are very active they have involved themselves mainly in occupational activity which provides the chances of social interaction. Moreover, most of them are devoting some time to their hobbies and religious activities also. Whereas moderately active are devoting some time to hobbies, social interaction and religious activities.

Our findings about the Chandigarh and Jabalpur respondents regarding the variables discussed above are little different, although the trend of facts is same in both the cities. About the class of service of the respondents having high degree of activeness we find little difference, while in Chandigarh majority of them have retired from class I Govt. services, in Jabalpur, a considerable proportion of them have class II service background. The reason for this difference is quite understandable by considering the fact that in the sample of Jabalpur city itself the number of the respondents retired from class I services is very less. Therefore, this difference does not affect the idea about comparatively high level of pre-retirement socio-economic status of the highly active respondents than the less active ones.

Regarding the level of social interaction we find that while in Chandigarh the majority of moderately active respondents have moderate level of interaction with non-family members, in Jabalpur they have higher level of social interaction. It shows that in the traditional society people interact more with neighbours and relatives than in the modern society. Reverse is the situation regarding involvement in hobbies. In Chandigarh the majority of highly active retirees are having high level of involvement in hobbies, whereas in Jabalpur a considerable number of them have no involvement in hobbies which can be explained by their lower strata and present occupation. In the case of religious activities while majority of highly active Chandigarh retirees are having low religious involvement, majority of them in Jabalpur are having high religious involvement which can be explained by their traditionality. In this way by keeping in mind the characteristics of both the cities, i.e. highly developed and less developed places, this difference seems to be quite understandable. Highly educated people prefer hobbies whereas less educated people depend upon social interaction and find pleasure in religious activities.

Now we are in the position of deriving certain conclusions on the basis of our findings regarding the variables discussed above, about the three different life styles of the retired people. By considering the pre-retirement socio-economic status and health condition as the basic variables we can say now that who are the people who adopt low, moderate and high degree of activeness willingly in their life after retirement and remain satisfied. The concept of time and leisure are the cultural products (Little, 1984 : 17), therefore, we find the difference in activities of the aged people also. Regarding the less active well-adjusted respondents in both the cities it has been found that most of them are the Government amployees retired from class IV services, grouped with low educational qualification and low pre-retirement socio-economic status, having bad health condition at present, having monthly income of Rs. 400 and below but quite adequate to meet their required expenditure. They have adopted a life of low activity and interaction and are quite satisfied with it. They have not indulged themselves in any occupational activity again after retirement due to various reasons. Firstly, though their income is less, it is quite sufficient to meet their expenditure due to the absence of dependents probably, secondly, their physical condition does not permit them to take up the occupational activity which also provides the source of passing the time and interaction along with money, and thirdly, due to their belief in traditional values and norms they want to relax in this period of life. The people from the lower caste group of the Indian society are not supposed to have religious involvement like people of upper caste group according to the traditional values and norms. Since most of the class IV workers are the migrants of rural traditional society and that too from the lower social strata, they do not devote time in worshipping, prayers or reading of the religious books. Moreover the socialization of the people of this strata is such that they do not get much education and become the earning members so soon in their lives that they do not get opportunity to develop any hobbies in their busy and hard-schedule. These are the retirees who spend some time of the day in the light household jobs and interaction with the family members. Most of the day they spend in idling down or taking rest. Sometimes they do meet with their next door neighbours and gossip with them while sitting together in the outer portion of their houses and occasionally they meet and interact with their relatives.

Regarding the moderately active well-adjusted respondents our data of both the cities reveals that most of them are the Government employees retired from class III services, grouped with moderate educational qualification, i.e. matriculation or so and medium pre-retirement socio-economic status, having at present fair health condition, i.e. only physical weakness, and monthly income between Rs. 401 to Rs. 800 which is quite sufficient to meet their required expenditure. They have willingly adopted the life of moderate activeness and interaction and are quite satisfied with it. They have not involved themselves in any occupational activity again after retirement due to various reasons. Firstly, their income is sufficient to meet their expenditure due to the investment of their saving to get some return in the form of house rent as well as small number of dependents, probably only the wife, secondly, their physical weakness, although they are not diseased, does not allow them to take up this activity which along with money provides the source of passing the leisure time and opportunity of social interaction with the people other than the family members, and thirdly, due to their traditional values and norms they want to relax in this period of life. Apart from some household jobs including the marketing they spend some time everyday in religious activities as well as in hobbies like paper reading or walking also. Along with the interaction with the family members they do meet almost everyday with their next door neighbours among whom they select their friends also and sometimes they meet and interact with their relatives.

As far as the respondents, having high degree of activeness is concerned, our data regarding their socio-economic status in both the cities shows a little difference. As the table 4.26 also shows that while in Chandigarh majority of the most active well-adjusted retirees have retired from class I services, in Jabalpur relatively a larger proportion of them were holding the class II positions in Government services before retirement. By considering the fact, that in Chandigarh the number of the respondents having class I service background is larger than those retired from class II services and in Jabalpur the number of retirees from class I services is less than half than those having class II service background, this difference can easily be ignored. And by combining both the class of services together, we can say that most of the very active well-adjusted retirees are those who have higher pre-retirement socio-economic status, retired from either class I or class II Government services, having higher educational qualifications i.e. graduation and above and enjoying good health at this age.

They have taken up the occupational activities again after retirement which provides them money and the opportunity to remain engaged and interact with the people other than the family members. Regarding the occupational activity the difference between the retirees from class II and class I Government services is, that while most of the respondents having class II service background, have gone for the services again, most of the respondents having class I service background have preferred self-employment in the form of private practice of the profession, farming, business, industry etc. The reason for this difference is that the class II retirees may not be having so much of extra money to invest it somewhere at the risk of losing it. Anyway the point here is that the retirees from both the upper classes of services have kept themselves busy in the gainful activity which provides them opportunity of social interaction too. As the table 4.26 shows though a considerable proportion of highly active retirees are not financially comfortable, a majority of them are having their monthly income of above Rs. 400/- in most of the cases either quite sufficient to meet their expenditure or more than the requirement. The point worth noting here is that a considerable proportion of the respondents of this category in both the cities are having quite a comfortable financial position and it became possible only due to their present occupational activity in most of the cases. By virtue of their belongingness to the higher caste group, most of these highly active well-adjusted retirees, specially those who are self employed, alongwith their occupational activity. devote some time everyday to religious activity. They are also spending enough time on their hobbies like reading, gardening, walking, music listening etc. They meet with their neighbours and relatives sometimes but with their friends they meet quite often. Apart from this, quite a few of them have taken the membership of voluntary organizations where they get the chance of meeting and interacting with variety of people. In this way we find in our study that the most active retirees are those who have taken up the occupational activity again after retirement, devoting some time towards religious activities, enough time on hobbies and interaction with various groups of people. They are the people who have not changed their life style after retirement and performing all the activities of middle age.

Since the number of highly active respondents among the well-adjusted respondents is much larger than those having moderate and low activeness, we can certainly say that our study supports the activity theory and the active life style is quite desirable after retirement. But still we cannot say that it will be satisfying to each and every aged person. As we have discussed above, although the number is not very significant but some retirees are quite satisfied and leading a happy life with moderate and even low activity, they are contented with the interaction only with their near and dear ones, provided they have got enough income to meet their expenditure even if there health condition is not very good. The reason for their satisfactioni nspite of ill health may be firstly, that they may be taking it as a natural phenomenon of aging and secondly, they are in the position to spend some money for their treatment.

From this finding we can certainly say that in the Indian society, especially among the lower middle and lower class of people, if the financial condition of the aged people remains comfortable without working in this age, most of them will be able to lead a satisfying life without much activity and interaction. Thus, financial condition has emerged out as the most important intervening variable between the activity and adjustment. A careful look and thought towards the state of affairs of the respondents of these three categories demonstrates the fact, which we have stated earlier also that high activity and interaction with various groups of people contributes to the higher morale and happiness of an aged person only when his health condition and financial condition are comfortable. And this finding seems to be quite logical also.

In this way we can say that every retiree chooses his life style i.e. active, disengaged or the mid-way, by considering his health and financial condition at the time of retirement, of course his socialization and educational background guides him to do so. Although the personality traits of an individual also play an important role while selecting the life style but they are also connected with the educational and socio-economic background of the individuals to a large extent. Lazy and introvert type of people do not enjoy the activity and social interaction even in middle age. Such people feel relaxed after retirement if their income is good. The values and attitudes of the people differ from class to class in the society. It is observed that normally the aged belonging to the lower and middle strata of the society have traditional values and attitudes which conform to the complete rest in old age. Therefore, we have found that all those having moderate and low degree of activeness belong to the lower class of services. If such people are forced by the circumstances to work again after retirement they get upset mentally and become unhappy, On the contrary the people from upper strata of the society, having modern values and norms hate idleness and want to 'die with the boots on'. They take up the occupational activity to remain engaged in some gainful activity and interaction with others even if it is not required financially. Therefore, we have found that quite a few of the well-adjusted highly active respondents income is more than their requirement, Thus, one stable element in the choices of behaviour is personal values (International Encyclopedia of the Social Science, 1968 Vol. I, P. 182).

On the basis of above discussion the criticism of the two opposite theories of successful aging, that both offer an over simplified view of aging and its effect on the individual seems to have some weightage, and it seems proper that a developmental approach should be adopted towards the desired life style of the aged, since it recognizes both stability and the change for successful aging.

Lastly, on the basis of our findings, an effort has been made to prepare a chart, showing the probability of adopting the 'Developmental Approach' regarding successful aging. In our study three processes of good adjustment or three types of life style regarding the level of activity have emerged. They are the adoption of high, moderate and low level of activity in retired life. It has been tried to establish here that the people having certain characteristics are more likely to adopt a particular life style and involve themselves in particular activities in later years of life to remain happy. These characteristics, to some extent, have been ascribed but to a large extent have been achieved during the gradual development of life, due to which they have become capable of leading their desired life style in old age.

5

CONCLUSIONS AND SUGGESTIONS

The sample of the earlier study of the Chandigarh retirees was not adequately representative in dimensions as it did not represent all the aged people of the uraban Indian society. It confined only to the retirees living in the highly developed and modern city of Chandigarh and because of the higher cost of living in Chandigarh, mostly the higher categories of the Government employees have settled down there after retirement. This limitation of the study made it difficult to generalize the findings for all the urban aged people in Indian society, because the problem of adjustment may have different characters in the developed or under-developed societies. It is because of this reason the city of Jabalpur was selected for the present study along with Chandigarh. In Jabalpur mostly the lower class of Government employees have settled down after retirement. These two cities are existing at two different levels of development and represent atleast two different socio-cultural. ethos. As a matter of fact Jabalpur represents the larger section of Indian urban society because most of the cities of India have characteristics of a developing city like Jabalpur. After the completion of present study now we are in the position to generalize our findings for the whole Indian urban society without any hesitation. On the basis of some striking findings a few conclusions can be drawn and some broad trends of the study may be regarded as generally applicable. Further, considering that the practical purpose of gerontology, especially the studies of adjustment in old age, is to provide information facilitating proper social planning and programming for the welfare of the aged, some suggestions can be given on the basis of our findings.

The present investigation shows that old age has started emerging as a social problem in Indian society due to the socio-cultural changes brought about by the industrial revolution. The findings clearly indicate that the increasing importance of achieved properties, the caanging social structure especially the family structure, individualistic and materialistic values, negative attitudes of the younger generation towards the aged and compulsory retirement from the economic activity are the main contributing factors for the emergence of the social problem of old age. Among both the groups of Chandigarh and Jabalpur respondents we have found that those respondents are better adjusted who are leading a life resembling the life of the aged people in the pre-industrial society in terms of having financial and physical security, satisfactory family relationship, social interaction and association with various groups of people, involvement in useful and creative activities.

In the present investigation we find that the proportion of well adjusted retirees is more in Chandigarh than the proportion of well adjusted retirees in Jabalpur. It is quite understandable by considering the fact that in Coandigarh most of the respondents are the retirees from class I and class II Government services whereas in Jabalpur most of the respondents are the retirees from class III and class IV Government services. It may reasonably be extrapolated that the proportion of the mal-adjusted aged will be much more among the non-pensioners and non-earners belonging to the lower classes of society. It may be anticipated that the number of such socially problematic old people will keep on increasing with the advancement of industrializatlon. If proper steps are not taken to check it, the problem may become very serious and endanger the society itself.

This problem cannot be handled adequately at the individual and familial levels. So it calls for the concrete efforts of society for its solution. The mal-adjusted people are unable to solve their problems themselves and they do not get help from the family members also. As a result, they look forward to social assistance which can and should be given by planning the programmes for the welfare of the aged. Our national goal is to bring improvements in the levels of our national welfare through five year plans. Article 41 of the constitution of India lays down, as one of the Directive Principles of State policy, that the state shall within the limits of its economic capacity and development, make effective provision for securing the right to work, to education and to public assistance in cases of unemployment, old age, sickness and disablement and in other cases of underserved wants.' India has declared itself as a welfare state which keeps making continuous efforts for the maximum welfare of the maximum number of people in the state. As far as the welfare of the old people is concerned, India has not so far developed any comprehensive and universal old age security system.

The findings about the association between the situational factors and the level of adjustment in both the groups of respondents reveal that for good adjustment in old age the importance of acquired properties like education, social status, income and the physical fitness is increasing, whereas the ascribed properties like age or seniority are losing their significance. The information about the femily life of the retired people has revealed some important facts. The types of household of the respondents of both the groups have clearly shown that with the advancement of the society towards modernism the joint family system is disappearing and the nuclear family system is emerging. Therefore we find that in comparison to Jabalpur respondents a larger number of Chandigarh respondents are living in nuclear families. But in Jabalpur also the number of those living in joint families is less than those living in nuclear families and same the case in Chandigarh too. The unfavourable attitude towards the nuclear family system expressed by the majority of the respondents of both the groups indicate that the old people want to live with their children. But the finding that the living with children is positively associated with the level of adjustment of the Chandigarh respondents, having higher socio-economic status, but it is not so in the case of Jabalpur respondents, having lower socio-economic status clearly indicates towards the fact that financially well off aged people are more likely to get proper care, respect and position of authority in the family than the poor ones. This fact is substantiated by the finding that the frequent conflict of a considerable proportion of the Chandigarh respondents and majority of the Jabalpur respondents with their family members are due to the financial problem. It is observed that the family members do not normally oppose the aged if his financial condition is very good. This fact is supported by our finding that in the case of financially well off Chandigarh respondents the number of those having satisfactory relationship with the family members living with them as well as with the children living separately is more than the Jabalpur rcspondents, suffering from financial hardships. On the whole, the information about the family life of the respondents of both the cities demonstrates that quite a few of the aged people are unable to enjoy a financially and physically secured-life within the family system. When the old people do not get proper care and protcction from their family, their needs have to be met by outsidc agencies. Thus, the duty of providing financially, physically and socially secured life to the needy aged people is being transferred to the state automatically in thc present society. Though there is an awareness of this problem, Indian society is not yet well-equipped to meet such an eventuality.

The Government employees get much less amount of money as pension compared to thcir last pay drawn. It is not sufficient to meet their exprnditure and maintain the pre-retirement standard of living. This change immediately after retirement gives them a shock. A higher proportion of the Chandigarh respondents and a great majority of the Jabalpur respondents have reported about the inadequacy of their monthly income. They do not get proper medical assistance while more medical facilities, free of charge, at the door step, are needed in old age than in middle age. There are many drawbacks and inconveniences for the aged in the existing medical services, such as difficulties at out-patient departments of hospitals. They get discouraged from seeking medical aid unless it is very essential, due to these inconveniences as well as the financial problem. Their physical weakness and ailments prevent them from creative and useful social activities and if they have to indulge themselves in such activities, is does not contribute to their psychological well being i.e. happiness, as we have found in the case of Jabalpur respondents that interaction with various groups of people has no statistically significant positive association with the level of adjustment of retirees. The positive association between the finadcial and health condition on the one hand and the adjustment of both the groups of retirees on the other shows that financial and medical needs are the basic needs of the aged people and fulfilment of these needs is very essential for better adjustment. In a Kerala study of the problems of the pensioners also it has been found that health problem and financial difficulties over shadow the other problems such as loneliness, fear of death, helplessness etc. (Bose, 1982 : 13).

On the basis of these findings it can be suggested that the Government or society should concentrate first on giving sufficient financial and physical security to the aged people, while preparing the policies and programmes for their welfare. These aspects of life should be given top priority in the list of the agencies working for the welfare of the aged. It will not only satisfy their physical needs but also enable them to satisfy their socio-psychological needs. Our data shows that with the comfortable financial condition even with the less activity and interaetion some retirees have achieved a higher level of adjustment.

By keeping in view the anticipated accute problem posed by the size and the structure of the aged people some suggestions regarding few short and long term measures to be taken, can be made for providing social assistance to the old people to improve their financial condition. In the case of the Government pensioners, especially those who have retired from the lower class of services, there should be an increase in the amount of pension commensurate with the cost of living and to maintain atleast a minimum standard of living.

The financial condition of those retired earlier remains worse than those retired later because their pension is less than those retired later, whereas the cost of living is same for every one (Tripathy, 1980 : 5-6). Quite a few respondents of Jabalpur have reported that their pension is not sufficient even to give them two square meals a day. Due to the various problems faced by the retirees an 'All India Federation of Pensioners' Association came into existence in 1958 for demanding the help from the Government of India but its efforts have brought a negligible relief from financial worries to the pensioners. For non-earners and non-pensioners destitutes, although some states and Union territories have introduced the old age pension scheme' (India, A Reference Annual, 1981, P. 116), the amount of money they get every month is very little and due to various reasons very little number of them are able to get it (Parthasarthy, 1980 : 385 ; Bose, 1982 : 11). The suggestion, given by Soodan (1975 : 185-196) about the pension for the self-employed people and for the employees working in private establishments from the fund collected by the employees as well as the employers, is also quite reasonable. Thus the social security pattern of America may be considered. Extension of 'Employees State Insurance Scheme' to take care of the retired non-pensioners industrial workers as suggested by Bose (1982 : 17) may also be thought off. National Board for the care of the aged should be established. The provision of a uniform old age pension scheme for the destitutes to maintain a minimum standard of living as also suggested by Chowdhary (1981 : 56) and Hardikar and Bhatia (1983 : 91), may also be considered. As cited by Freyberg (1982 : 5), International Labour Organization has recommended that state pension should be between 65 to 80 per cent of the working wages. By keeping in mind the poor economy of the country apart from giving some financial assistance to the aged, provision of facilities for part time jobs requiring less physical and mental strain as they are available in Japan (Pinge, The Economic Times, 30th May 1982); and Czechslovakia (Social Welfare 1980 : 176), may also be tried. Chowdhary (1981 : 56) has also suggested about the employment opportunities to the able bodied aged to have economic security. Their services may be of great use to the society also as it has happened in the case of Gujrat Industrial and Technical Consultancy Organization which has been successfully involving the retired technocrates and managers in the task of reviving hundreds of sick units in the small and medium scale sector (Rao, The Economic Times, 30th May 1982). At the time of retirement most of the aged people remain physically and mentally fit. The present investigation has also revealed that most of the respondents of both the cities are healthy. Our data also shows that a considerable number of the retirees are involved in occupational activity. Quite a few of them have still to fulfill the parental responsibilities of educating and marrying off their children. These findings suggest that increase in the pensionable age by a few years, as it has happened in America (Cruik Shank, 1980 : 14), will enable the employees to complete their responsibilities before retirement. The United Nations (1959, 134 : 153) has reported, that in a European Seminar on the individual and social importance of activities for the elderly people, it has been recommended that if the old people wish and are capable of doing hard work, they should be allowed to work, otherwise large pensions should be given to them. Uhlig (1952 : 90-93) has found that most of the people aged above 60 years do not want to retire but to continue their employment as long as possible. Quite a few studies have shown as cited in The Economic Times (23rd January 1982, P. 4-5) that 75 per cent of the aged remain physically fit and no change occurs in the mental faculties of the aged people. Clauge (1951 : 152-153), Townsend (1961 : 153) and Bortz (1963 : 157-160) have also favoured employment for the older people. As noted by Blyton (1984 : 69-83), the application of 'Partial Pension Scheme' on a national scale in 1976 and in some firms of the European countries including Britain is also a wounderful idea for the easy preparation of retirement. 'Phased' or 'Partial' retirement seeks to case the transition between work and retirement as it has happened in Czechoslovakia (Cruik Shank, 1980: 16).

About the medical assistance, it can be suggested that it

should be made absolutely free for all old people. In hospitals the old people should be given preference in all respects, especially in the out patient departments. As suggested by Soodan (1975 : 187), membership of the National Health plan fund by elderly people and home nursing services by private practitioners and trained nurses to people having chronic diseases and acute physical weakness may also be considered. The provision of the separate hospital for the aged people, which is at the planning stage at present according to the information given by the Chairman . 'Age care India' (Nav-Bharat, 9th July 1994 : P 4 Col. 1) need to be materialized immediately. Suggestions given by Chowdhry (1981 : 61-62) about the infirmaries for chronically ill, suffering from incurable diseases and disabled aged people and, Hardikar and Bhatia (1983 : 91) about the geriatric hospitals at district places and geriatric units in sub-centres are very sensible, and serious thoughts should be given in this direction. As Bose (1982, 1-19) has cited, in some intensive studies of the urban aged, it has been found that 50 per cent of the aged die a 'natural dealth' in the absence of 'medicated survival' facilities available to them, more or less same proportion of them do not have any income of their own, and reliance on sons is the only strategy of survival for them.

It is generally observed as expressed by Chowdhry (1981 : 55) also that even if the children want to provide a secured life to their aged parents, they are unable to do so mainly due to financial constraints (India, A Reference Annual, 1981, P. 116). And if they are forced by the circumstances to keep their parents with them, their relations with parents become tense and conflicts take place in the family. In this situation, it can be said that if the Government or welfare agencies share the children's responsibility of looking after the aged by providing the supportive services, i.e. the financial and medical assistance to the aged people it will encourage their respectful living with their children. This solution of the problem of old age will be more satisfactory for the emotional and psychological adjustment of the aged people as our study has shown. It will be more economical for society also in the long run (D'Souza, 1976 : 27) and suits Indian society as it cannot afford to spend much money on the care of the aged due to its poor economy. Some views regarding the care of the aged in India have also been expressed by Statch (The Illustrated Weekly of India, 25th December 1982, P. 17) on behalf of 'Helpage India'. Because as expressed by Neysmith and Edwardh (1984 : 25), low economic status of countries of third world forces them to make policy which functions to maintain national elites at the expense of the majority, and India is not the exception in this regard. Whereas it is required that the third world countries must find the resources to meet the needs of the persons over 60 as, their number in such countries is going to be more than their counterparts in industrialized countries in near future. The cost of residential care for the elderly has steadily increased throughout the post-war period due to inflation and price rise. Policy decisions regarding the care of the aged have always been based in part upon the cost of caring them in homes. India at present cannot bear the total financial burden of the care of aged (Dorton and Knapp, 1984 : 157-183). In the situation encouragement of their living in joint families by providing supportive services to the family seems to be quite appropriate.

Extra facilities for owning spacious houses to the aged may also help them in leading a happier life by attracting their children to live with them. On the basis of various findings, Donahue (1969 : 42) has concluded that if the older generations remain in their own homes and their children come to stay with them, their adjustment is better than when the reverse situation obtains. Self-esteem plays an important role in adjustment. The level of self-esteem changes with the living arrangement in ordinary housing, residential homes and special sheltered housing. Very high level of self-esteem has been found in elderly people living independently in the community than in the other groups of living arrangements (Goleman, 1984 118-135). It has also been found that the people living in their own homes have the most advantageous position in terms of health, economic position, family constellation, activities or attitudes. The man who lives in others' homes rank next, while those who live in boarding houses and and hotels deviate further in many respects (Cavan, 1949 : 71-83). Therefore as Chowdhary (1981 : 56-61) and Stach (The Illustrated Weekly of India, 26th December, 1982, p. 17) have also suggested only for such financially and physically weak old people who neither can manage their own affairs nor can they live with their children due to some reasons, the institutional care and protection should be provided by opening homes for the old people. For others, greater emphasis should be laid on the development of non-institutional care, i.e. the supportive services within the family. Townsend (1963 : 427-437) has also suggested gradual abandoning of communal homes for the aged people in Britain. As cited by Russell (1979 : 400) a number of studies has indicated that institutionalization develops certain negative characteristics, including low morale, negative self-image, pre-occupation with the past, feeling of personal insignificance, intellectual ineffectiveness, docility and withdrawal, anxiety and fear of death (International Encyclopedia of the Social Sciences, 1968, Vol. I, P. 83 ; Biley and Foner, 1968 ; Tobin and Lieberman, 1976). Therefore the institutions i.e. the homes for the aged which are being opened in India by Government and voluntary organizations (India, A Reference Annual, 1981, P. 116), should be last resort when other alternatives have failed (Russell, 1979, 433). The ordinary housing of old people is a growing concern for most of the countries now. The recently emerged programme of 'staying put' in U.K., which focuses specifically on housing assistance for elderly people, who remain in conventional domestic housing, to make their houses comfortable for old age (Wheeler, 1982 : 299-329), is also a very good idea which can be adopted. As, keeping old people in their own homes has been strongly advocated as both the right and the cheapest way of care for them. An overwhelming majority of the aged people want to stay in their own houses rather than to move in institutions but at the same time it is tragic to hear that old man was found dead alone in slum (Population Review, 1977, 21, 1-2, 158-160). This situation calls for the encouragement of their living arrangement with children. Government policies in China also provide a secure future for the over sixties by ensuring that they remain in their families (Aerial. The Economic Times, 30th May 1982).

The findings regarding the positive relationship of attitudlnal factors on the one hand and the level of adjustment on the other among both the groups of respondents show that people having positive attitudes towards various social changes (nuclear family system, inter-caste marriage, abolition of the purdah system, equal rights to women, widow remarriage and divorce) and non-interfering attitudes towards the personal affairs of the grown-up children (taking important decisions, going out in the evening, outing for entertainment and sitting with friends) have better adjustment than those havins traditional or conservative attitudes towards these matters. Most of our Chandigarh respondents have modern attitudes whereas most of our Jabalpur respondents have conservative attitudes towards social changes taking place in Indian society. Therefore we find that the number of well adjusted aged people is more among the Chandigarh respondents than the Jabalpur respondents. On the basis of these findings, it can be suggested that welfare centres should be opened for the aged where facilities for socializing them according to new values and norms may be provided. Counselling services can be provided in these centres where consultants can advise them on various matters and help them in solving their problems, espeically those created by the generation gap. They can be educated through organized lectures and literature, pointing out the disadvantages of holding the traditional values and norms in the changing society and advantages of new values and norms which conform to the changing conditions of present society. Their traditional attitudes can be changed and positive attitudes towards the new social order can be general to some extent. It will facilitate them to have better adjustment with the younger generation. Because as Bose (1982 : 14) has noted the aged in India still receive respect and warmth of affection from the family, due to the difference of opinion sometimes conflicting situations arise. The finding about the absence of any relationship between adjustment and strength of religious beliefs (existence of gods and goddesses, concepts of 'Pap' and 'Punya', 'Karma' and rebirth, and hell and heaven in the case of Chandigarh respondents and negative association between these variables in the case of Jabalpur respondents demonstrates that these baliefs have either no role or negative role regarding adjustment in old age. This unclear finding about the link between religion and old age does not encourage us to suggest that faith in religious beliefs should be generated among the old people by imparting religious instructions.

As Bnatia (1976 : 317) has also mentioned, social scientists have been busy for quite some time discussing the relative significance of the two current apparantly opposite approaches for a policy, based on real social situations for successful aging. The findings regarding the relationship of various behavioural factors on the one hand and the level of adjustment of both the groups of respondents on the other show that the 'active' type of life is more desirable for good adjustment. The old people do not want to disengage themselves from society. They like to remain fully integrated in the social network and enjoy association and interaction with various groups of people. Lack of activity and social interaction is neither desired nor enjoyed by them. Therefore, when they are forced to lead a disengaged life, initially due to retirement and then due to physical weakness they become frustrated and disturbed. This finding is substantiated by the study of Bhatia (1976 : 317) also who has found out that quite a few of them who had disengaged were unhappy and suffering from loneliness. Though in the present study the theories of successful aging have not been tested through controlled observation, still it can be said that our findings among both the groups of respondents support the activity theory. In the case of Chandigarh respondents all the behavioural factors, which indicate the activeness and social interaction of the respondents, are found to have a positive association with their adjustment. But in the case of Jabalpur respondents interaction with family members, friends, neighbours and relatives have no statistically significant positive association with adjustment due to the physical ailments and accute financial problems of those, leading a completely retired life, whereas the occupational activity, showing the activeness and social interaction both, has higher degree of positive association with adjustment since it is carried out, mostly by the physically fit people and it provide financial security to them. This involvement in religious activities, which shows the withdrawal of an aging individual from the world is found to have no relationship and negative relationship with the adjustment of Chandigarh and Jabalpur respondents respectively. Accordlng to Indian religious preachings, the aged people are recommended to detach themselves from the materialistic world and to attach with the spiritual world. We really do not know to what extent these preachings were practiced by the general population, but in mythological stories, consisting of life histories of well known kings, we do find that after getting grey-haired as the symptom of old age they used to give their rulership roles to their grown-up sons willingly, devoted more time to religious activities and remained contented with the disengaged type of life style. But our findings show that religious activities either do not play any role or play negative role in the adjustment in old age. The activities connected with the present life are more satisfactory for them than those connected with the imaginary life after death. This finding does not suggest that more religious institutions should be opened by society where the aged people can involve themselves in religious activities. Of course this sort of facilities should exist in the soeiety to some extent for those who adopt willingly a disengaged life style.

By considering the importance of behavioural factors regarding adjustment in old age it may be suggested that facilities for such sources of activities, as Tibbitts (1954 : 301-308) has said, which replace the earlier sources of status, social contacts, companionship and affection to the aged, may be provided by society. Aged people should be enabled to participate fully in the main stream of collective life (Parthsarathy ; 1980 : 381-88). The positive association between the involvement in occupational activities and the adjustment again suggests that part-time jobs for the physically fit aged people will not only solve their financial problem but also keep them busy, create the sense of usefulness and provide the chance of social interaction. In a study of aged in Delhi it was found that 50 per cent of them are very active but not in gainful work, which shows the immense scope for working out programme for active retirement (Bose, 1982 : 10).

The aged persons need to be 'retyred' instead of retired. The chronological age is not necessarily the biological age. Fixing the age of retirement chronologically is both, unjust and unscientific. The suggestion of Garg, et al. (1980 : 9), that some score system should be evolved on the basis of physical and mental capacities for the aged for his retirement, is a very goed idea. If it is not possible due to unemployment problem of the younger generation, they should be given proper amount of money in the form of pension to keep them free from economic want. Friendly societies for the aged can solve their problems of sickness and loneliness to a great extent (Mangamal, 1980 : 8). Chowdhry (1981 : 69) has also suggested the provision of employment opportunities for the able bodied aged people. The positive association between the involvement in hobbies and the adjustment also suggests that society should provide some facilities for passing the leisure time in more satisfying ways. According to the report of the United Nations (1959 ; 134-153), in a European seminar on the individual and social importance of activities for the elderly people, it has been recommended regarding entertainment and other facilities that the leisure time activities, such as planned holiday excursion, library, sport club, lecture, cinema, television show, craft workshop, etc. should be organized by public and private agencies through clubs. Regarding the Indian aged people, it can be said that interest in voluntary organizations should be created among them. Our findings show ihe lack of interest of the retirees of both the groups in voluntary organizations. But those who are interested in voluntary organizations are certainly better adjusted than those who are not, More voluntary organizations should be opened and the membership fees for the aged should be very less. The membership of voluntary organizations gives a sense of belonging and opportunities for social participation to an individual. Special organizations for the welfare of the aged may be opened, such as hobby centres, libraries, day centres, old persons' clubs, so that they get a chance for passing the leisure time in healthy recreational activities as well as for developing friendly relations wlth their age group. While Hardikar and Bhatia (1983 ; 91) have emhhasized on geriatric clubs and libraries, Chowdhry (1981 : 56) has suggested the day care centres or old persons clubs for those who live with their families. This will help them to overcome their feeling of emptiness and loneliness. It will also be helpful in avoiding the conflicts with family members which come from an idle mind. Opportunities should be given to the healthy people for serving society through charitable organizations. In the case of retirees, prer-retirement training and the plannlng of retirement, five to ten years before retirement may prove to be very beneficial in all the aspects of their life. The suggestions made by Soodan (1975 : 188) and D'Souza, (1982 : 61) regarding some special services, such as home-maker/home help service, cheap hot meals facilities, friendly visits, night attendants on nominal charges or free of charge and visiting nurse serviccs for help in small matters, and pensions at home, delivery of purchases at home, special entertainment facilities in the community as it happens in Russia (Menon, 1980 : 13) should also be considered for those who cannot manage their personal and household activities and go out due to physical weakness. On the whole, our data demonstrate that the aged people like to remain active and involved in social interaction with other people. The existence of the positive relationship between the activeness and social interaction on the one hand and the level of adjustment on the other suggests that soeiety should provide full opportunities to its aged people to remain socially active. The fact that people do not like to be segregated from the rest of society, does not allow us to suggest the establishment of special colonies for the retired or aged people as we find in the western countries. Family is the primary vehicle of social security and social assistance to the aged. However, current social assistance schemes for the aged, since they have the character of a'destitution allowance', do not strengthen the capacity of the family to look after the aged, but rather have the effect of replacing the family. On the contrary as Chowdhry (1981 : 53) Stach (1982 : 17) and Bose (1982 : 14) have also suggested, by avoiding the ill effects of urbanization and industrialization, as far as possible through the provision of the supportive services, designed to help the families to take care of the aged within their own environment, their living in the joint families should be promoted.

The progress of a nation may be marked by the care which it provides for the aged (Mani, 1980 : 4). No plan for economic and social development would be justified if it fails to satisfy the special need for the aged in regard to security and care (Parthasarathy; 1980 : 381-88). 'Helpage India' a voluntary association for the care of the aged is trying to create a wider awareness that old age is a national problem which India should plan to meet (The Editorial, Voluntary Action, 21, (9), 1979, PP. 3-4). No doubt as Parathasarthy (1980 : 382) has noted, social welfare measures will have to be doubled in near future as compared to measures required in 1971 for a 9.9 million population above 70 years of age, which is going to be 19.1 million in 1991. Since the failure of the system of institutional arrangements for taking care of the aged in the developed countries is a well known fact, the question of its application in the developing and transitional society like India does not arise. Only in the case of non-availability of the family protection the aged should be provided institutional care and for rest of the aged masses the imotional support of the family should be utilized. The primary responsibility for care of the aged must coutinue to rest on the family but there is a growing need for domiciliary services to help the family in the tas£ (The Editorial, Voluntary Action, 21(2), 1972, PP 3-4). Considering, the social welfare services should be directed not to iddividuals but to the individuals in the family (D'Souza, 1982 : 61). Thus, the best course of action for India will be the 'half way house' as suggested by Bose (1982 : 17) where the efficiency of modern institutions can merge with the warmth of the family ties of the older days. Later on as it has happened in Latin America as noted by Tapia-Videla and Parrish (1982 : 31-55) the services for the aged people in public health, social security and other civic amenities can be broadened and improved with the increased economic development of country.

United Nations Economic and Social Commission for Asia and Pacific organized the world Assembly on Aging in Vienna in 1982 (Taylor, 1982 : 5). The purpose of holding this assembly was to understand the problems of the aged, to consider the development and humanitarian issues and to provide welfare services to the aged. Launching of an action oriented programme to guarantee old people the right to participate fully in their society, to contribute to its growth and to be protected by it', was the main aim of this assembly. United Nations Assembly had selected the 'Banyan' trees as the official logo because it symbolizes longevity, self-reliance, continuing growth and a community meeting place. The integration of the aged in the main stream of population is being recognized in the whole world. The message of World Health Organization for the aged people was 'Add life to the years, not years to the life'. This will be possible especially in the Indian context, only when they are treated with dignity and love in the families. Since present urban Indian families need supportive services to look after their aged members, they should be provided and the burden of looking after the aged people should be shared by the society.

APPENDIX I

TABLE—A

Percentage of Population 65 Years Old and Over for Selected Countries

Country	1900	1970-76
France	8.2	13.6
U.K.	4.7	13.8
Sweden	8.4	14.5
West Germany	4.9	13.9
U.S.A.	4.1	10.3
Italy	6.2	10.9
Canada	5.1	8.3
Netherlands	6.0	10.4
Czechoslovakia	—	11.6

Source :—United Nations, Demographic Year book, 1974, United Nations, The Aging of Populations, Population Studies, No. 26, Noted by Robert Havighurst' Aging in Western Society' in *The Social Challenge of Ageing*. Edited by Hobman David. London. CroomHelm Ltd. 1978 : 16.

TABLE—B-1

Indian Population in Various Age-groups of Old Age in Different Census Years 1911 to 1971

Age Group	Percentage Distribution in					
	1911	1921	1931	1951	1961	1971
61-66	2.81	2.82	1.86	2.07	2.56	2.61
66-70	0.77	0.80	0.88	1.38	1.11	1.24
70—	1.58	1.69	1.29	2.21	1.26	2.28

TABLE—B-2

Indian Population Above Certain Age-points of Old Age in Different Census Years (1911 to 1971)

Age Points	Percentage Distribution in					
	1911	1921	1931	1951	1961	1971
60+	5.16	5.31	4.03	5.66	4.85	6.13
65+	2.35	2.49	2.17	3.59	2.29	3 52
70+	1.68	1.69	1.29	2.21	1.96	2.28

Source :—Table B—1 and B—2 have been taken from Pathak, K.B. (1973) 'On the Age Composition of the Indian Population from 1911 to 1971, *Interdiscipline* 10 (Summer) : 35-42.

TABLE—C

Indian Population Aged 60 Years and Above in Different Census Years from 1961 to 1981

Age Group	1961	1971	1981
60-64	2.56	2.62	2.73
65 to 69	1.11	1.28	1.43
70 and Above	1.96	2.06	2.33
Total (60 and Over)	5.63	5.96	6.49

Source :—Census of India, 1981. Series—I, Part II Special Reports and and Tables Based on 5 per cent Sample Data, Chapter 3—Age Distribution.

APPENDIX II

ITEM ANALYSIS OF THE STATEMENTS OF THE SATISFACTION INDEX

Item Analysis of the Statements Regarding the First Component of Life Satisfaction Index i.e. Resolution and Fortitude.

Items are :

1. My age does not bother me and my life is as useful and meaningful as it was in middle age.
2. Quite often thoughts about death worry me a lot.
3. Even at the time of difficult situations I do not lose self-confidence and courage.
4. I believe in destiny and I know that I cannot get a bit more than what I am destined for.
5. Either blame others or curse myself for creating any problem which I have to face.
6. I believe and practise the 'try again' type of approach in my life.

Comparison of the Mean Response of Each of the Above Mentioned Items in Upper and Lower Quartiles

Item No.	Mean of Lower Quartile	Mean of Upper Quartile	Value of 't'
1	1.4	4.2	13.5
2	1.96	4.4	9.5
3	2.6	4.4	7.6
4	1.4	2.4	2.7
5	3.4	4.7	6.6
6	2.56	4.5	7.4

Item Analysis of the Statements Regarding the Second Components of Life Satisfaction Index i.e. Goodness of Life.

Items are :

1. I have got much more than what I expected out of my life.
2. I feel that due to the lack of opportunities I am unable to fulfil my ambitions.
3. As I grow older, things seem better than I thought they would be.
4. I think that due to various reasons I am unsuccessful in achieving most of my goals.
5. It gives me a feeling of great satisfaction that I am getting most of my desired things.
6. I with that some interesting and pleasant events should take place in my life.

Comparison of the Mean Response of Each of the Above Mentioned Items in Upper and Lower Quartiles.

Item No.	Mean of Lower Quartile	Mean of Upper Quartile	Value of 't'
1	1,32	4.48	7.9
2	1.2	3.8	9.6
3	1.4	4.4	11.8
4	2.5	3.9	3.8
5	2.2	3.8	4.1
6	1.2	4.1	12.6

Item Analysis of the Statements Regarding the Third Component of Life Satisfaction Index i.e. Positive Self Concept.

Items are :

1. Even at this age I feel young.
2. I cannot do so many things which I want to do due to various reasons.
3. Compared to other people of my age I make a good appearance.
4. I feel old and somewhat tired.
5. I cannot get along very well with the people of younger generation because they do not value my advice and give no proper respect.
6. I feel that I am quite capable of doing things that are expected from me by others.

Comparison of the Mean Response of Each of the Above Mentioned Items in Upper and Lower Quartiles.

Item No.	Mean of Lower Quartile	Mean of Upper Quartile	Value of 't'
1	1.4	4.2	11.1
2	1.5	4.1	9.8
3	2.1	4.3	7.8
4	1.36	3.88	8.7
5	2.12	3.52	4.02
6	2.24	4.44	9.6

Item Analysis of the Statements Regarding the Fourth Component of Life Satisfaction Index i.e. Mood Tone.

Items are :

1. I am just as happy and satisfied as I was when I was young.
2. Quite often I feel blue and depressed.
3. There are many things which interest me and keep me busy, therefore, I do not feel empty and lonely.
4. I very easily get upset and irritated when things do not happen according to my wish.

5. I do not find any reason to remain frustrated and sad in the present life.
6. My life has become monotonous and boring and quite often I feel lonely and isolated.

Comparison of the Mean Response of Each of the Above Mentioned Items in Upper and Lower Quartiles.

Item No.	Mean of Lower Quartile	Mean of Upper Quartile	Value of 't'
1	1.00	4.36	29.7
2	1.00	3.96	12.3
3	2.36	4.48	8.8
4	1.40	3.60	6.9
5	1.44	4.00	9.1
6	1.60	4.40	11.1

Item Analysis of the Statements Regarding the Fifth Component of Life Satisfaction Index i.e., Zest for living.

Items are :

1. These are the best years of my life.
2. Quite often I feel there is no point in living.
3. I have made several plans for things I intend to do in future.
4. This is the dreariest time of my life.
5. I get pleasure out of my activities and my experiences are quite interesting.
6. When I was young there were reasons to be optimistic about life but now there is nothing to look forward to.

Comparison of the Mean Response of Each of the Above Mentioned Item in Upper and Lower Quartiles.

Item No.	Mean of Lower Quartile	Mean of Upper Quartile	Value of 't'
1	1.00	3.72	12.00
2	1.76	4.36	8.70
3	1.40	3.08	4.33
4	1.16	4.04	12.40
5	1.16	4.20	12.70
6	1.08	3.80	8.00

APPENDIX III

INTERVIEW-SCHEDULE FOR THE STUDY OF SOCIAL ADJUSTMENT IN OLD AGE

(A Case Study of Retired Government Employees Living in Chandigarh and Jabalpur)

Sr. No.————

Identification Date :

1. (a) Name———————
   (b) Address——————
   (c) Age—————————
   (d) Marital Status————
   (e) Religion———————
   (f) Caste————————

2. (a) Education———————
   (b) Designation in Government service at the time of retirement————————
   (c) Class of service at the time of retirement I/II/III/IV ————————
   (d) Type of post held at the time of retirement : Gazetted/Non-gazetted————————
   (e) Date of retirement———————

3. (a) Home Town——————————Tehsil———————————
   District—————————————State——————————————
   Country——————————————

(b) Main reason for not settling down in hometown after retirement.

———————————————————————

———————————————————————

———————————————————————

4. (a) What is your monthly income ?———————

(b) What are the sources of income ?

1————————

2————————

3————————

4————————

5————————

(c) How many persons depend on you for financial support ? ——————————

(d) Whether your monthly income is less, same or more than your required monthly expenditure ?—————

——————————

(e) If your monthly income is less than the required expenditure, how do you handle the situation of financial crisis ?

1. Withdrawal from savings.
2. Help from the sons/daughters/other relatives.
3. Cutting down the expenditure.
4. Any other.

8. (a) Do you have any of the following physical ailments ?

1. Difficulty in seeing and reading.
2. Difficulty in hearing.
3. Digestive complaints.
4. General weakness.
5. Trembling.
6. Sleeplessness.
7. Pain in joints or difficulty in walking.
8. Breathlessness.
9. Blood pressure, high/low.

10. Asthma.
11. Kidney trouble.
12. Heart trouble.
13. Diabetes.
14. Pain in chest.
15. Any other.

(b) On the whole, how seriously are you suffering from all the ailments you have got ?
Not applicable/Very mildly/Mildly/Seriously/Very seriously.

(c) During the last one year how many days did you spend in bed due to illness ?——————

(d) How will you evaluate your health condition these days ?
Very good/Good/Undecided/Bad/Very bad.

6. Please state the type of your attitude regarding some changes taking place in society.

(a) The nuclear family system.
Unfavourable/Indifferent/Favourable.

(b) Inter-caste and inter-community marriages.
Unfavourable/Indifferent/Favourable.

(c) The abolition of the purdah system.
Unfavourable/Indifferent/Favourable.

(d) Eqaul rights to women.
Unfavourable/Indifferent/Favourable.

(e) Widow remarriage.
Unfavourable/Indifferent/Favourable.

(f) Divorce.
Unfavourable/Indifferent/Favourable.

7. (a) In your opinion what the grown-up children should do :

1. While taking important decisions, whether they should take parents' permission/take the

parents' advice inform the parents' about the decision ?

2. Before going out in the evening, whether they should take the parents' permssion/inform the parents before going out/may go without informing the parents ?

(b) In your opinion what the parents should do :

1. Whether they should go out with their grown-up children for the purpose of entertainment. Most of the time/Sometimes/Rarely ?
2. Whether they should sit in the drawingroom with the friends of grown-up children. Most of the time/Sometimes/Rarely

8. How strong your belief is in :

(a) The existence of gods and goddesses. Weak/Moderate/Strong

(b) The concept of 'Punya' and 'Pap' Weak/Moderate/Strong

(c) The concept of 'Karma' and 'rebirth'. Weak/Moderate/Strong

(d) The concept of hell and heaven. Weak/Moderate/Strong.

9. (A) *Family composition* : (Persons living in the same household) :

Sr. No.	Relationship with the Respondent.	Age	Sex	Marital status	Education	Occupation	Monthly income from Occupation
1.							
2.							
3.							
4.							
5.							
6.							

(b) On an average, how will you evaluate your relationship with the family members living with you ?
Unsatisfactory/Satisfactory/Very Satisfactory.

(c) How often do you have conflicts with your family members living with you ?
Quite Often/Sometimes/Rarely.

(d) What is the main reason for these conflicts most of the time ?

....

....

(e) Daily what portion of the day you spend approximately in face to face interaction with the family members living with you ?
Quarter of the day/Half of the day/Most of the day.

10\. (a) Do you have any children staying away from you ?
No/Yes

(b) If yes, how often you meet your children staying away from you ?
Less than once in a year/Once in a Year/More than once in a year.

(c) On an average, how will you evaluate your relationship with the children staying away from you ?
Unsatisfactory/Satisfactory/Very satisfactory

11\. (a) How many intimate friends do you have in this city ?

....

(b) What is the frequency of mutual visits between you and your intimate friends ?
Quite often/Sometimes/Rarely.

12. (a) How many families of neighbours do you meet ?

....

(b) What is the frequency of mutual visits between you and your neighbours.
Quite often/Sometimes/Rarely

13. (a) How many families of relatives do you have in this city ?

(b) What is the frequency of mutual visits between you and your relatives ?
Quite Often/Sometimes/Rarely

14. (a) Are you holding the membership of any voluntary organization located in this city ?
No/Yes

(b) If yes, what is the number of such organizations.
———

(c) What is the frequency of your attendance at the meetings of these organizations ?
Quite often/Sometimes/Rarely.

15. (a) Do you have any occupation at present ?
No/Yes.

(b) If yes, what type of occupation do you have ?
Service/Business/Private practice/Farming/Any other.

16. (a) Do you have any hobbies (special interest in some activities) ?
No/Yes

(b) If yes, what are they ?
1. ......
2. ......
3. ......
4. ......

17. What are the main activities in your routine excluding compulsory activities like taking bath, dressing, eating etc. and how much time do you spend approximately on those activities daily ?

Sr. No.	Name of the Activity	Time spent on the activity daily	
		Hours	Minutes
1.			
2.			
3.			
4.			
5			
6.			
7.			
8.			
9.			
10.			

LIFE SATISFACTION INDEX

Please express degree of your agreement with the following statements :

SA=Strongly agree
A=Agree
U=Undecided
D=Disagree
SD=Strongly disagree

S. No.	Statements	SA	A	U	D	SD
1.	My age does not bother me and my life is as useful and meaningful as it was in middle age.	5	4	3	2	1
2.	I feel that due to the lack of opportunities I am unable to fulfil my ambitions.	1	2	3	4	5
3.	Compared to other people of my age I make a good appearance.	5	4	3	2	1
4.	Quite often I feel blue and depressed.	1	2	3	4	5
5.	I have made several plans for things I intend to do in future.	5	4	3	2	1
6.	Quite often thoughts about death worry me a lot.	1	2	3	4	5
7.	As I grow older things seem better than I thought they would be.	5	4	3	2	1
8.	I cannot do so many things which I want to do due to various reasons.	1	2	3	4	5
9.	I am just as happy and satisfied as I was whem I was young.	5	4	3	2	1
10	Quite often I feel there is no point in living now.	1	2	3	4	5
11.	Even at the time of difficult situations I do not lose self-confidence and courage.	5	4	3	2	1

S. No.	Statements	SA	A	U	D	SD
12.	I wish that some interesting and pleasant events should take place in my life.	1	2	3	4	5
13.	Even at this age I feel young.	5	4	3	2	1
14.	I very easily get upset and irritated when things do not happen according to my wish.	1	2	3	4	5
15.	These are the best years of my life.	5	4	3	2	1
16.	I believe in destiny and know that I cannot get a bit more than what I am destined for.	1	2	3	4	5
17.	It gives me a feeling of great satisfaction that I am getting most of my desired things.	5	4	3	2	1
18.	I feel old and somewhat tired.	1	2	3	4	5
19.	There are many things which interest me and keep me busy, therefore, I do not feel empty and lonely.	5	4	3	2	1
20.	Either I blame others or curse myself for creating any problem which I have to face.	1	2	3	4	5
21.	I have got much more than what I expected out of my life.	5	4	3	2	1
22.	I cannol get along very well with the peonle of younger generation because they do not value my advice and give me proper respect.	1	2	3	4	5
23.	I do not find any reason to remain frustrated and sad in the present life.	5	4	3	2	1
24.	When I was young there were reasons to be optimistic about life, but now there is nothing to look forward to.	1	2	3	4	5

S. No.	Statements	SA	A	U	D	SD
25.	I believe and practise the 'try try again' type of approach in my life.	5	4	3	2	1
26.	I think that due to various reasons I am unsuccessful in achieving most of my goals.	1	2	3	4	5
27.	I feel that I am quite capable of doing things that are expected from me by others.	5	4	3	2	1
28.	My life has become monotonous and boring and quite often I feel lonely and isolated.	1	2	3	4	5
29.	I get pleasure out of my activities snd my experiences are quite interesting.	5	4	3	2	1
30.	This is the drearest period of my life,	1	2	3	4	5

BIBLIOGRAPHY

(A) REFERENCES—CITED

Aging in South Asia. *Social Action*. Vol. 32 (1) 1982. January-March.

Aggrawal, S.N. 1973. *India's Population Problems*. Bombay : Tata McGraw-Hill Publishing Company Limited.

Anderson, J.E. 1959. 'The Use of Time and Energy'. pp. 769-793 in *Handbook of Aging and the Individual : Psychological and Biological Aspects*, edited by James E. Birren. Chicago : University of Chicago Press.

———. 1963 'Environment and Meaningful Activity' PP. 223-245 in *Process of Aging, Vol. I*, edited by Richard H, Williams, Clark Tibbitts and Wilma Donahue. New York : Atherton Press.

Arthur, Julietta K. 1960. *How to Help Older People*. New York : J.B. Lippincott Company.

Bhatia, H.S. 1964. 'Rural Social Change and the Problem of the Aged'. *Social Welfare* XI (July) ; 5-6.

———. 1976. '*Aging and Social Adjustmcnt*'. A sociological Study of the Retired Public Servants'. Ph. D. Thesis. University of Udaipur.

Bengston, Vern L. 1973. *The Social Psychology of Aging, New York* : The Bobbs—Merrill Company, Inc.

Bose, A.B. and Saxena, P.C. 1964. 'Some Characteristics of the Aged Population in Rural Society'. *The Journal of Family Welfare*. 10 (June) : 33-39.

Bose, Ashish, 1982. Aspects of Aging in India' *Social Action* 32 (a) 1982 Jan-March, 1-19.

Baumert, Garhard, 1960. 'Changes in the Family, and the Position of Older Persons in Germany'. *International Journal of Comparative Sociology*. 1 (March) : 202-210.

Bortz, Edward L. 1963. *Creative Aging*. New York : The Macmillan Company.

Burns, Bobert K. 1954. 'Economic Aspects of Aging and Retirement'. *American Journal of Sociology*. LIX (January) : 384-390.

Burgess, Ernest W. 1950. 'Personal and Social Adjustment in Old Age' PP. 138-166 in *The Aged and Society*, edited by Milton Derber. Industrial Relations Research Association, U.S.A.

———. 1951. 'The Problem of Aging'. PP. 7-25 in *Living Through the Older Years*, edited by Clark Tibbitts. Ann Arbor : University of Michigan Press.

———. 1954. 'Social Relations, Activities and Personal Adjustment'. *American Journal of Sociology*. LIX (January) : 352-360.

———. 1957. 'The Older Generation and the Family'. PP. 158-171 in *New Frontiers of Aging*, edited by Wilma Donahue and Clark Tibbitts. Ann Arbor ; The University of Michigan Press.

———. 1960. 'The Transition from Extended Families to Nuclear Families'. PP. 77-82 in *Handbook of Social Gerontology*, edited by Clark Tibbitts. Chicago : The University of Chicago Press.

Baron, Milton L. Streib Cordon And Suchman, Edward A.1952. 'Research on the Social Disorganization of Retirement'. *American Sociological Review* 17 (August) : 479-482.

Crawford, Marion P. 1973 Retirement : 'A Rite De Passage'. '*The Sociological Review*. 21 (August) : 447-461.

Champion, Dean J. 1968. *Basic Statistics for Social Research*. Scranton, Pennsylvania : Chandler Publishing Company.

Cumming, Elaine and Henry, William B. 1961. *Growing Old : The Process of Disengagement*. New York : Basic Books. Inc.

Cottrel, L.S. Jr. 1942. 'The Adjustment of the Individual to His Age and Sex Roles'. *American Sociological Review* ? (October) : 617-620.

Chiriboga, David, A. 1982. Consistency in Adult Functioning : The Influence of Social Stress. *Aging and Society*. 2. I (March) 7-29.

Chellan, Raju. 1982. 'Problems of Old Age : Science of Gerontology'. *The Economic Times* : 30 May 82 : 4-8.

Census of India. 1971. Series-25. Chandigarh, Part III. Establishments Report and Tables.

Census of India. 1981. Series-I. India, Paper I of 1981 Provisional Population Totals, India.

Census of India. 1981. Series-II. Madhya Pradesh Supplement, Paper I, 1981 Provisonal Population Totals.

Cavan, Ruth Shonle. 1949. 'Family Life and Family Substitutes in Old Age'. *American Sociological Review* 14 (February) : 71-83.

Cruik Shank, Nelson, H. 1980. 'The Greying in America. *Social Welfare*. 27 (4) July 14-15.

Clauge, Ewan. 1951. 'Aging and Employability (PP. 141-153) In *Living Through the Older Years*, edited by Clark Tibbitts, Ann Arbor : University of Michigan Press.

Chowdhry, Paul D. 1981. *A Handbook of Social Welfare*. Delhi : Atma Ram and Sons.

D'Souza, Victor S. 1962. 'Social Grading of Occupations in India'. *The Sociological Review* 10 (July) : 145-159.

———. 1968. *Social Structure of a Planned City* : *Chandigarh*. New Delhi : Orient Longmans Limited.

———. 1971. 'Changes in Social Structure and Changing Roles of Older People in India'. *Sociology and Social Research*' 55 (April ; 297-304).

———. 1976. 'Aging in India : An Emerging Social Problem'. *Science Today*, 11 (October) : 26-27.

D'Souza, Alfred. 1982. 'The Social Organization of Aging Among the Urban Poor'. *Social Action* 32 (1) Jan. March : 53-64.

Desai, K.G and Naik, R.D. 1973. *Problems of Retired People in Greater Bombay*. Bombay : Tata Institute of Social Sciences, Series No. 27.

Dorton, Robin and Knapp, Martin. 1984. 'The Cost of Residential Care for the Elderly : The Effects of Dependency Design and Social Environment. *Aging and Society* 4, II (June) : 157-183.

District Census Handbook : 1971 (a) Series-25, Chandigarh, Part X-A.

———. 1971 (b) Series-25, Chandigarh Part X-B.

District Census Handbook. 1982. Directorate of Economics and Statistics.

District Census Handbook, Jabapur, 1971.

Donahue, Wilma ; Orbach, Harold L. And Pollak, Otto. 1960. 'Retirement : The Emerging Social Pattern'. PP. 330-406 in *Handbook of Social Gerontology*, edited by Clerk Tibbitts Chicago : The University of Chicago Press.

Donhahue, Wilma, 1969. 'Living in the Four-generation Family'. PP. 37-51 in *Living in the Multigeneration Family*, edited by Wilma Donahue, Joyce L. Kornbluh and Lawrence Power, Ann Arbor : The University of Michigan, Division of Gerontology.

Dubey, S.N. 1982. *Madhya Pradesh : In Quest of Infrastructure for Growth* in Souvenir of Indian Economic Association.

Eaton, Walter H. 1947. 'Alternative Meanings of Adjustment'. *American Sociological Review* 12 (February) : 75 : 81.

Estes, Carroll, L. Swan, James, H and Gerard, Leboree. 1982. 'Dominant and Competing Paradigms (Perspectives) in Gerontology Towards a Political Economy of Aging *Aging and Society*. 2, II (July : 151-164).

Eswaran, Lalita. 1982. 'Disturbing Future Trend'. *The Economic Times*, 23rd May 1982 : 4-5.

Edwards, Allen L. 1960. *Techniques of Attitude Scale Construction*. Bombay : Vakils, Feffer and Simons.

Encyclopedia of Social Sciences, 1968.

Folsom, Joseph K. and Morgan, Margaret C. 1937. 'The Social Adjustment of 381 Recipients of Old Age Allowances'. *American Sociological Review*, 2 (April) : 223-229.

Freyberg, Ewa. 1982. 'Aging Women'. *The Economic Times*, 23rd May 1982 : 4-5.

Francher, J. Scott. 1969. 'American Values and the Disenfranchisement of the Aged'. *Eastern Anthropologist* 22 (January) : 29-36.

Gaullier, Xavier. 1982. 'Economic Crisis and Old Age Policies in France : *Aging and Society*. 2, II (July) :165-182.

Gordon, Margaret S. 1960. 'Aging and Income Security'. PP. 208-260 in *Handbook of Social Gerontology*, edited by Clark Tibbitts. Chicago : The University of Chicago Press.

Gard, B.S, Gupta, S.C, Mishra, V.N. and Singh R.B. 1980. 'To be Aged, Sick and Disabled in a City'. *Social Welfare* : 27 (4) July 1980 : 6-7.

Gursharan Kaur. 1964. *The Problems of Aged Women in Batala*. An unpublished Master's Thesis. Punjab University, Chandigarh.

Goleman, Peter, G. 1984, 'Assessing Self Esteem and its sources in Elderly People'. *Aging and Society* 4, II (June) : 117-135.

Goodman, Leo A. and Kruskal, William M. 1963. 'Measures of Association for Cross Classifications. III : Approximate Sampling Theory'. *The Journal of the American Statistical Association* 58 (June) : 310-364.

Hardikar, S.N. and Bhatia G.G. 1983. 'Old Age—A Medical and Social Review' in *Disabled in India*, edited by S.N. Gajendragadkar. Bombay : Somaiya Publications Pvt. Ltd.

Hauseri Phillip M. 1954. 'Changes in the Labour Force Participation of the Older Workers'. *American Journal of Sociology* LIX (January) : 312-323.

Hazan, Maim. 1984. 'Religion in old Age Home'. *Aging and Society*. 4, II, (June) : 137-156.

Havighurst, Robert J. 1954. 'Flexibility and the Social roles of the Retired'. *American Journal of Sociology* LIX (January) : 309-311.

———. 1956. 'Research on Personality and Social Adjustment'. PP. 15-16. in *Psychological Aspects of Aging*, edited by John E. Anderson. Washington : American Psychological Association, Inc.

———. 1957 (a) 'The Leisure Activities of the Middle Aged'. *American Journal of Sociology* LXIII (September) : 153-162.

———. 1957 (b) 'Personal and Social Adjustment in Old Age'.

PP. 173-179. in *New Frontiers of Aging*. edited by Wilma Donahue and Clark Tibbitts. Ann Arbor : The University of Michigan Press.

———. 1959. 'Social and Psychological Needs of the Aging'. PP. 439-447 in *Readings in the Psychology of Adjustment*, edited by Leon Corlow and Walter Katkovsky, New York : McGraw-Hill Book Company.

Havighurst, Robert J. 1962 (a) 'The Nature and Values of Meaningful Freetime Activity'. PP. 899-904 in *Aging Around the World : Social and Psychological Aspects of Aging*, edited by Clark Tibbitts and Wilma Donahue. New York; Clumbia University Press.

———. 1962 (a) 'The measurement of successful Aging'. P. 664 in *Aging Around the World : Social and Psychological Aspect of Aging*. edited by Clark Tibbitts and Wilma Donahue. New York : Columbia University Press.

———. 1963. 'Successful Aging' PP. 299-320 in *Process of Aging Vol. I*. edited by Richard H. Williams, Clark Tibbitts and Wilma Donahue. Chicago : Atherton Press.

———. 1978. 'Aging in Western Society' In *The Social Challenge of Aging* edited by David Hobman, London : Croom Helm Ltd.

Hyman, Herbert. 1960. *Survey Design and Analysis*. Glencoe : The Free Press.

Help the Aged : Editorial. *Voluntary Action*. 22 (9) September 1979 : 3-4.

Howell, Trevor, H. 1953. *Our Advancing Years*. London Pnoenix House Ltd.

Hunter, Woodrow, W. 1969. *Preparation for Retirement*. Ann Arbor : The University of Michigan, Division of Gerontology.

Hochschild, Arlie Russell, 1973. *The Unexpected Community*. New Jersy : Prentice-Hall, Inc.

International Encyclopedia of Social Sciences. Vol. I. 1968, U.S.A. The Macmilian.

Indra, Rajinder. 1963. *Problems of the Old Women in a Village*. An unpublished Master's Thesis, Panjab University, Chandigarh.

India, 1981, A Reference Annual, Compiled and edited by Research and Reference Division, Ministry of Information and Broadcasting, Government of India.

Jagjit Singh. 1962. *Problems of the Old Men in Burail.* An unpublished Master's Thesis, Punjab University, Chandigarh.

Kapadia, K.M. 1959. *Marriage and Family in India.* Bombay : Oxford University Press.

Kaplan, Max 1960. 'The Uses of Leisure' PP. 407-443 in *Handbook of Social Gerontology*, edited by Clark Tibbitts, Chicago The University of Chicago Press.

Katz, Fred E. 1966. 'Social Participation and Social Structure'. *Social Forces* 45 (December) : 199-210.

Kurian, George, 1972. 'Aging in India and Canada : A Comparative Perspective'. *Social Action* 22 (July) 222-230.

Komarovsky, Mirra. 1946. 'The Voluntary Associations of Urban Dwellers'. *American Sociological Review* 11 (December) : 686-698.

Kuhlen, Raymond G. 1959. 'Aging and Life Adjustment'. PP-852-892 in *Handbook of Aging and the Individual*, edited by James E. Birren. Chicago : The University of Chicago Press.

Katz, Daniel, 1953. 'Field Studies' PP 56-97 in *Research Methods in Behavioural Sciences.* edited by Leon Festinger and Daniel Katz. New York : Holt, Rinehard and Winston Inc.

Kooy, Gerrit A. 1963. 'Social System and the Problem of Aging'. PP-43-60 in *Process of Aging Vol. II*, edited by Richard H. Williams, Clark Tibbitts and Wilma Donahue. Chicago : Atherton Press.

Koening, Samuel, 1963. *An Introduction to the Science of Society* New York : Barnes and Noble.

Little, Virginia, C. 1984. 'An Overview of Research Using the Time-Budget Methodology to study Age-related Behaviour' *Aging and Society* 4, Part I (March) : 3-20.

Lipman, Aaron and Sterne, Richard S. 1969. 'Aging in the United States : Ascription of a Terminal Sick Role'. *Sociology and Social Research* 53 (January) : 194-203.

Landis, Judson T. 1942. 'Social Psychological Factors of Aging'. *Social Forces* 20 : 468-470.

Lawton, George. 1951. 'Aging Creatively'. PP-113-130 in *Living Through the Older Years*. edited by Clark Tibbitts. Ann Arbor : University of Michigan Press.

Louis, Lowy, 1979. '*Social Work with the Aging*'. The challenge and Promise of Later Years. New York : Harper and Row, Publishers.

Marulasiddaiah H.M. 1966. 'The Declining Authority of Old People'. Indian *Journal of Social Work* XXVII (July) : 175-185.

Mani, Mahajan, P. 1980. 'Probing the Mind of the Old' *Social Welfare*. 27 (4) July 1980 : 4-5.

Messer, Mark. 1968. 'Age Grouping and the Family Status of the Elderly'. *Sociology and Social Research* 52 (April) : 271-279.

Mangamalchari, S.K, 1980. 'Friendly Societies for the Aged' *Social Welfare*, 27 (4) July 80 : 8-9.

Mather, William G. 1941. 'Income and Social Participation'. *American Sociological Review* 6 (June). 380-383.

Menon, L. 1980. 'Helping the Retired to Lead Active Life !' *Social Welfare* 27 (4) July 80 : 12-13.

Macchiwalla, Ashraf I. 1983. 'Voluntary Organizations and Their Participation' *Disabled in India*, edited by S.N. Gajendragadkar. Bombay : Somaiya Publications Pvt. Ltd.

Making Old Age Content. *Population Review*, 21 (1-2) January-December, 1977 : 157-59.

Maddox, George and Risdorfer, Carl. 1962. 'Some Correlates of Activity and Morale Among the Elderly'. *Social Forces* 40 (March) : 254-260.

Maddox, George L. 1963. 'Activity and Morale' : A Longitudinal Study of Selected Elderly Subjects : *Social Forces* 42 (December) : 195-234.

———. 1969. 'Themes and Issues in Sociological Theories of Human Aging'. PP. 11-14 in *Proceedtngs of* the *8th International Congress of Gerontology*. Washington : International Association of Gerontology.

Neysmith, Shelam, M. and Edwardh, Joey, 1984. 'Economic Dependency in 1980s : Its Impact on Third World Elderly' *Aging and Society* 4, I (March) : 21-44.

Narang, Taranjit. 1968. *Adjustment of the Aged with Special Reference to Family Types.* An unpublished Master's thesis, Punjab University, Chandigarh.

Nair, G. Ravindran, 1980. 'The Prime of Senility'. *Social Welfare.* 27 (4) July 1980 : 20-21.

Orbach, Harold L. 1962. 'Normative Aspects of Retirement'. PP. 53-63. In *Aging Around the World , Social and Psychological Aspects of Aging,* edited by Clark Tibbitts and Wilma Donahue. New York : Columbia University Press.

Pandit, Manohar, 1982. *The Cultural Heritage of Jabalpur,* in the Souvenir of Indian Economic Association.

Pathak, K.B. 1973. 'On the Age composition of the Indian Population from 1911-1971. *Interdiscipline* 10 (Summer) 35-42.

Philibert, M. 1969. 'Historical and Theoretical perspective on current Developments in Social Gerontology'. PP. 23-26 in *Proceedings of the 8th International Congress of Gerontology.* Washington : International Association of Gernotology.

Parathsarathy, M.B. 1980. 'On some Aspects of Aging in India' *Indian Journal of Social Work* : 40 (i) Jan. 80, 381-388.

Pan, Ju-Shu. 1951. 'Factors in the Personal Adjustment of Old people in Protestant Homes for the Aged.' *American Sociological Review* 16 (June) : 379-381.

Pocket Compendium of Madhya Pradesh Statistics, 1982. Issued by Directorate of Economics and Statistics, Madhya Pradesh.

Poorkaj, Houshang, 1972. 'Social Psychological Factors and Successful Aging.' *Sociology and Social Research* 56 (April) : 289-300.

Palmora, Erdman and Whittington, Frank, 1971. 'Trends in the Relative Status of the Aged. Social Forces 50 (September) : 84-91.

Ramamurti, P.V. 1968. 'A Study of Some Factors related to adjustment of Urban aged men. 'Ph.D. Thesis, Sri Venkateswara Unieersity, Tirupati.

Ramamurti, P.V. 1970. A study of certain Socio-Economic variables as related to Adjustment in Old Age, *Journal of psychological Researchers* 14, 3 (Sep) : 91-94.

Reissman, Leonard, 1954. 'Class, Leisure and Social Participation'. *American* Sociological Review 19 (February) : 76-84.

Raju, B.K. 1982. 'Problems of the Aged, A report of Manila Meet. *Yojana*, XXVI-3 : 16 Feb. 1982 p. 14-15.

Rao, Padma H. 1982. 'Gujarat Example'. The Economic Times. 30th May, 1982 : 4-8.

Rose, Arnold M. 1960. 'The Impact of Aging on Voluntary Associations'. pp, 666-697, in *Handbook of Social Gerontology*, edited by Clark Tibbitts. Chicago : The University of Chicago Press.

Reichard Suzanne ; Livson, Florine and Peterson, Paul, G. 1962. *Aging and Personality*. New York : John Wiley and Sons. Inc.

Reichard, Suzanne, 1962. Personality and Adjustment to Aging'. pp. 666-669 in *Aging Around the World : Social and Psychological Aspects of Aging*, edited by Clark Tibbitts and Wilma Donahue. New York : Columbia Univesity Press.

Rogers, Tommy, W. 1979. 'One Aged Familial Relationships' *Journal of Social and Economic Studies* 7 : 199-218.

Rosow, Irving, 1963. 'Adjustment of the Normal Aged'. pp. 195-223 in *Process of Aging*, Vol. II, edited by Richard H. Williams, Clark Tibbits and Wilma Donahue. Chicago : Atherton Press.

———. 1967. *Social Integration of the Aged*. Now York : Free Press.

Russel, Ward A. 1979. *The Aging Experience*. An Introduction to Social Gerontology. New York : J.B. Lippin Cott Company.

Streib, Gordon F. and Thompson, Wayne E. 1957. 'Personal and Social Adjustment in Retirement'. pp. 180-197. in *New Frontiers of Aging*, edited by Wilma Donahue and Clark Tibbitts. Ann Arbor : The University of Michigan Press.

Sethi, Patanjali, 1982. 'New Horizons'. *The Economic Times*. 30th May 1982 : 4-8.

Soodan, Kirpal Singh. 1972. 'Changing Roles of the Aged.' *Indian Journal of Gerontology* 4 (April) : 50-52.

———. 1975. *Aging in India.* Calcutta : The Minerva Associates.

Sharma, K.L. and Jain U.C. 1969. 'Religiosity and Fear of Death in Young and Retired Persons'. *Indian Journal of Gerontology* 1 (October) : 110-114.

Sharma, P.S. 1980. 'Treat them with dignity and love'. *Social Welfare*, 27 (4).

Shanas, Ethel, 1959. 'Some Sociological Research Findings about Older People : Pertinent to Social Work'. pp. 49-58 in *Towards Better Understanding of the Aging* : A Report of the Seminar on the Aging, Aspen Colorado 1958. New York : Council on Social Work Education.

Shanas, Ethel ; Townsend, Peter Frlis, Dorothy Henning ; Milhoj, Stehouwer, Ja. 1968. *Old People in Three Industrial Societies.* London : Routledge and Kegan Paul.

Skrabanek, R.L. 1969. 'Adjustment of Former University Faculty Members to Retirement'. *Proceedings of the South Western Sociological Association* 19 (April) : 65-69.

Simpson, Ansel p. 1961. 'Social Class Correlates of Old Age' *Sociology and Social Research* 45 (January) : 131-139.

Schmidt, John Frank. 1951. 'Pattern of Poor Adjustment in Old Age'. *The American Journal of Sociology* LVII (July): 33-42.

Statistical Abstract of Punjab, 1972. Economic and Statistical Organization's Publication.

———. 1975. Economic and Statistical Organization's Publication.

Sauvy, Alfred, 1963. 'Demographic Ageing.' *International Social Science Journal* XV (July-September) : 355-365.

Simmons, Leo W. 1945. The Role of the Aged in Primitive Society. London : Yale University Press.

———. 1959. 'Aging in Modern Society. pp. 4-8 in *Towards Better Understanding of the Aging*, A report of the seminar on the Aging, Aspen, Colorado 1958, New York : Council on Socil Work Education.

———. 1960. 'Aging in Pre-industrial Societies.' pp. 62-91 in *Handbook of Social Gerontology*, edited by Clark Tibbitts. Chicago : The University of Chicago Press.

Steglits, Edward J. 1951. 'The Personal Challenges : Biological Changes and Maintenance of Health.' pp-43-62, in *Living Through the Older Years*, edited by Clark Tibbitts. Ann. Arbor. University of Michigan Press.

The Greying of Nations. *The Economic Times* (May) 23rd May 1982 : 4-5.

The Tribune. 1976. Dated 9th May, Para 3, Column 1.

Tapia-Videla, Jorge, I. and Parrish Charles, J. 1982. Aging Development and Social Service : Delivery systems in Latin America : Problems and Perspectives. *Aging and Society*. 2, 1 (March) : 31-55.

Thompson, Wayne, E. and Streib, Gordon F. 1962. 'Meaningful Activity in a Family Context'. pp. 905-912. in *Aging Around the World : Social and Psychological Aspects of Aging*, edited by Clark Tibbitts and Wilma Donabue. New York Columbia University Press.

Tripathi, K.P. 1980. 'Problems of Pensioners'. *Indian Worker*. 98 (41) 14th July 1980 : 5-6.

The Gentle Art of Aging '*The Economic Ttimes* (Mag)30 May 1982, P.V. : 4-8.

Taylor, Debbie. 1982, 'Headover Heels at 80 ; *The Economic Times* (Mag) 23rd May 1982 : 4-5.

Tibbitts, Clark, 1954. 'Retirement Problem in American Society *American Journal* of Sociology LIX (January) : 301-308.

———. 1960 (a) 'Origin, Scope and Fields of Social Gerontology', pp. 3-36, in *Handbook of Social Gerontology*. edited by Clark Tibbitts. Chicago : The University of Chicago Press.

———. 1960 (b) 'Aging as a modern social Achievement.' pp. 3-63 in *Aging in To-day's Society*, edited by Clark Tibbitts and Wilma Donahue. Englewood Cliffs RJ : Prentice–Hall Inc.

———; 1963. 'Introduction to Social Gerontology : Origin, Scope and Trends'. *International Social Science Journal* XV (July-September) : 339-354.

Townsend, Peter. 1961. '*The Family Life of Old People* : London : Routledge and Kegan Paul.

———. 1963. 'The Argument for gradually Abandoning Communal Homes for the Aged'. *International Social Science Journal* XV (July-September) : 427-437.

Talmon, Yonina. 1961. 'Aging in Israel : Planned Society.' *The American Journal of Sociology* LXVII (November) : 284-295.

Tissue, Thomas, 1972. 'Old Age and the Perception of Poverty'. *Sociology and Social Research.* 56 (April) : 331-344.

United Nations. 1959. A Report of the European Seminar on the Individual and Social Importance of Activities for the Elderly. Konigewinter, Jr. Bonn. German Federal Republic 19-28 October, 1958.

Uhlig, Richard H. 1952. 'Employment and Retirement of a Group of Older Males'. *American Sociology Review* 17 (February) : 90-93.

Verzer, F. 1969. 'The Phenomenon of Aging.' *Indian Journal of Gerontology* 1 (October) : 94-98.

Wright, Verne, 1942. 'Summary of Literature on Social Adjustment'. *American Sociological Review.* 7 (June) 407-422.

Woltereck, Heinz. 1958. *A New Life in Old Age.* London : Max Beinardt. Limited.

Wormel, Michael T. and Gelbaum Selma. 1945. 'Work and Retirement in Old Age'. *American Journal of Sociology* LI (July) : 16-21.

Wenger, G. Clare. 1982. 'Aging in Rural Communities : Family contacts and Community Integration'. *Aging and Soeiety* 2, II, (July) : 211-229.

Wheeler, Bose, 1982. 'Staying put : A New Development in Policy' *Aging and Society*, 2, II (July) : 299-329.

(B) References-Consulted

Agnihotri, Borendra Kumar, 1976. 'Problems of the Old Age' *Agra University Journal Research*, 24 (2) July 1976 : 74-94.

Arkin, Herbert and Bolron, Raymond B. 1969. *Tables for Statisticians.* New York : Barnes and Noble, Inc.

Amesur, C.A. 1959. 'Welfare Services for the Aged and the Infirm'. *Indian Journal of Social Work*, 20 (3) December 1959 : 157-62.

Annonymous. 1960. *Facing Retirement.* London : George Allen and Unwin Ltd.

Anantharaman R.N. 1982. 'A Study of Institutionalized and Non-institutionalized Older People'. *Psychological Studies* 25 (1) Jan. 80. 31-33.

Bahr, Howard M. 1970. 'Aging and Religious Disaffiliation'. *Social Forces* 49 (September) : 59-71.

Barreto, Petrocinio. 1980. 'Homes for the Aged and Poor'. *Goa Today* 14 (12) July, p. 11.

Burr, James J. 1969. 'Financial Support of the Aged by Their Relatives'. pp. 60-67 in *Living in the Multigeneration Family* edited by Wilma Donahue, Joycer, Fornbluh and Lawrence Power. Ann Arbor : University of Michigan, Division of Gerontology.

Barron Milton L. 1961. *The Aging American* : An Introduction to Social Gerontology and Geriatrics, New York : Thomasy Crowell Company.

Britton, Joseph H. Mather, William and Lansing, Alice K. 1962. 'Expectations for Older Persons in a Rural Community : 'Community Participation'. *Rural Sociology*. 27 (December) : 387-395.

Bellin, Seymour S. and Hardt, Robert H. 1958. Marital status and Mental Disorders Among the Aged'. *American Sociological Review*. 23 (April) : 155-162.

Bunzel, Joseph H. 1972. 'Attitudinal Conflicts in the Post-Employment Years Among Three Low Fixed-Income Groups'. *Indian Journal of Gerontology* 4 (January-April) : 31-49.

Birren James E., Eiegel, Klans F. and Morrison, Donald F. 1963. 'Intellectual Capacities, Aging and Man's Environment'. pp. 9-44 in *Process of Aging*, Vol, I., edited by Richard H. Williams, Clark Tibbitts and Wilma Donhaue, Chicago : Atherton Press.

Binstock, Robert H. and Shanas Ethel. 1976. *Eds. Handbook of Aging and the Social Sciences*. Chicago : Van Nostrand Reinhold Company.

Birren James E. 1964. *The Psychology of Aging*. New Jersey : Prentice-Hall, Inc. Cliffs.

Busse, Edward W. 1957, 'Mental Health in Advanced Maturity'. pp. 143-151 in *New Frontiers of Aging*, edited by Wilma

Donahue and Clark Tibbitts. Ann Arbor : The University of Michigan Press.

Barfield, Richard and Morgan, James. 1969. *Early Retirement. The Decision and the Experience.* Ann. Arbor : Braun-Brumfield, Inc.

Burgess, Ernest. W. 1950. Aging in Western Society, Chicago : The University of Chicago Press.

Breen, Leonard Z. 1960. 'The Aging Individual'. pp. 145-162 in *Handbook of Social Gerontology*, edited by Clark Tibbitts. Chicago : The University of Chicago Press.

———. 1963. 'Retirement Norms, Behaviour and Functional Aspects of Normative Behaviour'. pp. 381-388 in *Process of Aging* Vol. II. edited by Richard H. Williams, Clark Tibbits and Wilma Donahue. Chicago : Atherton Press.

Bultona, Gordon L. 1969. 'Rural-Urban Differences in the Familial Interaction of the Aged'. *Rural Sociology* 34 (March) : 5-15.

Blau, Zena Smith. 1961. 'Structural Constraints on Friendships in Old Age'. *American Sociological Review* 26 (June) : 429-439.

Behrends, Hanna. 1969. 'The Role of Public Relations in the Service for the Elderly with Special Reference to Advisory Services'. pp. 509-512 in *Proceedings of the 8th International Congress of Gerontology* Washington: International Association of Gerontology.

Bennett, Ruth. 1969. 'Recent Developments-Social'. pp. 19-22 in *Proceedings of the 8th International Congrcss of Gerontology.* Washington : International Association of Gerontology.

Boresford, John C. and Riblin Alice M. 1960. 'The Multi-generation Family' pp. 1-36 in *Living in the Multi-generation Family*, Edited by Wilma Donahue, Joyce L. Kornbluh and Lawrence Power. Ann. Arbor : The University of Michigan, Division of Gerontology.

Bischof, Ledford, J. 1969. *Adult Psychology.* New York : Harper and Row, Publishers.

Clark, M.M. 1968. 'Changing Value Systems and Intergenerational Conflict : American Subcultural Comparisons'. pp. 425-427 in *Proceedings of the 8th International Congress of*

Gerontology. Washington : International Association of Gerontology.

Charles R. Manley Jr. 1954. 'The Migration of Older People'. *American Journal of Sociology* LIX (January) : 324-331.

Chowdhury, Rafiqul, Huda. 1982. 'The Aged in Bangladesh. *Social Action* 32 (1) Jan. March 82 : 20-38.

Cucio, Viktorija. 1973. 'Some Psychological Aspects of Old Age'. pp. 105-113 in *GERONTOLUSVRI ZECRNIK*. BEOGRAD : INSTITUT ZA SOCIJALNU POLITIKU.

Chaudhury, S.R. 1982. *Social Security in India and Britain*. Calcutta : The World Press.

Case Work with the Aging : Proceedings of the Seminar held at Columbia University. *Social Case Work* : XLII No. 5-6 May June 1961.

Covan, R.S. et al. 1949. *Personal Adjustment in Old Age*. Chicago : Science Research Associates.

Clauge, Ewan. 1951. 'Aging and Employability'. pp. 141-155 in *Living Through the Olders Years*. edited by Clark Tibbitts. Ann. Arbor ; University of Michigan Press.

Cese-Bianchi, Marcello and Trentini, Clan-Cario. 1962. A Further Contribution to the Study of Adjustment in Old Age'. pp 623-627 in *Aging Around the World : Social and Psychological Aspect of Aging*, edited by Clark Tibbitts and Wilma Donahue. New York : Columbia University Press.

Chandra, Suresh. 'The Social Challenges of Old Age'. *Social Welfare*. 17 (6) Sep. 1970 : 20-23.

Chevan, Albert and Henry Korson J. 1972. 'The Widowed Who Live Alone : An Examination of Social and Demographic Factors'. *Social Forces* 51 (September) : 45-53.

Cottrell, Fred, 1960 (a). 'The Technological and Societal Basis of Aging.' pp. 92-119 in *Handbook of Social Gerontology*, edited by Clark Tibbitts Chicago : The University of Chicago Press.

———. 1960 (b) 'Governmental Functions and the Politics of Age'. pp. 624-665 in *Handbook of Social Gerontology*, edited by Clark Tibbitts, Chicago : The University of Chicago Press.

Confrey, Eugene A. and Goldstein, Marcus S. 1960. 'The Health Status of Aging People'. pp. 165- 207 in *Handbook of Social Gerontology*, edited by Clark Tibbitts. Chicago : The University of Chicago Press.

Crawford, Marion P. 1971. 'Retirement and Disengagement'. *Human Relations* 24 (June) : 255-278.

Cumming, Elaine ; Dean Lois R. and Hewell, David S. 1960. 'Disengagement : A Tentative Theory of Aging'. *Sociometry* 23 (March) : 23-36.

Cumming, Elaine, 1963. 'Further Thoughts on the Theory of Disengagement'. *International Social Science Journal* XV (July-September) : 377-393.

Clemente, Frank and Summers, Cenef, 1973. 'A Comment on Palmore and Whittington's relative Status of Aged'. *Social Forces*. 51 (June) : 494-495.

David, B.P. et al. 1971. *Variations in Services for the Aged*, London G. Bell and Sons.

Donahue, Wilma. 1951. 'Changes in Psychological Processes with Aging'. pp. 63-85 in Living Through the Older Years, edited by Clark Tibbitts. Ann Arbor : The University of Michigan Press.

——. 1957. 'Emerging Principles and Concepts : A Summary'. pp. 198-206 in *New Frontiers of Aging*, edited by Wilma Donahue and Clark Tibbitts. Ann Arborr : The University of Michigan Press.

——— 1963. 'Rehabilitation of Long Term Aged Patients'. pp. 541-565 in *Process of Aging Vol. I*, edited by Richard H. Williams, Clark Tibbitts and Wilma Donahue. Chicago : Atherton Press.

Dumagedier, Joffre and Ripert, Aline. 1963. 'Retirement and Leisure'. *International Social Science Journal* XV (July-September) : 438-447.

Dovenmueble, R.H. and Associates. 1962. 'Depressive Reaction in the Elderly'. p. 63 in Aging *Around the World* : *Medical and Clinical Aspects of Aging*. edited by Herman T. Blumenthal, New York : Columbia University Press.

Epstein, Lenore A. and Murray, Janet H. 1967. *The Aged Population of the United States*. Washington : United States Government Printing Office.

Edward L. and Bortz, M.D. 1963. *Creative Aging*. New York : The Macmillan Company.

Frohlich, Moses M. 1951. 'Mental Hygiene of Old Age'. PP. 85-98 in *Living Through the Older Years*, edited by Clark Tibbitts. Ann. Arbor : University of Michigan Press.

Friis, Henning et al. 1971. *Old People in Three Industrial Societies*. London : Routledge and Kegan Paul.

Friedmann, Eugene A. 1960. 'The Impact of Aging on the Social Structure'. PP. 120-162 *in Handbook of Social Gerontology*, edited by Clark Tibbitts. Chicago : The University of Chicago Press.

Gligorijevic, B. 1973. 'The Households of the Residents of Belgrade Aged 60 and Over'. PP. 87-104 in *GERONTO-LUSVKI ZBORNIK*. BEDGRAD : INSTITUT ZA SOCIJALNU POLITIKU.

Clenn, Norval D. 1969. 'Aging Disengagement and Opinionation', *Public Opinion Quarterly* 33 : 1 : 17-33.

Garrett, Henry E. 1967. *Statistics in Psychology and Education*. Bombay : Vakils, Feffer and Simons Private Ltd.

Glenn, Norval D. and Grimes, Michael. 1968. 'Aging, Voting and Political Interest'. *American Sociological Review* 33 (August) : 563-575.

Gupta, J.P. 1977. 'Social Welfare Services for the Aged'. *Social Welfare* 24(7) October '77 : 1-3.

Hoar, Jere. 1961. 'A Study of Free Time Activities of 200 Aged Persons'. *Sociology and Social Research* 45 (January) : 157-163.

Hepner, Harry W. 1969. *Retirement : A Time to Live Anew*. New York : McGraw-Hill Book Company.

Harlan, William H. 1964. 'Community Adaptation to the Presence of Aged Persons : St. Petersberg, Florida' *American Journal of Sociology* LIX (January) : 332-339.

Herman, E. and Hilleboe, M.D. 1857. 'A Modern Pattern for Meeting the Health Needs of the Aging'. PP, 45-62 in *New Fronti ers of Aging*, edited by Wilma Donahue and Clark Tibbitts Ann. Arbor : The University of Michigan Press.

Hughes, Fielden, 1974. 'Enjoying Your New Leisure' in *A Lively Retiremcnt*. edited by William Living. London : Queen Anne Press.

Hamovitch, Maurica B. 'Social and Psychological Factors in

Adjustment in A Retirement Village.' PP. 115-125 in *The Retirement Process.* A Report of Conference, December 1966, Gaithersburg, Md., edited by Frances M. Carp. Betheada, Md. National Institute of Child Health and Human Development.

Hoyl, G.G. 1954. 'The Life of the Retired in a Trailer Park'. *American Journal of Sociology*, LIX (January) : 361-370.

Jacobs, Ruth Harrieta. 1979. *Life After Youth : Female Forty-What Next ?* Boston : Becon Press.

Jaksic, Slobodan. 1975. 'The Position of Old People and the System of Values'. PP. 60-66 in *GERONTOLOVSKI ZBORNIK.* Belgrade : Society of Gnrontology of the SR of Serbia.

Kalathil, Jose. 1980. 'Ozanam Home'. *Social Welfare.* 27 (4) July '80 : 10-11.

Kidd, Charles V. 1951. 'Economic Security for Older Persons'. PP. 155-178 in *Living Through the Older Years.* edited by Clark Tibbitts. Ann Arbor : University of Michigan Press.

Kreps, J.M. 1969. 'Income and Leisure Issue in Advanced Economics' PP. 473-476 in *Proceedings oj the 8th International Congress of Gerontology.* Washington : International Association of Gerontology.

King, Charles E. and Howell, William H. 1965. 'Role Characteristics of Flexible and Inflexible Retired persons'. *Sociology and Social Research* 49 (January) : 153-165.

Kleemier, Robert W. 1954. 'Moosehaven : Congregate Living in a Community of the Retired'. *American Journal of Sociology* LIX (January) : 347-351.

———. 1962. 'The Use and Meaning of Time in Special Settings'. PP. 9-13 in *Aging Around the World : Social and Psychological Aspects of Aging,* edited by Clark Tibbitts and Wilma Donahue. New York : Columbia University Press.

Lowenthal, Marjorie Fiske. 1963. 'Some Social Dimensions of Psychiatric Disorders'. PP. 224-246. *Progress of Aging, Vol. II,* edited by Richard H. Williams, Clark Tibbitts and Wilma Donahue. Chicago : Atherton Press.

Lewton, George. 1956. *Aging Successfully.* New York : Columbia Univrrsity Press.

Lehr, U. 1969. 'Consistency and Change of Social Participation in old Age', PP. 444-447 in *Proceedings of the 8th International Congress of Gerontology, Vol. I. Washington* : International Association of Gerontology.

Leeb, Rita, 1974. 'Aging in Open and Closed Societies'. *Sociology and Social Research.* 58 (July) : 392-398.

McMeely, R.L. and Colen, John V 1983. *Aging in Minority Groups*, edited by R.L. Moneely and John V. Colen. New Delhi : Sage Publications.

Moore, Flon H. 1959. *The Nature of Retirement*, edited by Gordon F. Streib. New York : The Macmillan Company.

Mangat Rai, E.N. 1973. 'Problems of Old Age and Retirement ! *Illustrated Weekly of India.* 94 (2) 25 March '73 : C-13.

Maves, Paul B. 1960. 'Aging, Religion and the Church'. PP. 698-749 in *Handbook of Social Gerontology*, edited by Clark Tibbitts. Chicago ; The Udiversity of Chicago Press.

Mansukhani, Ashok. 1972. 'Old Age can only be Postponed'. *Times of India* 2 April '72 : 6-7.

Milhoj, P. 1969. 'Trend of Retirement in an Industrial Society.' PP. 317-319 in *Proceedings of the 8th International Congress of Gerontology.* Washington : International Association of Gerontology.

Mercer, Jane, R. and Butler, Edger W. 1967. 'Disengagement of the Aged Population and Response Differentials in Survey Research'. *Social Forces* 46 (September) : 89-96.

Mladenovic, Marko. 1973. 'The Position of Old People in the Family of an Industrial Society.' PP. 34-71 in *GERONTOLOSKI ZBORNIK*, BROGRAD : INSTITUT ZA SOCIJALNU POLITIKO.

———, 1975. 'The Old Family and Society'. PP. 9-19 in *GERONSOLSKI* ZBORNIK. Belgrade : Society of Gerontology of the S.B. of Serbia.

Martin, John and Doran Ann. 1966. 'Evidence Concerning the Relationship Between Health and Retirement'. *The Sociological Review 14* (November) ; 329-343.

Mcconnell, John W. 1960. 'Aging and the Economy'. PP. 489-520 in *Handbook of Social Gerontology*, edited by Clark Tibbitts. Chicago : The University of Chicago Press.

Marris, Peter, 1958. *Widows and Their Families*. London : Routledge and Kegan Paul.

Murray, Ramond W. and Flyna, Frank T. 1938, *The Treatment of the Aged*. New York : Appleton-century-cratis Inc.

Nedeljkovic, Yves. 1970. *Old People in Yugoslavia*. Report of the Investigation sponsored by the Institute of Social Policy. Beograd.

Nair, K. Sumumaran, 1970. 'Loneliness in Old Age'. *Social Welfare*. 16 (11) Feb' 1970. 13.

National Old People's Welfare Committee. 1949. *Age is Opportunity : A New Guide to Practical Work for the Welfare of Old People*. London : National Council of Social Service.

Neugarten, Bernice L. 1963. 'Personality and the Aging Process'. PP. 321-334 in *Process of Aging*. Vol. I, edited by Richard H. Williams, Clark Tibbitts and Wilma Donahue. Chicago : Atherton Press.

Overstreet, Harry. A. 1951. 'A Comprehensive Programme for Personal and Social Adjustment in Old Age.' PP. 179-190 in *Living Through the Older Years*, edited by Clark Tibbitts. Ann. Arbor : University of Michigan Press.

Ostergaard, F. 1969. 'The significance of the Multigenerational Family in Providing Services to the Aged.' PP. 494-497 in *Proceedings of the 8th International Congress of Gerontology* Vol. I. Washington : International Association of Gerontology.

Orbach, Harold L. 1969. 'Social Values and the Institutionalization of Retirement'. PP. 389-402 in *Process of Aging Vol. II*: edited by Richard Williams, Clark Tibbitts and Wilma Donahue. Chicago : Atherton Press.

Omachi, C. 1969. 'Meaningful Free Time Activities'. PP. 513-514 in *Proceedings of the 8th International Congress of Gerontology Vol. I*. Washington : International Association of Gerontology.

Panchanadikar, K.C. and Panchanadikar J. 1970, *Determinants of Social Strueturc and Social Change in India.* Bombay : Popular Prakashan

Plan Your Old-Age Life. *The Hindustan Times* 8th April 1982 : 3.5.

Powys, Cowper John. 1944. *The Art of Growing Old.* London : Johnthan Cape Ltd.

Petrovic, Zivojin, 1975. 'Family and Old People'. PP. 75-83 in *GERONTOLOSKI ZBORNIK.* Belgrade ; Society of Gerontology of the SR of Serbia.

Pakusch, D.N. 1969. 'Time and Meaningful Activity' PP. 502-504 in *Proceedings of the 8th International Congress of Gerontology,* Washington : International Association of Gerontology.

Preston, Caroline F. 1970. 'A Cross-National Comparison of Subjective Agedness'. *International Journal of Comparative Sociology* 11 (March) : 64-67.

Rabinozitz, Patricia M. 1951. 'Living Arrangements for Older People'. PP. 131-140 in *Living Through the Older Years,* edited by Clark Tibbitts. Ann Arbor : University of Michigan Press.

Rao, B. Sridhar. 1975. 'Old Age can be Made Happy' *Social Welfare* 21 (ii) Feb. 1975 : 9-10.

Rosenmayr, Leopold and Kockeis, Eva. 1963. 'Propositions for a Sociological Theory of Ageing and the Family'. *International Social Journal* XV (July-September) : 419-426.

Rosen, George, 1960. 'Health Programme for an Aging Population'. PP, 521-538 in *Handbook of Social Gerontology,* edited by Clark Tibbitts. Chicago : The University of Chicago Press.

Riesman, David, 1954. 'Some Clinical and Cultural Aspects of Aging'. *American Journal of Sociology* LIX (January) 324-331.

Richardson, Ian. M. 1963. 'Occupation and Health'. PP. 459-477 in *Process of Aging Vol. II,* edited by Richard H. Williams, Clark Tibbitts and Wilma Donahue. Chicago : Atherton Press.

Rucker, Allen W. 1957. 'The Coming Economic Challenge of Longevity'. PP. 76-88. *in New Frontiers of Aging,* edited by

Wilma Donahue and Clark Tibbitts. Ann Arbor : The University of Michigan Press.

Sharma, Prayag and Sharma, Raj. 1982. 'Old Age in Nepal : Some Preliminary Observations'. *Social Action* 32(1) Jan. March ,82 : 39-64.

Srinivas, M.N. 1964. 'Social Structure'. *Sociological Bulletin* XIII (March) : 12-21.

Singh, R.R. 1969. 'The Changing Social Structure and the Aged'. *Indian Journal of Gerontology* 1 (October) : 118-124.

Singh, R,R. 1970. 'Welfare of the Aged'. *Indian Journal of Social Work*. 30 (4) January 1970 : 327-33.

Stryker, Sheldon, 1956. 'Relationships of Married Offspring and Parents : A Test of Mead's Theory' *American Journal of Sociology* LXII (November) : 308-319.

Strehler, Bernard L. 1962. *Time, Cells and Aging*. New York : Academic Press.

Smith, David Horton, 1966. 'The Importance of Formal Voluntary Organizations for Society'. *Sociology and Social Research* 50 (July) : 483-494.

Saul, Shura. 1974. *Aging : An Album of People Growing Old*. New York : John Wiley and Sons, Ine.

Sheps, Cecil G. 1957. 'Health in Middle and Later Years'. 129-142 in *New Frontiers of Aging*, edited by Wilma Donahue and Clark Tibbitts. Ann. Arbor : The University of Michigan Press.

Soodan, Kirpal Singh. 1971. 'Programmes for the Welfare of the Aged'. *Social Wclfare*. 18 (1) April : 24-26.

Soodan, Kirpal Sing. 1973. 'Economic Status of the Aged'. *Social Welfare*. 20 (6) September : 22-23.

Srivastava, P.C. 1964. *Social Securiiy in India*. Allahabad : Lokbharati Publications.

Suri, G.K. 1962. 'Old Age Security with Special Reference to India'. *Indian Jonrnal of Labour Economics*. 4 (4) 308-16.

Steinger, Peter O. 1957. 'Income and Employment'. PP. 89-98 in *New Frontiers of Aging*, edited by Wilma Donahue and Clark Tibbitts. Ann Arbor : The University of Michigan Press.

Stern, James. 1957. 'For the Employment of the Aging'. PP. 28-44 in *New Frontiers of Aging*, edited by Wilma Donahue and Clark Tibbitts Ann Arbor : The University of Michigan Press.

Streib, Gordon F. and Thompson, Wayne F. 1960. 'The Older Person in a Family Context'. PP. 447-488 in *Handbook of Social Gerontology*. edited by Clark Tibbitts. Chicago : The University of Chicago Press.

Slavick, Fred and Wolfbein, Seymour L. 1960. 'The Evolving Work Life Pattern'. PP. 298-329 in *Handbook of Social Gerontology*, edited by Clark Tibbitts. Chicago : The University of Chicago Press.

Sheldon, Henry D. 1954. 'Who are the Aged'. P. 12 in *Housing the Aging*, edited by Wilma Donahue. Ann. Arbor : University of Michigan Press.

———. 1957. 'Future Trends in Our Older Population' PP. 65-77 in *New Frontiers of Aging*', edited by Wilma Donahue and Clark Tibbitts. Ann Arbor : The University of Michigan Press.

———. 1960. 'Changing Demographic Profile.' PP. 27-61 in *Handbook of Social Gerontology*, edited by Clark Tibbitts. Chicago : The University of Chicago Press.

Tindall, Ralph H. 1959. 'Relationships Among Measures of Adjustment'. PP. 107-115 in *Readings in the Psychology of Adjustment*, edited by Leon Gorlow and Walter Katkovsky. New York : McGraw-Hill Book Company.

Talland, George A. 1968. Editor *Human Aging and Behaviour*. New York : Academic Press. Inc.

Tartler, Rudolf. 1963. 'The Older Person in Family, Community and Society'. PP. 61-76 in *Process of Aging*, Vol. II, edited by Richard H. Williams, Clark Tibbitts and Wilma Donahue. Chicago : Atherton Press.

Taskar, M.S. 1953. 'Problem of the Aged'. *Social Service Quarterly*, 38 (3) Jan. 1953 : 83r87.

Treanton, JanerRene. 1962. 'Some Sociological Considerations on the Problem of Adjustment in Older People'. PP. 665 in *Aging Around the World : Social and Psychological Aspect of Aging*, edited by Clark Tibbitts and Wilma Donahue. New York : Columbia University Press.

———. 1963. 'The Concept of Adjustment in Old Age'. PP 292-298 in *Process of Aging Vol. I*, edited by Richard H. Williams, Clark Tibbitts and Wilma Donahue. Chicago : Atherton Press.

Thomae, Hans, 1963. 'Aging and Problems of Adjustment. '*International Social Science Journal* XV (July-September) 366-376.

VUKOVIC' ZARKO. 1974. 'Some Aspects of Free Time and Recreation in Old Age'. PP. 122-126 in *GERONTOLOSKI ZBORNIK*, Belgrade : Society of Gerontology of the SR of Serbia,

Vivrett, Walter K. 1960. 'Housing and Community Setting for Older People'. PP 549-623 in *Handbook of Social Gerontology*, edited by Clark Tibbitts, Chicago : The University of Chicago Press.

Waterman, Leroy. 1951. 'Religion and Religious Observance in Old Age'. PP. 99-112 in *Living Through the Older Years*, edited by Clark Tibbitts. Ann. Arbor : University of Michigan Press.

Wilson, Thomas. 1974. *Pensions, Inflation Grow in : A Comparative Study of the Elderly in the Welfare State*. London : Heinemann Educational Books.

Williams, Richard H. 1963. 'Styles of Life and Suceessful Aging ! PP. 335-371 in *Process of Aging Vol. I* edited by Richard H. Williams, Clark Tibbitts and Wilma Donahue. Chicago : Atherton Press.

Webber, Irving L. 1954. 'The Organized Social Life of the Retired : Two Florida Communities'. *American Journal of Sociology* LIX (January) : 340-346.

Walter C, Mc. and Kain J.R. 1957. 'Aging and Rural Life', PP. 118-128 in *New Frontiers of Aging*, edited by Wilma Donahue and Clark Tibbitts. Ann Arbor : The University of Michigan Press.

Warner, Bloomberg J.R. 1957. 'Antomation Predicts Change'. PP. 10-27 in *New Frontiers of Aging*, edited by Wilma Donahue and Clark Tibbitts. Ann Arbor : The University of Michigan Press.

Wedderburn, Dorothy Cole. 1963. 'Economic Aspects of

Ageing'. *International Social Science Journal* XV (July-September) : 394-409,

Wedderburn, Dorothy, 1969. 'Income Maintenance in Old Age'. PP. 505-508 in *Proceedings of the 8th International Congress of Gerontology*, Washington : International Association of Gerontology.

Weller, Carlv. 1951. 'Biological Aspects of the Aging Process'. PP 27-42 *in Livlng Through the Older Years*'. edited by Clark Tibbitts. Ann Arbor : University of Michigan Press.

Wolybein, Seymour L, 1957. 'Employment outlooks for Older Workers'. PP. 99-117. in *New Frontiers of Aging*, edited by Wilma Donahue and Clark Tibbitts. Ann Arbor, The University of Michigan Press.

Williams, Richard H. 1960. 'Changing Status, Roles and Relationships'. PP. 261-297. in *Handbook of Social Gerontology*, edited by Clark Tibbitts. Chicago : The University of Chicago Press.

Young, Michael and Geertz, Hildee. 1961. 'Old Age in London and San Francisco : Some Families Compared'. *The British Journal of Sociology* XII (June) : 124-141.

Yarrow, Marion Backe 1963. 'Appraising Environment'. PP 201-223 in *Process of Aging*, Vol. I, edited by Richard H. Williams, Clark Tibbitts and Wilma Donahue. Chicago : Atherton Press.

Zivkovic, M. 1973. 'Roots, Constitution and Heritages of Gerontology'. PP. 1-33 in *GERONTOLOSKI ZBORNIK* BEGRAD : INSTITUT ZA SOCIZALNN POLITIKU.

———. 1974. "Connections Between Old Parents and Their Children'. PP. 8-21 in *GERONTOLOSKI ZBORNIK.* Belgrade : Society of Gerontology of the SR Serbia.

INDEX